Africa Bears Witness

Africa Bears Witness

Mission Theology and Praxis in the 21st Century

Edited by
Harvey Kwiyani

© 2024 Harvey Kwiyani

Published 2024 by Langham Global Library
An imprint of Langham Publishing
www.langhampublishing.org

Langham Publishing and its imprints are a ministry of Langham Partnership

Langham Partnership
PO Box 296, Carlisle, Cumbria, CA3 9WZ, UK
www.langham.org
Originally published 2021 by African Theological Network Press (ATNP)

ISBNs:
978-1-83973-892-0 Print
978-1-83973-982-8 ePub
978-1-83973-983-5 PDF

Harvey Kwiyani hereby asserts his moral right to be identified as the Author of the General Editor's part in the Work in accordance with sections 77 and 78 of the Copyright, Designs and Patents Act 1988.

All rights reserved. No part of this publication may be reproduced, stored in a retrieval system or transmitted, in any form or by any means, electronic, mechanical, photocopying, recording or otherwise, without the prior written permission of the publisher or the Copyright Licensing Agency.

Requests to reuse content from Langham Publishing are processed through PLSclear. Please visit www.plsclear.com to complete your request.

All Scripture quotations, unless otherwise indicated, are taken from the Holy Bible, New International Version®, NIV®. Copyright ©1973, 1978, 1984, 2011 by Biblica, Inc.™ Used by permission of Zondervan.

Scripture quotations marked (NRSV) are taken from the New Revised Standard Version Bible, copyright © 1989 National Council of the Churches of Christ in the United States of America. Used by permission. All rights reserved.

British Library Cataloguing-in-Publication Data
A catalogue record for this book is available from the British Library

ISBN: 978-1-83973-892-0

Cover & Book Design: projectluz.com

Langham Partnership actively supports theological dialogue and an author's right to publish but does not necessarily endorse the views and opinions set forth here or in works referenced within this publication, nor can we guarantee technical and grammatical correctness. Langham Partnership does not accept any responsibility or liability to persons or property as a consequence of the reading, use or interpretation of its published content.

Dedicated to
Andrew F. Walls
Missionary, Scholar, Pioneer, Mentor, Friend

Contents

Contributors ix

Foreword xiii

Preface xv

Acknowledgements xvii

Introduction 1
    Kyama Mugambi and Harvey Kwiyani

1 Africa Bears Witness 5
    Harvey Kwiyani

2 Mission in Prophetic Dialogue: Exploring the Ethos of
    Transformative Encounters in Africa 17
    J. N. J. (Klippies) Kritzinger

3 Mission as New Catholicity, Afro-Westernization
    and Globalization 33
    Jean Luc Enyegue, SJ

4 In the Power of the Spirit: Towards a Pentecostal Theoretical
    Framework for Missiology in Africa 45
    J. Kwabena Asamoah-Gyadu

5 Kenosis as Missional Strategy for a Church in Need of Conversion:
    Reimagining Mission in Post-Apartheid South Africa 61
    J. Frederick Marais

6 Catalytic Church Mission and Peacebuilding in Africa: A Review
    of the Church's Prophetic Role in Socio-Political Change 75
    Elias O. Opongo, SJ

7 Mission and Development 89
    Rowanne Sarojini Marie

8 African Charismatic Movements and Urban Missiology 103
    Ignatius Wilhelm (Naas) Ferreira and Joseph Bosco Bangura

9 Neo-Prophetism and Rebranding of *Missio Dei* in African
    Christianity 115
    Chammah J. Kaunda

10   Contextualized Missions and Theological Education in the
     Global South: A Case Study from East Africa 129
     Peter Maribei and Kyama Mugambi

11   The *Pambio* in Mission: Meaning and Significance in African
     Christianity 145
     William O. Obaga

12   Missiology for a Youthful Continent 159
     Joseph Ola

13   African Women in Mission Challenging Gender-based Violence
     in East Africa. 173
     Linda Ochola-Adolwa and Harvey Kwiyani

14   African American Presbyterian Mission Work as an Exercise in
     Recognizing and Redefining Identities, 1916–1935. 187
     Kimberly Hill

15   African Christians and Missionaries in Europe 199
     Harvey Kwiyani

     Conclusion: Tending and Attending to an African Missiology 213
     Harvey Kwiyani and Angus Crichton

Contributors

J. Kwabena Asamoah-Gyadu, PhD, is the President of the Trinity Theological Seminary, Legon, Ghana. He is also the Seminary's professor of contemporary African Christianity and Pentecostal theology. Prof. Asamoah-Gyadu is from Ghana, and has published widely on the intersection between contemporary expressions of Christianity and new trends in missiology in Africa.

Joseph Bosco Bangura, PhD, is a senior researcher in missiology and African Pentecostalism at the Evangelische Theologische Faculteit, Belgium. Dr. Bangura also teaches at the Protestant Theological University, Groningen, Netherlands. He grew up in Sierra Leone, and currently lives and works in Belgium.

Angus Crichton, PhD, is from the UK and has spent the last twenty years learning about Christianity in Africa, particularly Uganda. Dr. Crichton taught in a theological college and has developed a publishing initiative with Ugandan colleagues. He is a research associate at the Cambridge Centre for Christianity Worldwide, UK.

Jean Luc Enyegue, SJ obtained his STL in systematic theology from Boston College School of Theology, and his PhD in church history from Boston University, Massachusetts, USA. Originally from Cameroon, Rev. Dr. Enyegue teaches church history at Hekima University College, Nairobi, Kenya. He is Director of the Jesuit Historical Institute in Africa (JHIA) also based in Nairobi, Kenya.

Ignatius Wilhelm (Naas) Ferreira, PhD, is South African and a senior lecturer at North West University, South Africa.

Kimberly Hill is a historian of in African American missions and Black internationalism. She is an associate professor of US and African American history at the University of Texas, USA, and the author of *A Higher Mission: The Careers of Alonzo and Althea Brown Edmiston in Central Africa* (University Press of Kentucky, 2020). Her PhD is from the University of North Carolina, USA.

Chammah J. Kaunda, PhD, is a Zambian scholar working as assistant professor at the United Graduate School of Theology, Yonsei University, South Korea. He is also Extraordinary Professor in the department of religion and theology at the University of the Western Cape, South Africa. Dr. Kaunda has authored scores of peer-reviewed journal articles and book chapters on Christianity in Africa.

J. N. J. (Klippies) Kritzinger is an emeritus professor of missiology at the University of South Africa (UNISA). He was dean of the faculty of theology and religious studies at UNISA from 1999 to 2001, and editor of *Missionalia* from 1992 to 2009. He is an emeritus minister of the Uniting Reformed Church in Southern Africa (URCSA), which he served from 1993 to 2015. He is involved in the Northern Theological Seminary in Pretoria, which equips ministers for the URCSA.

Harvey Kwiyani, PhD, is a Malawian theologian at the Church Mission Society in Oxford, UK, where he leads the Centre for Global Witness and Human Migration, and manages the world Christianity and diasporas programs. He founded and continues to serve as Executive Director of Missio Africanus, an intercultural mission training initiative that seeks to equip and empower the global church for mission in Europe. Having long-served in mission in Europe and North America, he writes on cross-cultural mission and leadership, and has authored several books, including *Sent Forth: African Missionary Work in the West* (Orbis Books, 2014) and *Multicultural Kingdom: Ethnic Diversity, Mission and the Church* (SCM Press, 2020).

J. Frederick Marais, PhD, is South African, and an ordained pastor of the Dutch Reformed Church in South Africa, having served in two congregations for more than fifteen years. Dr. Marais is the director for theological education for the Dutch Reformed Church at the Faculty of Theology, Stellenbosch University, South Africa. He helped found the South African Partnership for Missional Churches. He researches and has written several books on missional theology and ecclesiology, and is also involved with the Andrew Murray Centre for Spirituality in Wellington, South Africa.

Peter Maribei is originally from Kenya, and currently serves as the associate director of education abroad at Miami University, Ohio, USA. Dr. Maribei has been engaged in leadership development initiatives at a missions agency and in church plants across Eastern and Southern Africa. He has a PhD in Leadership Studies from University of San Diego, California, USA.

Rowanne Sarojini Marie holds a PhD in Theology and Development from the University of KwaZulu-Natal (UKZN), South Africa. She is passionate about issues of development, gender justice, and ministerial formation. Dr. Marie, a South African, is the President of the Seth Mokitimi Methodist Seminary (SMMS) in Pietermaritzburg, South Africa.

Kyama Mugambi, PhD, is a World Christianity scholar from Kenya. He is assistant professor of World Christianity at Yale Divinity School, Connecticut, USA, and the author of *A Spirit of Revitalization: Urban Pentecostalism in Kenya* (Baylor University Press, 2020).

William O. Obaga is a Kenyan church historian, church musician, choral conductor, composer, and musicologist. He holds a PhD in church history from Luther Seminary, Minnesota, USA. He is the associate director for Africa at the World Mission Prayer League, Minnesota, USA, Nairobi.

Linda Ochola-Adolwa is a Kenyan ordained Anglican minister and serves as the executive director of Hatua Trust, a faith-based organization whose mission is to catalyze Christians for social transformation. She has a PhD from Fuller Seminary, California, USA, and works as church partnership coordinator with International Justice Mission, Kenya.

Joseph Ola has a DTh from University of Roehampton, UK, and is a pastor and editor at The Apolistic Church (LAWNA), UK. He is the founder of Alive Mentorship Group, an online mentoring platform for young adults with membership spanning over sixty nationalities, and he also serves on the board of Missio Africanus. He comes from Nigeria.

Elias O. Opongo SJ, PhD, is a lecturer at Hekima Institute of Peace Studies and International Relations, Hekima University College, Kenya. Rev. Dr. Opongo is also the director of the Centre for Research, Training, and Publication at Hekima. He researches and teaches transitional justice, social ethics, post-conflict reconstruction, community peacebuilding, religious extremism, extractive industries, and conflict.

Foreword

Christianity in Africa is diverse and flourishing. This book celebrates the growth of the church on the continent. It also reflects theologically on the ways the church fulfils the mission of God and how it might better follow Christ in mission through the many social and ecclesial challenges. Those working in churches in Africa and the diaspora will find much to ponder here. It is also a valuable resource for those, like me, who wish to understand and learn from Christian sisters and brothers across the globe.

Harvey Kwiyani has brought together an excellent range of scholars and reflective practitioners from across the African continent, the USA, and Europe. They are people on the move, who bring their experiences of living in different countries to bear on their work. They write in an accessible style. They provide metaphors, proverbs, and biographies to illustrate their arguments. Among the contributors are three women. A range of denominations are represented, including Lutheran, Anglican, Methodist, Dutch Reformed, and Pentecostal-Charismatic ministries. It is particularly pleasing to see two articles by Catholic theologians, both Jesuit priests. Sometimes commentary on Christianity in Africa can be siloed, with Catholics and Protestant-Pentecostals writing separately. Pentecostal ministries have seen huge and well-documented growth in Africa over the past 50 years. Yet other Christian denominations are also growing.[1] The Catholic Church remains the largest ecclesiastical institution and has a significant infrastructure of medical, educational, and development facilities. This book provides a glimpse into the range of theology and practice among and between denominations, whilst its contributors share a common missiological endeavour.

The focus of most of the chapters is firmly on the African continent, but the questions and concerns are pertinent to the African diaspora, discussed in the final chapters, and to other parts of the Christian church. For example, the question of how to deal with a historic legacy of disproportional benefit from authority, power, and wealth comes from the Dutch Reformed Church. The answer, however, which is drawn from a re-reading of Philippians to better understand the humility of Christ, is pertinent beyond its immediate context.

---

1. For details see, Gina A Zurlo, *Global Christianity: A Guide to the World's Largest Religion from Afghanistan to Zimbabwe* (Grand Rapids: Zondervan, 2022), pp. 6–7.

The consideration of what it means to be Christian peacebuilders – a point of general concern – is addressed through an assessment of different types of conflict on the African continent. Likewise, the enquiry of the proper role of African churches in development proposes some important general principles, such as: development requires the empowerment and participation of all people, rather than top-down imposition. Other enquiries in this book seek to understand the appeal of charismatic ministries preaching the prosperity gospel and the rise of neo-prophetic churches who offer a contextual response to difficulties. Significant factors include the socio-economic plight of urban dwellers whose fabric of communal support is stretched thin, the lack of state infrastructure in the growing African cities, and deeply rooted expectations of charismatic leadership. The sympathetic analyses of the social situations are followed by theological and biblical critiques of the theological premise of prosperity preaching and prophetism. The chapters warn about misleading preaching and the dangers of prophets who see themselves as embodiment of God's mission. The contributors' concerns about appropriate Christian leadership and the contexts of socio-economic marginalisation, political mismanagement, and gender-based violence are well made. The critiques, however, do not come from a lofty judgemental position but from a profound appreciation of the attraction of ministries they disagree with, and a deep understanding of the daily difficulties that ordinary Christians face. In the chapters there are also stories of great hope. They come from different quarters, including those whose prophetic stance in recent years has been dialogical and life-giving, and African women who, from the early church, have inspired others to be strong.

Much of the African church is vibrant, youthful, newly urban, and growing. It is situated in low and middle-income countries whose populations are set to grow significantly over the next decades. This may seem to be a very different situation than the continent of Europe, yet, with this collection, we see African missiologists setting vital questions that have human resonance. They are reflecting upon local, regional, transnational, and intercontinental factors of mission. Europe and North America have, for so long, tried to set the agenda for the Christian church worldwide. It has often done so by assuming that the western context is universally applicable. We may expect to see more agenda-setting from the African church. We "outsiders" may learn more of the contextual struggles faced by our brothers and sisters as well as their perspectives on common human problems. We may all learn from the theologies of reconciliation and hope that are emerging from their midst.

Emma Wild-Wood, PhD
Centre for the Study of World Christianity,
University of Edinburgh, UK

Preface

This book comes into print in the twenty-fourth year of the twenty-first century, a century when world Christianity became a given – something that can easily be taken for granted. In a sense we are still at the beginning of the century. Yet, the missiological trends that will shape our discourses in this century are emerging with some clarity. The most prominent among those is the worldwide presence of followers of Jesus Christ contributing to the phenomenon of world Christianity. That Jesus Christ has disciples in every country in the world has serious implications for the way we engage in mission. These disciples, wherever they are, can only be faithful to their calling by engaging in God's mission.

When Christ calls us to the faith, he calls us to mission. Some may be called to foreign lands. Others may be called to some specialized cross-cultural form of mission. Yet, everyone is called to mission. God has called African, Asian, and Latin American Christians all to participate, and this ought to be foundational to the way we think about mission in the twenty-first century. Mission today cannot continue to be only about the West sending missionaries to the rest of the world. The time for that way of thinking about mission is gone. This book's main argument is that mission theology itself has to reflect this polycentric and multidirectional nature of mission in the twenty-first century. As with everything else, theological cross-pollination about mission will enrich the ways we understand and participate in God's mission in the world.

There is no doubt at all in my mind that we need to discover new ways of participating in and talking about God's mission in the world today. The world has changed significantly since William Carey left the shores of England to go to serve in mission in India, since David Livingstone went to South Africa, or since James Hudson Taylor went to China. Indeed, it has changed even more since the end of the Second World War. The many mission societies that followed Carey's Baptist Mission Society, sending numerous Europeans and North Americans in mission around the world since the 1800s, now find themselves in a strange world, wondering how they continue to serve God in a world less enthusiastic about Western missions. Thus, they need to think themselves into a new life by engaging Christians from other parts of the world. I have become convinced after working in Europe and North America for more than two decades that this mission theology will energize God's church in the world, and catalyse it afresh for mission. Such theology must also listen to the missiological discourses from Africa, Asia, and Latin America.

This book is about mission theology and practice taking place in Africa today. Its purpose is two-fold. First, it articulates aspects of mission theology coming out of Africa. Thus, it wants to make accessible both to Africans (in the continent and in the diaspora), and to the rest of the body of Christ, how Africans are thinking theologically about mission in the twenty-first century. This is of great importance as, since 2018, Africa is the continent with the most Christians in the world. I dare to add, it is the continent with the most mobile Christians in the world. African diaspora Christianity exhibits two hallmarks of African Christianity in the twenty-first century – spiritual revivals and migration. African Christianity may lead in mission in this century. Second, the book tells stories of Africans engaging in mission in Africa and overseas. The narrative and the theological essays work together to paint an image of how mission looks in Africa when made sense of and articulated by Africans. The book is intentional in the diversity of its contributors who represent all regions of sub-Saharan Africa, with the exception of the Horn of Africa. Consequently, the reader will come out with a fuller understanding of mission in the twenty-first century Africa.

It is my sincere hope that, in reading this book, you will find something to enrich your theology of mission.

Harvey Kwiyani
Liverpool, 2024

Acknowledgements

Though this book bears my name on the front cover, it has been a group effort. I have enjoyed the friendship and support of Kyama Mugambi (with whom I co-wrote the introduction) and Angus Crichton (and with him, I co-wrote the concluding chapter of the book). Their hard work made this book possible in more ways than just contributing to these two chapters. In his role as editorial manager at the African Theological Network Press, Kyama received the manuscript from me and turned it into the book you are holding now. Without him, this would not have happened in the joyful ways it did. Angus took numerous hours editing and proofreading the manuscript. His eagle-eyed editorial work made the text flow more pleasantly. As the editor of the book, it was my responsibility to make sure the book reads well. I bear responsibility for any shortcomings you will find here.

I am also deeply grateful to all contributors. This book has been in the works for a long time, made even longer by the COVID-19 pandemic that slowed us all down since early 2020. All contributors were patient and responsive when called upon.

A great deal of content in this book reflects my work, teaching missiology to numerous students in Britain. Their perceptive questions helped me understand the issues being discussed here much better. I feel the need to mention two students in particular, John Neate and Joseph Ola. As a British student studying African Christianity, John helped me understand how an African missiology would speak to non-Africans. Joseph contributed an essay to this book on a missiology for a youthful continent. I am always grateful to these two and many other students I have worked with at Liverpool Hope University, Church Mission Society, and Birmingham Christian College.

I am grateful to my family for nurturing my passion. My parents, Jonathan and Hilda Kwiyani, pray for my work each day. Their prayers help me continue to write. My wife, Nancy, and my two daughters, Rochelle and Roxanne, have always been gracious to allow me time to reflect and write. Even though writing is a lonely endeavour, it has communal implications, and these three ladies deal with it gracefully.

Finally, I thank God for giving this Malawian a gift to share with the world.

Introduction

Kyama Mugambi and Harvey Kwiyani

This is a book about the mission of God among Africans, both in Africa and in the African Diaspora. It celebrates the explosion of Christianity in Africa as evidence that Africans are bearing witness of Christ to one another, especially in the sub-Saharan part of the continent. It has only been fifty years since most African countries gained independence, and it is now well understood that Africa has been evangelized by Africans. African Christians are engaging in God's mission – and as will be argued in this book, they are involved in evangelizing not only Africa but also many other parts of the world. This book reflects on how Africans speak and think theologically about mission, how they actually engage in mission, and how God's mission is shaping the continent.

Harvey Kwiyani's opening essay establishes the foundational argument of this volume that mission belongs to God and not to the church. However, the church is God's human agent for mission, and it must engage the numerous points of contact found in the rich diversity of the African context. Mission, for instance, engages in "prophetic dialogue" in Africa, as J. N. J. Kritzinger demonstrates. Through such dialogue, a creative tension is maintained between transformation and identification, and between speaking and listening in the context of mission. Through such prophetic practices, communities of hope find their voice and have missional influence in their contexts, especially as their missional leaders take risks for what they believe. Kritzinger's chapter gives examples of what such faithful witness looks like in the midst of difficult challenges and painful legacies in Africa.

God's mission in Africa is always about God's dynamic engagement with Africa's present realities. Jean-Luc Enyegue illustrates how mission cannot be locked in a past temporal-geographic-cultural milieu. The continuing interface between Christianity and the African context incorporates elements of Africa's diverse cultures today. The mission of God also casts a glance at the global context and applies itself to what globalization has to offer. It is not a *for-or-against* tension with Westernization but a *with-and-for* engagement. This dynamic mission-shaped encounter between the gospel and African cultures can be seen in all African Christian expressions but is particularly marked in the Pentecostal-charismatic strands. Kwabena Asamoah-Gyadu shows how the word and Spirit animate this pneumatic Christianity's soteriology, crucicentrism, and biblicism towards mission.

As sketched in these first four chapters, mission is, in essence, practical. The remaining chapters of the book lay out the practical ways in which mission acts. Frederick Marais presents *kenosis* as a framework for mission in confronting the effects of apartheid, one of the most painful and debilitating legacies in modern Africa. The church, in this case the Dutch Reformed Church, performs introspection, using *kenosis* as the guiding paradigm, to interrogate its relationship with power and privilege in order to become effective in mission for its world today. This chapter demonstrates that while mission can have a historical dimension, it needs to be efficacious in its contemporary role.

Mission necessarily engages the religiously pluralistic and cosmopolitan context Africa finds itself in today. Elias Opongo shows that in the fractious, often violent encounters that are the product of Africa's religious and ethnic diversity, mission is about peacebuilding. The church in mission becomes the moral voice that protects and promotes the common good and with it human dignity. Similarly, the socio-economic disparities found within the continent present an opportunity for mission. Rowanne Marie makes the point that mission and development go together. Pushing beyond the stereotypes of development NGOs as mission, Marie illustrates that mission is also a confrontation of the structural injustices that produce the inequalities evident on the continent today. Highlighting the rapid urbanization of the continent, Ignatius Ferreira and Bosco Bangura show how mission is a quest to bear witness to the reign of God in Africa's cities. The chapter points to the immense potential for urban mission in African pneumatic Christianity.

Chammah Kaunda takes a particular aspect of African Pentecostal Christianity to draw lines of continuity with Africans' traditional worldview. He shows that African prophetism is a socially constructed religious innovation whose dependence on socio-cultural contexts has implications for worship and mission. Innovation is also found in the pedagogy of emerging African Christian expressions. Peter Maribei and Kyama Mugambi explore one particular example of how churches democratize urban missions beyond the clergy through indigenously developed programmes. The result is programmes that go further than earlier Western models in inspiring missional engagement among African Christians. William Obaga examines another instance of innovation. Using *Pambio*, a popular form of music, he contemplates the impact of the arts in mission, particularly among Africans in the Diaspora.

As a young continent, any discussion of mission would not be complete without a discussion about the role of the youth. Using research from the Nigerian context, Joseph Ola explores the engagement between the youth and leadership. His findings point to the need for a vision of mission that incorporates the youth in releasing the future missionary potential of African Christianity. Similarly, there is an urgent need to reflect on the role of women in mission. Linda Ochola-Adolwa and Harvey Kwiyani discuss the missional fortitude of African women who continue to bear witness for Christ, defying great odds against them. The lives of women in Africa are evidence of the hope that the gospel brings in the face of such challenges as gender-based violence.

Identity is an important theme in mission. Kimberly Hill revisits early twentieth-century mission by African Americans to Africa to expose valuable lessons about how identity, unity, and shared perspectives form the basis for long-lasting mission initiatives. The book concludes with reflections on the important role of the Diaspora in reinvigorating Christianity in the Western world. Kwiyani explores the present and future of Africa's role in mission beyond the continent. It is our sincere hope that the collection of essays presented in this book will encourage further missiological discourse and research in African Christianity.

1

Africa Bears Witness

Harvey Kwiyani

My study of mission history was largely informed by Kenneth Scott Latourette (1884–1968).[1] His seven-volume collection entitled *The History of the Expansion of Christianity*[2] (published between 1937 and 1945) still sits calmly on a bookshelf right in front of my desk, always waiting for me to pick one of the volumes up, as I usually do, to find some hidden information about a missionary who worked in some distant part of the world, and Latourette never disappoints. The first three volumes are not very big, yet they cover the first 1800 years of mission history. Volume 1 covers *The First Five Centuries*, of Christian growth throughout the Roman Empire and beyond. It pays considerable attention to the missionary work of the early North African church, showing how important Egypt and the Maghreb were to both the establishment and the expansion of Christianity. Volume 2 is devoted to *The Thousand Years of Uncertainty*, between 500 AD and 1500 AD. He, somehow, manages to fit in a thousand years of mission history in one volume while giving his readers enough details that actually leave them informed about all the major events of that period. Volume 3 discusses mission in what he calls the *Three Centuries of Advance*, from 1500 AD to 1800 AD. Of course, this period

---

1. Kenneth Latourette is one of the most recognized mission historians of the twentieth century. Earlier in his life, he served as the Travelling Secretary of the Student Volunteer Movement for Foreign Mission. After a short time in China, he returned to the US, and after several years of teaching in Oregon and Ohio, he joined Yale University Divinity School in 1921, first as the D. Willis James Professor of Missions and World Christianity (1921–1949), and later, the Sterling Professor of Missions and Oriental History (1949–1953). He retired in 1953. His publication list is long. He is celebrated both as a historian of Christianity and world mission and China.

2. Kenneth Scott Latourette, *A History of the Expansion of Christianity*, 7 vols. (London: Harper and Brothers, 1937).

focuses on the emergence of the expansion of European Christendom, first in the Americas and later in Africa and Asia. These three hundred years also mark the rise of the Western domination of the world which was, to a large extent, made possible by the coupling of *mission* (a word that first appeared in Christianity's history in the sixteenth century)[3] and *colonialism*. As expected, Latourette is as informative about Bartolomé de las Casas in Latin America as he is about Mateo Ricci and Francis Xavier in Asia.

After this, Latourette devotes *three* volumes (Volumes 4, 5, and 6) to what he calls *The Great Century of Christian Mission*, spanning from 1800 to 1914, with the first of the three volumes dedicated to mission history in *Europe and the United States of America*, the second (and visibly the largest) volume to *The Americas, Australasia, and Africa* while the third focuses on *Northern Africa and Asia*. They are followed by a smaller volume, Volume 7, which is entitled, *Advance Through Storm: A.D. 1914 and After, With Concluding Generalizations*. Of course, Volumes 1 to 3 read like a prelude to these three volumes of nineteenth-century mission history. Whatever happened in the first eighteen hundred years of Christianity seems to only be setting the stage for what we have seen in the past two hundred years. In terms of volume, Latourette's work appears to suggest that many more historical events in mission take place in the nineteenth century than all the other centuries put together, even though that may actually point to the historiographical challenges that shape our understanding of the story of mission. After this seven-volume series, Latourette published another multi-volume series entitled *Christianity in a Revolutionary Age*[4] which essentially rehashes some of the same history in the three volumes of *The Great Century*. The series adds some new materials discussing the subsequent emergence of a world Christian community as far as could be told in the 1960s. His work is thorough and has informed many other mission history books for decades. It is impossible to talk seriously about mission history (or even church history) without mentioning Latourette's work. However, it is decidedly eurocentric. His telling of mission history, especially going back to 500 AD, is essentially a history of European missionary work in the world. In his writing, mission is what the Europeans (and their American descendants) did in other parts of the world. His mission history reads like an extended compendium of Western missionary biographies, and he manages

---

3. Timothy C. Tennent, *Invitation to World Missions: A Trinitarian Missiology for the Twenty-first Century* (Grand Rapids: Kregel Publications, 2010).

4. Kenneth Scott Latourette, *Christianity in a Revolutionary Age: A History of Christianity in the Nineteenth and Twentieth Centuries*, 1st ed., 5 vols. (New York: Harper, 1958).

to capture them all, including those obscure missionaries who did not survive malaria, yellow fever, or dysentery on the mission field. Latourette is not the only one who wrote mission history in this manner. Stephen Neill's *A History of Christian Missions*[5] and *Colonialism and Christian Mission*[6] are not too different. J. Herbert Kane's *A Concise History of the Christian World Mission*[7] fails to avoid these pitfalls.

As a matter of fact, almost all books on the history of Christian missions published between 1870 and 1970 told the story from a Western perspective, and were characterized by a combination of celebration of the achievements of Western missionaries in evangelizing the world and a concern that the "younger churches" that emerged around the world could not survive without their presence, especially when it became clear that European colonization of Africa and parts of Asia was coming to an end. Mission history books from that era did not pay adequate attention to the stories of the indigenous people who were being evangelized, as long as they were being converted, and this was usually held as a measure of the missionaries' effectiveness. For instance, we know a great deal about the Reverend David Clement Scott who worked in Kabula (later named Blantyre) in southern Malawi between 1881 and 1898. His incomings and outgoings in the area that later became Nyasaland (and later, Malawi) are recorded in the history books.[8] We, however, know next to nothing about his Malawian translator and partner in the ministry, my great-great grandfather, Mtimawanzako Nacho, who was the first Malawian to go to Scotland at the age of 16 (with the help of Scott, of course) for education at Stewarts Melville College in Edinburgh in 1885.[9]

On his own, Nacho was of no real historical value. After returning from Scotland, he briefly served as a translator for the British in the armed pacification of Malawi in the 1890s. He also led, almost single-handedly, the mission at Chiradzulu as an outpost of the Blantyre Mission. After this, he disappeared from the story. There are no real records of his work in Malawi

---

5. Stephen Neill and Owen Chadwick, *The Pelican History of the Church, VI: A History of Christian Missions* (New York: Penguin Books, 1986).

6. Stephen Neill, *Colonialism and Christian Missions* (New York: McGraw Hill, 1966).

7. J. Herbert Kane, *A Concise History of the Christian World Mission: A Panoramic View of Missions from Pentecost to the Present* (Grand Rapids: Baker, 1982).

8. Andrew C. Ross, *Blantyre Mission and the Making of Modern Malawi*, Kachere Monograph Series (Blantyre: CLAIM, 2018). Also earlier on, Bridglal Pachai, *Malawi: The History of the Nation* (London: Longman, 1973). In addition, Alexander Hetherwick, *The Romance of Blantyre: How Livingstone's Dream Came True* (Norwich: Lassodie Press, 1931).

9. John McCracken, *A History of Malawi, 1859–1966* (Boydell & Brewer Ltd, 2012).

as well as in Scotland. Our Malawian mission history fails to explore the significance of Nacho's work as a missionary among his own people until 1945 when he took his own life after exhausting conflicts with his colonial neighbours (the A. L. Bruce Estates, which belonged to Alexander Low Bruce, David Livingstone's son-in-law but were run by Alexander Livingstone Bruce, David Livingstone's grandson until 1948) because, of course, that is *not* mission history. Indeed, names of indigenous people often come up in mission history only when they had something to do with the missionaries – the missionaries themselves were the subject of the history.

Needless to say, mission history was, for a very long time, the story of the expansion of a European religion. What Latourette calls *The Great Century* was great for European mission in the world because it was also a great century of European migration and colonial expansion. The success of the European (and North American) missionary movements depended, to a great extent, on the wider economic migration of millions of European Christians to the rest of the world which, in itself, was largely facilitated by colonialism. By the 1950s and 1960s, Latourette and his generation began to understand the changing religious landscape of the world. They saw the promised land of world Christianity from a distance; they had some theories about how it would emerge, but when it arrived, it looked different. By the end of the twentieth century, it was evident that world Christians had rejected not only the leadership of the European colonial agent, but also that of the Western missionary. Today, two decades into the twenty-first century, the mission historian must, of necessity, critique the subject's colonial history and begin to retell the story from the perspectives of the Latin Americans, Africans, and Asians.

As world Christians became aware of their call to serve in the mission of God, it also became clear that the emergence of a non-European missionary movement was on the horizon. Before long, we saw Latin American, African, and Asian Christians form their own missionary movements. Chronicling these movements started in the 1960s. In the ensuing decades, scholars like Andrew Walls, Lamin Sanneh, Kwame Bediako, Philip Jenkins, Jehu Hanciles and others provided a fuller commentary on the emergence of world Christianity. Even though there is evidence of growth in world Christianity in the first half of the twentieth century, the explosion has really happened in the fifty years between 1970 and 2020. In 1970, more than seventy percent of Christians in the world were White and lived in the West.[10] Gina Zurlo suggests that only

---

10. Gina A. Zurlo, Todd M. Johnson and Peter F. Crossing, "World Christianity and Mission 2020: Ongoing Shift to the Global South," *International Bulletin of Mission Research* 44.1 (2020).

about thirty percent of world Christians are White and live in Europe, North America, Australia and New Zealand in 2020 – and that percentage is still slowly decreasing.[11] In other words, seventy percent of world Christians today are currently not White and do not live in the West. They are Latin American, African, and Asian and are living in their home continents. Africa alone has almost 700 million Christians, up from 9 million in 1900.

Missiologically speaking, this rapid seismic shift in the distribution of Christians in the world has serious implications. We learn from the past two hundred years of church history that missionary movements hinge upon two key factors: *revivals* (which produce both the spiritual energy that makes mission possible and the increase in people willing to serve in mission); and *migration* (which moves energized Christians from one place to another where they bring their evangelistic faith).[12] In our world today, revivals are commonplace in Latin America, Africa, and parts of Asia. Across sub-Saharan Africa, for instance, the revivals that started in the 1970s are still going on. In Kenya, Tanzania, Uganda, as well as in Rwanda and Burundi, the aftermaths of the East African Revival can still be seen today. The same is true of migration. It is the Latin Americans, Africans, and Asians who are migrating around the world in large numbers. It should not be a surprise that Latin Americans, Africans, and Asians are becoming missionaries in large numbers even though many of them are not following the Western idea of both mission (which is to go to evangelize in a far-away country) and the missionary (the person who is separated to be a missionary, and is trained and sent by a mission agency to evangelize in a foreign country). Brazilians, Nigerians, and South Koreans now make a majority of missionaries in the world – they have the revivals and are also among the most mobile peoples in the world.

The word 'missionary' itself is evolving. Most African Christians, for instance, practice what I would call the *missionaryhood* of all believers. Every Christian is often encouraged to be an evangelist wherever he or she is. Thus, every Christian is encouraged to participate in God's mission – to be a missionary – in their context. To convert any person to Christianity is also to invite them to participate in God's mission wherever God calls and places them, and Africans do this well. The many thousands of Nigerian Christians in London consider themselves as missionaries, just like the European

---

11. Zurlo, Johnson and Crossing, "World Christianity and Mission 2020."

12. For a fuller argument, see Harvey C. Kwiyani, "Non-Western Missionary Movements," in *Missional Conversations: A Dialogue between Theory and Praxis in World Mission*, ed. Cathy Ross and Colin Smith (London: SCM Press, 2018).

missionaries who served in Nigeria in the nineteenth century. I know Chinese, Kenyan, Korean, Mexican and many other non-Western Christians who are serving God in Europe and North America. All these are missionaries too. Jehu Hanciles has often stated that every migrant Christian is a potential missionary,[13] and to this I add, every migrant Christian ought to be a missionary. Thus, with the rise of world Christianity, we are also witnessing the emergence of non-Western missionary movements. This has been long time coming – and what we have seen so far is just the beginning of a huge wave of Black and brown missionaries who will criss-cross the world and change the face of Christianity. This phenomenon will be reminiscent of the old missionary movements of African and Asian Christians in the early centuries of Christianity.

The emergence of non-Western missionary movements is good news. The death of Christendom, the ensuing slow recession of Christianity in Europe, following from the fast secularization of Europeans mean that European mission agencies will find it hard to keep recruiting and sending missionaries to the world. Of course, Europe herself needs to be re-evangelized. In many European cities, Christianity has become the religion of the immigrants. In London, more than sixty percent of church attendance is of African and Afro-Caribbean Christians (and Black people form only 14 percent of the city's population). In the United States, Christianity is deeply entangled in politics on the one hand, and shaped, to a large extent, by capitalism on the other hand. Therefore, American missionaries find their audience increasingly suspicious as they try to engage a world less enthusiastic about US militarism and influence. It is, therefore, needful and hopeful that world Christians are picking up the missionary baton. One hundred years ago, a typical missionary would most definitely be White, working in some distant place in Nigeria, Argentina, India, or China. Today, people of all races from all continents engage in God's mission. A typical missionary in this decade is most likely a Nigerian woman teaching in Northern Ghana, a Korean teenager leading a choreography team in London, an Angolan pastor leading a church in Portugal, an Eritrean refugee driving taxis in Minneapolis, an African-Belgian priest in charge of a parish in India, or indeed, a Brazilian football player working in Italy. Mission is slowly becoming a truly *from-everywhere-to-everywhere* phenomenon. Of the ten countries sending the most missionaries in 2010, three were in the global South – Brazil, South Korea, and India – and the second top ten includes six from the global South, including South Africa, the Philippines, Mexico, China,

---

13. Jehu Hanciles, *Beyond Christendom: Globalization, African Migration, and the Transformation of the West* (Maryknoll: Orbis Books, 2008), 296–302.

Colombia, and Nigeria.[14] Thus, nine out of twenty countries sending the most missionaries are in the Majority World. While the US still sends the highest absolute number of missionaries (using Johnson's definition), it is now Palestine that sends the most missionaries per million church members (followed by Ireland, Malta, Samoa, and South Korea).[15] As I have argued earlier, Africa sends more Christian migrants as missionaries around the world. If we could count all Nigerian pastors in Britain as missionaries, we could easily conclude that Africa has the most missionaries in the world. This leads us to the subject of this book; the theology and praxis of the African missionary movement.

The African Missionary Movement Has Arrived

The time for the African missionary movement is just beginning. The circumstances are perfect for this. If the current trends hold, African Christianity will continue to grow at extraordinary rates for the next few decades. Already, Africa has the most Christians among all continents. Of course, Africa is home to millions of displaced peoples, largely due to political conflicts, economic instability and poor living and health conditions. Most of these are displaced to neighbouring countries. For instance, there are three million Zimbabweans currently living in South Africa. In addition, many more Africans have migrated to many countries around the world into what has come to be known as the African Diaspora. A significant percentage of these have migrated to the West, to countries like Italy, France, Britain, and the United States. The extra-continental migrations have been so extensive that Africans are arguably the most mobile and constitute the most displaced continent.

At the time when Africans are migrating in all directions, the continent is experiencing a great spiritual awakening and fast becoming a Christian stronghold. Over the past fifty years, there have been more than ten million new conversions to Christianity taking place every year around the continent. Statistical projections suggest that by 2040, more than forty percent of Christians in the world will live in Africa. This explosion of Christianity in Africa is a result of African agency. Mission in Africa has been carried out

---

14. Centre for the Study of Global Christianity, *Christianity in its Global Context, 1970–2020: Society, Religion, and Mission* (South Hamilton: Gordon Conwell Theological Seminary, 2013), 76. www.globalchristianity.org/globalcontext. The authors do not count the thousands of Nigerian, Ghanaian, or Zimbabwean Christians living in Europe and North America because, of course, they are not registered as missionaries working with a mission agency and, thus, they are not identified as missionaries.

15. *Christianity in its Global Context*, 76.

mostly by Africans. Africans have not only evangelized their neighbours, they have also brought their faith along as they migrate one country to another.

Within the continent, African Christians rarely use the term "missionary" to identify themselves. When used, it generally refers to foreign missionaries (and these will usually be White Western missionaries). However, in the Diaspora, it is common to hear Africans call themselves missionaries. They believe they are the missionaries that God has sent to evangelize the world. Even though many call themselves missionaries in the Diaspora, very few of them are trained in cross-cultural mission or registered with a mission agency. Just like the Great European migration of the nineteenth century that brought many European Christians to the rest of the world, most African migrants are simply Christians caught up in migration and bringing their Christianity with them.

Overall, Africa already has contributed greatly to this Christian resurgence in the West. The largest congregation in Europe is the Embassy of God Church in Kiev, Ukraine, which was started and is still led by Sunday Adelaja, a Nigerian. It claims to have over 30,000 members, and its impact in Ukraine so far has been tremendous.[16] The second largest church in Europe, which is the largest in the UK, is Matthew Ashimolowo's Kingsway International Christian Centre, which claims to have over 12,000 members (an overwhelming majority of whom are Africans). There are many other wider networks of African churches in the Diaspora, for instance, the Redeemed Christian Church of God (RCCG) which seeks to "plant churches within five minutes walking distance in every city and town of developing countries and within five minutes driving distance in every city and town of developed countries."[17] The UK chapter of the RCCG currently has around 1000 congregations and is still planting churches at a very fast pace. In the USA, they are one of the fastest growing immigrant denominations, claiming over three hundred branches developed in the past fifteen years.[18] Out of Ghana come the Church of Pentecost and Lighthouse Chapel, which like the RCCG, have branches in almost every major city in

---

16. The Blessed Embassy of the Kingdom of God: History. http://www.godembassy.org/en/index.php.

17. Redeemed Christian Church of God, Our Mission. http://rccg.org/our-vision-mission/. Also see Hanciles, *Beyond Christendom*, 354–57.

18. Redeemed Christian Church of God, Our Origin. https://rccgna.org/the-church/our-origin/.

the West. From Ethiopia, we have the Mekane Yesus and the Oromo churches. The Mekane Yesus church is the fastest growing Lutheran church worldwide.[19]

In any attempt to articulate a mission theology in Africa, we must attend to two issues at the very least. First, the mission of God in Africa must connect with African theology in ways that make it truly African. God's faithfulness to the African context can only be seen in God self-identifying with the African. While I appreciate some aspects of the Western theology that came with the missionaries, and continues to shape most of our Western-educated theologians and many more African Christians through the media, I am convinced that only an African-shaped theology will transform the continent. After fifty years of independence, of attempts to decolonize both the church and theology, African Christians must now be able to articulate their own theology and missiology. Today, both the ways we participate in God's mission in Africa and the theology with which we understand it must look African. We will build on what we have learned from the West, to avoid their mistakes while contextualizing what has worked well.

Second, an African mission theology must start from a different premise from that which shapes Western discourses around *missio Dei*. Indeed, this is very necessary since our understanding of mission cannot be based on the circumstances that shaped the *missio Dei* movement in Europe and North America. Africans are not reacting to anthropocentrism or a crumbling imperialism as was the case in Europe in the 1940s. Nor is it facing any of the challenges that faced the missionary movement in the mid-twentieth century, such as China expelling all Western missionaries in the early 1950s. A faithful mission theology in Africa must detach mission from empires and colonialism.

Naturally, our mission theology in Africa has to start from the premise that mission belongs to God. It is God's mission – not ours, and not the missionary's. If mission belongs to God, the missionaries – or whatever we choose to call them – join God's ongoing mission in the continent. God's missionary presence in Africa precedes that of the church and the missionaries. The church is God's primary agent for mission, but it is not the only agent. So, to understand what the mission of God will look like in Africa, we need to ask, "What is God already doing here?" The answer to this question will vary according to the context in which it is asked and may point us towards God's wider life-giving

---

19. For a more extensive discussion of the African presence in Western Christianity, see Hanciles, *Beyond Christendom*, chapter 14. Also see Frieder Ludwig and J. Kwabena Asamoah-Gyadu, *African Christian Presence in the West: New Immigrant Congregations and Transnational Networks in North America and Europe* (Trenton: Africa World Press, 2011).

work in the world outside the church. For instance, *missio Dei* in Africa will look for God's presence and work in the context of poverty, diseases, bad governance, corruption, and ethnic conflicts.

To situate *missio Dei* properly in Africa, there is need to locate God's spirit at work already in the African context. For instance, I see in the Malawian concept of *umunthu*[20] points of contact where the mission of God might actually guide the African church to a missiology that is authentically African but also properly grounded in the Scriptures. *Umunthu*, which means 'personhood,' is an expansive philosophical, theological, and spiritual concept that actually puts human beings in a bonded community of life that includes God, spirits, and nature.[21] It describes a well-rounded philosophy of life in which to be a *munthu* – to have *umunthu*, or to have a spirit (as it is sometimes translated) – is to be at peace with oneself, God, the community around (which includes ancestors), and nature. For this reason, when Malawians say someone is a *munthu* (or has *umunthu*), they mean that the person is kind, sociable, caring, self-giving, generous, communal, hospitable, spiritual, and understanding, etc. Essentially, to have *umunthu* is to be someone who humanizes others through the life-affirming acts of hospitality, inclusivity, generosity, listening – acts that share one's *umunthu* with others, thereby enlivening them. To dehumanize others is to exclude or oppress them, which only reflects one's lack of *umunthu* and is equivalent to being a beast – *chinyama* or *chirombo*.[22]

---

20. In Chichewa (Malawi's national language), not unlike many other Malawian languages, *munthu* means person. Adding the prefix *u-* to make it *umunthu* transforms it to mean 'personhood' or 'humaneness'. Generally speaking, *umunthu* in Malawi is the same as *ubuntu* in South Africa. *Umunthu* is quite foundational in African life and very significant for understanding African theology. *Umunthu* is not a Christian concept, it precedes the advent of Christianity in Africa. As such, I am not arguing that *umunthu* is the *missio Dei* but that it is a cultural platform upon which the *missio Dei* can be explained and understood in Southern Africa.

21. Harvey J. Sindima, "Community of Life: Ecological Theology in African Perspective," in *Liberating Life* (Maryknoll: Orbis, 1990). Also see John Zizioulas, Contemporary Greek Theologians, iv: *Being as Communion: Studies in Personhood and the Church* (Crestwood: St. Vladimir's Seminary Press, 1985).

22. This is said of those people who terrorize their communities such as thugs, murderers, etc. For further reading on *umunthu*, see Harvey J. Sindima, "Bondedness, Moyo and Umunthu as the Elements of Achewa Spirituality: Organizing Logic and Principle of Life," *Ultimate Reality and Meaning* 14.1 (1991). Also, Gerard Chigona, *Umunthu Theology: Path of Integral Human Liberation Rooted in Jesus of Nazareth* (Balaka: Montfort, 2002). For Sindima, *umunthu* is the vital force (*moyo*). Also see Augustine C. Musopole, *Being Human in Africa: Toward an African Christian Anthropology* (New York: Peter Lang, 1994).

Missio Dei is primarily about humanizing others. The Triune God, the Great *Munthu*,[23] came to earth to restore human beings to their full humanity – their personhood, their *umunthu*. The culmination of this humanizing begins with regeneration whereby the Spirit (breath, Heb. *ruach* and Gk. *pneuma*) of God brings human spirits to life (Gen 2:7). Thus, the real *munthu* begins with salvation; the unregenerate *munthu* is only a shadow of the *munthu* that is made possible through Christ. The apostle Paul testified to this when he said, "we were once dead in our sins . . . but God made us alive together with Christ" (Eph 2:1–7, my paraphrase). Peter added that "you were once not a people, but now you are the people of God" (1 Pet 2:10). When the everyday acts of *umunthu* are soaked with prayers and faith, they become anointed avenues through which God's Spirit draws people to God's humanizing love. This is exactly what *missio Dei* is about. This humanizing principle of *missio Dei* rightly extends the concept of salvation in Africa to include many ways in which life and personhood is shared. Many scholars have shown how salvation in Africa is more than the saving of the soul.[24] Salvation must be holistic. The Greek word *sozo* which is translated "salvation," includes healing, deliverance, blessing, empowerment, liberation, feeding, clothing, etc.[25] All these are humanizing acts through which people can have the abundant life that Christ gave to humankind. In all these acts, plus many others, Christian witness is made and the gospel is shared, even sometimes without proclamation.

The implications of this interpretation of *missio Dei* are many and huge. For instance, by suggesting the possibility – or likelihood – of God's mission manifesting itself in *umunthu*, mission can be articulated in theocentric terms while also celebrating the priesthood of all believers. Every Christian is a missionary and God can use them anywhere, not just in church. It becomes possible to speak about holistic mission that pays attention to the whole human being, not just the person's soul. Such *missio Dei* is rooted in healthy, loving and humanizing relationships between Christians and the community in which they live and the nature that is their home. In this sense, *missio Dei* also leads to a Christian identification with the poor and the marginalized. Christian shepherds living by *umunthu* will be generous people who take good care of

---

23. See James H. O. Kombo, *The Doctrine of God in African Christian Thought: The Holy Trinity, Theological Hermeneutics and the African Intellectual Culture* (Boston: Brill, 2007).

24. See J. Kwabena Asamoah-Gyadu, *African Charismatics: Current Developments within Independent Indigenous Pentecostalism in Ghana* (Boston: Brill, 2005).

25. Strong's Concordance: Greek 4982 *sōzō* (from *sōs*, "safe, rescued") – properly, deliver out of danger and into safety; used principally of God rescuing believers from the penalty and power of sin – and into his provisions (safety).

their flock (including their lost sheep and not only the tithing members of their churches). Extortion for the sake of enriching themselves is thievery and a sign of lacking *umunthu*. In addition, *missio Dei* understood through *umunthu* encourages good stewardship of God's creation; for to have *umunthu* is to be in harmony with God, the spirits, the community, and nature. The desertification of the land and the exploitation of the lakes are contrary to *umunthu*, and therefore also contrary to *missio Dei*.

Conclusion

Missio Dei is a rather complex concept. In its basic sense, it says mission belongs to God and not to the church. This is not sufficient to help Christians understand how to carry mission out, especially in contexts where there is no doubt that mission is God's. To contextualize it in Africa, there is need to find "points" in African life where God is already at work. One such point of contact is the Malawian concept of *umunthu*. Through the Spirit of God, Christians have inherited God's personhood and therefore have the real *umunthu*. Through this, they ought to serve God to share it with the world and glorify God's Son. If we do well, our mission history for the century will look different from what we have had for the past two centuries.

2

Mission in Prophetic Dialogue

Exploring the Ethos of Transformative Encounters in Africa

J. N. J. (Klippies) Kritzinger

The term "prophetic dialogue" was made popular in missiological circles by Bevans and Schroeder.[1] It provides a helpful way of expressing the ethos of Christian mission, since it signals a creative tension between listening and speaking, identification and transformation, which is essential to credible mission.[2] This dialectical relationship between self-emptying presence and courageous witness has been expressed by other missiologists as an ethos of "bold humility"[3] or "disturbing presence,"[4] both of which are remarkably similar to "prophetic dialogue."

---

1. This is a shortened version of a paper presented to the American Society for Missiology on 15th June 2012. The original version was published as "Mission in Prophetic Dialogue," *Missiology* 41.1 (January 2013): 35–49. A longer version was later published as "Mission IN prophetic dialogue: Exploring the ethos of mission encounters in Africa," *Acta Missiologiae* 6 (2018): 81–100. It is published here with the permission of both *Missiology* and *Acta Missiologiae*.

2. Stephen Bevans and Roger Schroeder, *Constants in Context: A Theology of Mission for Today* (Maryknoll: Orbis, 2004) and *Prophetic Dialogue: Reflections on Mission Today* (Maryknoll: Orbis, 2011).

3. David J. Bosch, *Transforming Mission: Paradigm Shifts in Theology of Mission* (Maryknoll: Orbis Books, 1991), 489.

4. Anthony J. Gittins, *A Presence that Disturbs. A Call to Radical Discipleship* (Liguori: Liguori/Triumph, 2002).

Missiological Framework

To attain an adequate understanding of a particular mission praxis it is necessary to situate the ethos that characterizes it within a broader interpretive framework. To achieve a holistic understanding of mission praxis, one needs to explore the underlying ontology and epistemology as well as the relationship between theology and practice, as well as the nature of the transformative encounters taking place ("encounterology").[5]

The ethos of mission refers to the heart of the praxis, its inner logic, character or value system, which could also be called its axiology. It traces the inner "workings" that motivate, characterize and sustain a particular praxis. This essay shows how "prophetic dialogue" can be used as an axiological lens to explore transformative encounters in Africa.

The essay allows the meaning of prophetic dialogue to emerge by exploring two case studies. I therefore give only a working definition now, by saying that *dialogue* means embracing, listening and identifying, whereas *prophetic* means communication that unmasks evil while imagining hopeful alternatives. The case studies deal with mission encounters from two different regions of Africa, namely Burundi and South Africa. Since they took place in highly charged political situations, they are not representative of all mission encounters taking place across Africa. The essay does not claim to be representative; it only seeks to show that "prophetic dialogue" is a useful interpretive lens to explore the ethos of mission encounters in Africa.

Mission in Prophetic Dialogue – Exploring Two Encounters
Encounter 1: Maggy Barankitse (Burundi)
The context of the encounter

Marguerite (Maggy) Barankitse is a member of the Catholic Church in Burundi who played an important role in trying to heal that deeply broken society. Emmanuel Katongole explains how her ministry of reconciliation started during the civil war in October 1993, after witnessing the massacre of seventy-two people by Tutsi assailants.[6] Her seven adopted children – four

---

5. The full missiological framework that informs my approach is explained in the two publications in n.1 and in "A Question of Mission – a Mission of Questions," *Missionalia* 30.1 (2002): 144–73 and "Faith to Faith: Missiology as Encounterology," *Verbum et Ecclesia* 29.3 (2008): 764–90.

6. Emmanuel Katongole, *The Sacrifice of Africa: A Political Theology for Africa*, The Eerdmans Ekklesia Series (Grand Rapids: Eerdmans, 2011), 171.

Hutus and three Tutsis – miraculously survived the massacre, and she speaks of that experience as follows:

> As soon as I knew that my children had survived, I felt a strong will to live. I could think of one thing and only one thing: taking care of them; raising them beyond this hatred and the bitterness that I came to see in their eyes.[7]

As a result of that tragic event, Maggy committed herself to care for orphans as a religious calling, within a larger vision of raising children "beyond this hatred and bitterness." She established a centre for orphans called Maison Shalom (House of Peace) and embarked on a series of projects to protect, empower and reconcile Hutu and Tutsi children in the midst of ethnic hatred. She formulated her mission as follows:

> I wanted to break the cycle of hatred, to interrupt the chain of vengeance that was silently transmitting itself from generation to generation. . . . We need to uproot the sprout from which the hatred grew and festered. . . . We need to create a system in which the hatred, however ferocious, no longer exists. We need to invent a way of living without hate.[8]

Nurtured by a deep eucharistic spirituality, Maggy developed a "politics of love" with a strong emphasis on forgiveness, but she acknowledged that she had learnt most of that from the children and their amazing ability to forgive.[9]

The encounter

A significant encounter, between Maggy and a child soldier named Geraldo, is described as follows by Katongole:

> He stopped Maggy at a road block and ordered her out of her car, and ordered her to kneel down. Maggy refused, saying that she only knelt down before God. Then she noticed that the boy had a rosary around his neck. Maggy added, "But I will kneel down to pray if you kneel down with me." The boy hesitated. Maggy then asked him: "Why do you carry a gun and a rosary? The two you know do not go well together?" Then Maggy made the boy an offer: "If you give the gun back and come with me, I will give

---

7. Katongole, *Sacrifice of Africa*, 171.
8. Katongole, *Sacrifice of Africa*, 175.
9. Katongole, *Sacrifice of Africa*, 185.

you something better to do." The boy abandoned his weapon. He came with Maggy and is now Maggy's driver.[10]

There are many aspects of this dramatic event that could be analysed, but I limit myself to using prophetic dialogue as a lens to interpret the mission ethos expressed here.

Dialogue as embrace

In what sense was this encounter dialogical? It would have remained a monologue had Maggy not taken the initiative very early on. From a position of physical weakness she managed to exert a moral and spiritual power that changed the encounter into a dialogue.

What happened when she saw the rosary around his neck? She latched onto that scrap of evidence that he could be someone different. She saw the gun and the rosary – and opted to relate to him on the basis of the rosary. Since he was clearly an enemy, she was going to love him *as an enemy*, which meant loving him into becoming his better (rosary) self. The basis of all dialogue is a commitment to love, as Lochhead has pointed out: "To love one's neighbour as oneself is to be in a dialogical relationship with one's neighbour,"[11] and that commitment flows from the self-giving, kenotic love of Christ, revealed in openness and vulnerability.

And then Maggy suggested that if anybody was going to kneel, it was going to be both of them. She thereby invited him into a common act of faith, however distorted his Christianity had become by ethnic hatred and military power. She connected with him at a deep human level, saying Yes to him as a person, and on the basis of that affirmation of his humanity, she said No to his oppressive instructions. Using the terminology of Miroslav Volf's four step "drama of embrace,"[12] she opened her arms – and waited. When he had put down his gun and returned to her with empty hands, they could embrace. And then she opened her arms to let him go again, so that he could make his own contribution to God's mission of reconciliation in Burundi.

Maggy was deeply dialogical, since dialogue is not one activity among other activities, but "a quality that needs to pervade all our conversations and

---

10. Katongole, *Sacrifice of Africa*, 189f.

11. David Lochhead, *The Dialogical Imperative: A Christian Reflection on Interfaith Encounter* (Maryknoll: Orbis Books, 1988), 80.

12. Miroslav Volf, *Exclusion and Embrace: A Theological Exploration of Identity, Otherness, and Reconciliation* (Nashville: Abingdon, 1996), 140–47.

all our relationships."[13] Dialogue does not become such a way of life unless it is nurtured by a deep spirituality: "It is prayer that keeps me going. The Eucharist is my source of true courage."[14] Without immersing ourselves in the *yes* that God has spoken and embodied to us in Christ, we will not be able to sustain a dialogical, embracing *yes* to the people around us, particularly those filled with hatred and revenge.

Christian mission is in the first place an affirmation of humanity, saying *yes* to people in their concrete human existence. Much of the shame of mission in the modern era flows from the fact that Christian missionaries did not consistently say *yes* to people and cultures – in a listening, dialogical posture – before daring to say *no* to some beliefs and traditions – from a prophetic or "elenctic" posture that invites people to change.

Prophecy as unmasking and imagining
The prophetic dimension of Maggy's praxis in this encounter can perhaps best be formulated as the power of weakness to unmask the weakness of power. When Geraldo commanded her to kneel, she took the risk of challenging his authority, defying his arrogant claim to power. She said *no* to the power abuse of a young soldier on the basis of the *yes* to life that she lived every day. And because she knew that he was himself a victim of the violence and hatred engulfing their country, she committed herself to love him out of the clutches of that violence.

We see in this encounter that prophecy is more than saying *no*; it is an unmasking of power and a rejection of injustice for the sake of the humanity of everyone involved in the encounter. It is the unmasking of the contradictions in people's lives ("Why do you carry a gun and a rosary?") in order to bring healing and wholeness. Prophecy is also the courageous imagination of a vulnerable woman that a soldier could actually put down his gun and walk away from it into a new life. Prophecy is the hope-giving imagination that a different world is possible – and that it can begin right here, right now.

An important dimension in all this is the role of culture. I said earlier that Maggy took over the initiative early in the encounter. At the end of the encounter she was completely in charge, acting like a mother taking a lost son home. The authority with which she did that came from their shared cultural assumption that it takes a village to raise a child and that every child is every adult's responsibility. By becoming a soldier the young man Geraldo

---
13. Lochhead, *Dialogical Imperative*, 76.
14. Katongole, *Sacrifice of Africa*, 185.

had broken that positive cultural bond, but in this encounter it was being restored. Not every aspect of culture is healthy, but if we cannot mobilize every healthy aspect of culture in the struggle against violence and injustice, we have no hope of succeeding.

Prophetic dialogue as ethos

The dialogical and prophetic dimensions of a mission ethos are closely linked, as this encounter shows. The dialogical aspect is the careful observation and close listening to find an opening – a piece of common ground or point of contact – for making a prophetic, transformative move. In intentionally transformative praxis we encounter people who are involved in their own forms of praxis, so we open ourselves to their lives and try to resonate with their rhythms, hoping to get close enough that they may see, hear and feel something of the melody of the gospel in and through us, and begin to resonate with us – and with the music that sustains and directs us. It was her dialogical, incarnational lifestyle of careful attention, nurtured by a kenotic eucharistic spirituality, that enabled Maggy to notice the rosary – and to seize on it as a prophetic opportunity.

Another feature of an ethos of prophetic dialogue is the question of timing. In one sense prophecy is all about timing; about finding the right word or the clearest metaphor for the present moment. Biblical scholars have identified this as a key difference between true and false prophecy in the Hebrew Bible.[15] Mission praxis in service of the reign of God is living dialogically, in the moment, fully aware of every human being in the encounter, looking for opportunities to do good, to share hope, to confront evil. Only by being dialogically receptive, on the constant lookout for *kairos* moments, can one act prophetically as an agent of transformation. Similarly, only by being prophetically committed, fundamentally opposed to every form of sin – ethnic hatred, abuse of children, wanton violence, addiction to power, selfishness and greed – can one see and listen dialogically as an agent of transformation. Such a dialogical-prophetic ethos expresses a love that enables one to notice distortions of humanity and to grasp prophetic opportunities. It involves saying and living *yes* (dialogue) towards everyone controlled by sin and suffering, while saying and living *no* (prophecy) to whatever is controlling them and

---

15. See J. Davidson, "Orthodoxy and the prophetic word," in *Prophecy in the Hebrew Bible: Selected studies from Vetus Testamentum*, compiled by David E. Orton (Leiden: Brill, 2000), 9f; Walter Brueggemann, *Like Fire in the Bones: Listening for the Prophetic Word in Jeremiah* (Minneapolis: Fortress Press, 2006), 7.

making them less than fully human, so that a jointly imagined alternative may emerge – in which all the participants are transformed.

Mutual transformation

A dialogical-prophetic ethos involves mutual transformation towards the reign of God, not a one-way process where "missionaries" are "converting" others. So we also need to ask: how was Maggy changed by this encounter? She probably surprised even herself by the way she responded. The incident must have brought her into a deeper, closer relationship with God, grateful for the wisdom and courage that the Spirit had given her in that decisive moment. But there is more. Why would she continue exposing herself to unnecessary danger at road blocks if she could have a young ex-soldier driving her around? Love had taught her to be an inventor and innovator,[16] so she imagined a new role for him and he re-imagined himself into that role.

Another encounter

To limit a discussion of Maggy Barankitse's ministry to one dramatic encounter is to create a distorted impression. It falls into the trap of what some ethicists call a "decisionist" approach. Wells sketches an alternative: "Christian ethics is not about helping anyone act Christianly in a crisis, but about helping Christians embody their faith in the practices of discipleship all the time."[17] In other words, the emphasis should be on the character and enduring virtues of being a Christian community, which is – by its very nature – part of God's mission, not primarily on making good decisions in extreme situations. Maggy Barankitse's mission in Burundi should therefore not be reduced to a few dramatic events, like the one discussed above. The heart of her work was "the slow, painful work of repairing shattered lives and communities rent by hatred and violence."[18] She did this by setting up projects of education, social housing, farming, business development, hospitals, and entertainment. This patient process of "stitching back together" children's lives and doing "social repair" of communities is well captured by another encounter: Maggy's engagement with a five-year-old boy called Bosco, who lost his sight when his whole family was slaughtered before his eyes. Katongole describes how he was brought to

---

16. Katongole, *Sacrifice of Africa*, 178.

17. Sam Wells, *Improvisation: The Drama of Christian Ethics* (London: SPCK Publishing, 2004), 15.

18. Emmanuel Katongole, *Born from Lament: The Theology and Politics of Hope in Africa* (Grand Rapids: Eerdmans, 2017), 239.

Maggy but that no medical treatment could bring back his sight. However, he partially recovered his sight when, with Maggy's help, he started pursuing his dream of being a musician, becoming eventually one of the most popular musicians in Burundi.[19] His songs of lament, healing and reconciliation clearly embody the ethos of prophetic dialogue, as described by a fellow Burundian:

> They sing about the beauty of the country, but they go beyond that; not only to see what is there, but of something better. . . . It is more of a prophetic message . . . pointing out what is wrong (and thus causing a lot of trouble for the government), but it's also about what the country can become.[20]

It is evident that Maggy succeeded in drawing many young people into the ethos of her ministry and inspired them to pursue their own prophetic-dialogical ministries of reconciliation. However, the ugly reality of Burundian politics is that Maggy's outspoken opposition to President Pierre Nkururunziza's campaign for a third term forced her to flee into exile, after which the government shut down Maison Shalom programmes, closed their bank accounts and confiscated all the assets.[21] What made this tragedy even worse was that a prophetic musician like Bosco, a product of the Maison Shalom programmes, was targeted and killed in the process. It reveals the painful truth that a prophetic-dialogical ministry which works for reconciliation-with-justice is a dangerous option; it is not concerned in the first place with success, but with faithfulness and sometimes even with martyrdom.[22]

Encounter 2: Desmond Tutu (South Africa)

The second encounter took place in South Africa in the late 1970s and also concerns the role of Christians in a situation of violence and conflict. The fact that it took place more than forty years ago does not detract from its value as an example of mission done in prophetic dialogue.

---

19. Katongole, *Born from Lament*, 240.
20. Katongole, *Born from Lament*, 241.
21. Katongole, *Born from Lament*, 242.
22. Katongole includes an insightful chapter about martyrdom in his book (Katongole, *Born from Lament*, 243–59).

The context of the encounter

It is impossible for a South African to speak on the eve of 16 June about prophetic dialogue without reflecting on the struggle against racism.[23] 16 June is Youth Day in South Africa, a public holiday to commemorate the Soweto uprising of school children in 1976, which became a defining moment in South African history. In the aftermath of that uprising both the protest against apartheid and its repression escalated, leading to much further bloodshed. Another defining moment came the following year, when Steve Biko died in police detention on 13 September 1977. My second encounter takes us back to those troubled times, to the sermon preached at Biko's funeral on 25 September 1977 by Desmond Tutu, who was then the Anglican bishop of Lesotho.

The Victoria Sport Stadium in King William's Town in the Eastern Cape was packed with more than 15,000 mourners from all over South Africa who had come to bury Bantu Steve Biko, one of the founders of the Black Consciousness movement. There was intense anger in the audience, directed at the apartheid system for the murder of one of South Africa's most promising young leaders. Their attitude was defiant, exacerbated by the fact that hundreds of buses, taxis and motor vehicles had been stopped by security police and prevented from travelling to the funeral. There was also an atmosphere of deep dignity and pride when the large crowd sang the unofficial national anthem, *Nkosi sikelel' iAfrika (God bless Africa)* with raised fists. Speaker after speaker extolled Biko's courage, intellect and strong personality. And then a diminutive figure got up to preach a sermon.[24]

Opening identification

> When we heard the news "Steve Biko is dead" we were struck numb with disbelief. No, it can't be true! No, it must be a horrible nightmare and we will awake and find that really it is different – that Steve is alive even if it be in detention. But no, dear friends, he is dead and we are still numb with grief and groan with anguish "Oh God, where are you? Oh God, do you really care – how can you let this happen to us?"[25]

---

23. As mentioned already, this paper was first presented to the annual meeting of the American Society for Missiology (ASM) on 15th June 2012.

24. It is impossible to do justice to the whole sermon; I have selected a few sections from it that are pertinent to the ethos of prophetic dialogue. For the entire sermon, see Desmond Tutu, *Hope and Suffering: Sermons and Speeches* (Braamfontein: Skotaville, 1984), 12–16.

25. Tutu, *Hope and Suffering*, 12.

With these opening words, Desmond Tutu set the tone for his sermon. His opening words reveal a dialogical, embracing starting point. He identified with the mourning multitude by using "we," articulating the stunned disbelief of the whole Black community and affirming their anger and impatience with injustice. He had listened carefully to what people around him were saying about Biko's death and articulated their shared grief. He embraced the mourners around him as a fellow mourner. His praxis resonated with theirs, as he expressed his own sense of loss, establishing common ground with his audience from the start.

Appeal to White South Africans

A little later in the sermon, Tutu addressed the South African White community:

> I want again to appeal with all the eloquence that I can muster, to our White fellow citizens and our White fellow Christians. We, who today still advocate peaceful change and still talk about reconciliation and justice, are in grave danger. The danger is that our credibility is being seriously eroded; for whilst we speak of peace and non-violence we have the quite inexplicable action of the authorities in stopping those coming to mourn at Steve's funeral, an action that is most provocative. Why? . . . I want to say with all the circumspection and deep sense of responsibility that I can muster, that people can take only so much. As they say in English "Even the worm will turn." I have seen too much violence in other parts of the world to talk glibly about it, but I do want to issue a serious warning, a warning I am distressed to have to make.[26]

How did Tutu's rhetorical praxis interact with the praxis of White South Africans? He made an impassioned appeal to them to turn from the way of oppression and exclusion. On what basis did he make that appeal? Did he see a rosary, in addition to the gun? He addressed them as "White fellow citizens," affirming that all South Africans belonged to the same state and had to negotiate with one another to solve their problems. He also affirmed that White Christians were fellow believers, even though most of them did not exhibit neighbourly love towards the Black majority and even justified their racism on Christian grounds. For Tutu, White South Africans had a rosary

---

26. Tutu, *Hope and Suffering*, 14.

around their neck, and he would keep on appealing to that fact, however long it would take for them to put down the gun:

> When people are desperate then they will use desperate methods. Please, please, for God's sake listen to us whilst there is just a possibility of reasonably peaceful change. Nothing, not even the most sophisticated weapon, not even the most brutally efficient police, no, just nothing will stop people once they are determined to achieve their freedom and their right to humanness. For God's sake let us move away from the edge of the precipice. We may, all of us, Black and White, crash headlong to destruction. Let us avoid the alternative too ghastly to contemplate. Oh God, help us![27]

In this paragraph, Tutu identified himself as one of the people "who today still advocate peaceful change and still talk about reconciliation and justice." His praxis was aimed at reconciliation and justice. And he invited White South Africans to resonate with that, to transform their praxis to resonate with his. The ominous tone of this paragraph, suggesting an impending bloodbath, was not a rhetorical flourish to instill fear in Whites. He sensed an escalation of violence, and as an agent of peace, reconciliation and justice, he was trying his best to prevent it. At the same time he was inviting Black mourners to be (or remain, or become) part of the "we" who "still advocate peaceful change and still talk about reconciliation and justice." He acknowledged that the credibility of that group was wearing thin, but as an agent of reconciliation he stood between the rapidly polarizing factions, trying to achieve resonance with both.

Encouragement for the mourners

Tutu ended his sermon the way he began, by directly addressing the mourners in front of him. He started with a lament but ended with a word of hope:

> Despite all that points to the contrary, God cares. He cares about right and wrong. He cares about oppression and injustice. He cares about bulldozers and detentions without trial. And so we give thanks paradoxically for Steve and for his life and his death. Because you see, Steve started something that is quite unstoppable. The powers of injustice, of oppression, of exploitation, have done their worst and they have lost. They have lost because they are immoral and wrong and our God, the God of the Exodus, the liberator God is a God of justice and liberation and goodness. Our

---

27. Tutu, *Hope and Suffering*, 15.

> cause, the cause of justice and liberation must triumph because it is moral and just and right. Many who support the present unjust system in this country, know in their hearts that they are upholding a system that is evil and unjust and oppressive, and which is utterly abhorrent and displeasing to God. There is no doubt whatsoever that freedom is coming.[28]

This was a daring prophetic statement, in the face of the military might of the South African Defence Force and the security police, who had killed Steve Biko, and would ban seventeen political organizations and numerous individuals just a month later. Tutu dared to express his faith in a God of justice, liberation and goodness, who is moved by the suffering of the people and who will not allow that suffering to go on forever:

> The darkest hour, they say, is before the dawn. We are experiencing the birth pangs of a new South Africa, a free South Africa, where all of us, Black and White together, will walk tall, where all of us, Black and White together, will hold hands as we stride forth on the Freedom March to usher in the new South Africa where people will matter because they are human beings made in the image of God. We thank and praise God for giving us such a magnificent gift in Steve Biko and for his sake and for the sake of ourselves, Black and White together, for the sake of our children, Black and White together, let us dedicate ourselves anew to the struggle for the liberation of our beloved land, South Africa. Let us all, Black and White together, not be filled with despondency and despair. Let us Blacks not be filled with hatred and bitterness. For all of us, Black and White together, shall overcome, nay, indeed have already overcome.[29]

Only a prophet would risk saying such words at a highly charged political funeral of a Black political activist murdered by an oppressive White-dominated government. It is astoundingly inclusive and reconciliatory in scope: "Black and White together" is the refrain that rings out no less than six times in the paragraph, as a passionate appeal to the crowd of Black mourners not to be filled with hatred and bitterness, but to trust the promises of the God of justice, liberation and goodness by working for the realization of those goals through non-violent means, with the assurance of victory in their hearts and minds.

---

28. Tutu, *Hope and Suffering*, 15.
29. Tutu, *Hope and Suffering*, 15.

Mission in Prophetic Dialogue – Some Conclusions
Dialogue as Embrace

In both these encounters the Christian witnesses were dialogical; they embodied an ethos of affirmation and embrace. They carried out mission "in vulnerability, in humility . . . being open to be evangelized" by those whom they were evangelizing.[30] They expressed deep, even passionate, identification with the plight of the people around them. They exhibited what Jon Sobrino has called "orthopathy,"[31] a third dimension of Christian praxis in addition to orthodoxy and orthopraxis. That is what builds mutual trust, which is essential to any transformative encounter.[32]

Prophecy as Unmasking and Imagining

In both encounters, the Christian actors bore courageous, non-arrogant prophetic witness. Like the prophet Ezekiel of old, who immersed himself in the suffering of the exile community by sitting in stunned silence among them for seven days (Ezekiel 3:16), Maggy Barankitse and Desmond Tutu identified with the pain and loss of their communities. From that position of identification they strove to discern the will of God for their particular place and time, to read the signs of the times; to sense what was going on behind the scenes and under the surface. Being prophetic is a way of seeing, noticing what many others do not. Prophetic praxis begins with noticing strangers and outsiders, the marginalized and excluded, those trapped in various forms of addiction, greed and selfishness, those who do not accept the liberating lordship of Jesus Christ. Because prophetic praxis sees the heart breaking brutality of the world in the light of Christ, in the light of God's coming reign, it unmasks injustice and oppression. It expresses the *no* of God to evil, while imaginatively mediating the power of Christ's resurrection within that situation of wrong.

Seeing with prophetic imagination is to discern the will of God in everyday realities. The prophetic Spirit enabled Maggy to see the rosary around Geraldo's neck and in a split second to imagine him differently. Prophetic Christian praxis uses its imagination to express the will of God for society in compelling and mobilizing metaphors, thus providing bridges across which people can

---

30. Bevans and Schroeder, *Constants in Context*, 22.

31. Jon Sobrino, *Christ the Liberator: A View from the Victims* (Maryknoll: Orbis, 2001), 209f.

32. Bevans and Schroeder, *Constants in Context*, 31.

walk into new life. It is seeing the new reality already (in hope), as Desmond Tutu did in his sermon and Martin Luther King Jr in his "I have a dream" speech.[33] It is to believe that a more just and human world is possible, to imagine the shape of that future, and to show the way towards it.

That is why prophetic praxis is also about establishing communities of hope that anticipate the envisioned future. It is not about lone voices "crying in the wilderness." Every prophet is sustained by a support network, an "alternative community" that already embodies the anticipated future promised by God.[34] Prophetic praxis, as expressed in the lives of these two faithful witnesses, is inherently communal and public. It is the courage to call publicly on people to turn away from their self-centred, loveless and violent ways, towards the way of God. It includes the willingness to take risks and suffer for your convictions, without being intimidated by opponents or enemies. Prophecy does not show the way *out* of problems, but the way *in*: "In our time we may be unable to see the way out of the human problems of the world. But the way in is clearly evident. It is to invest our lives in the service of those problems as they bear upon people."[35]

Conclusion

To conclude the essay, three self-critical questions. First, could our describing the ethos of mission as "prophetic dialogue" lead us to emphasize doing at the cost of being, thus obscuring the mission of God – into which we are drawn by grace – thereby turning witnesses into impatient activists who need to "change the world?" That would make it a typically modernist enterprise. To avoid that, we need to emphasize that an ethos of prophetic dialogue describes not only our encounters with others, but primarily our ongoing encounter with the Other, who calls and sends us. In this regard Maggy Barankitse is a role model. Katongole explains how a month long withdrawal to a monastery in May 1996 to mourn a massacre of 400 Tutsi refugees became a turning point in her ministry.[36] She said that she then "began to understand God on the cross" and changed her approach from one of being "angry, tense and determined to

---

33. Martin Luther King, "I have a Dream," March on Washington, Washington, 28 August 1963. Numerous versions available online.

34. See the chapter on "The alternative community of Moses" in Walter Brueggemann's *The Prophetic Imagination* (Minneapolis: Fortress Press, 1978), 11–27.

35. Kenneth Cragg, *The Call of the Minaret* (New York: Oxford University Press, 1956), 214.

36. For this and the quotations that follow, see Katongole, *Born from Lament*, 231-2.

fight" into one driven by "the loving and forgiving God who invites us into the embrace of love as our true identity and calling." She described it as follows: "It is like a weight was taken off my back. God is God . . . I wanted to be a little instrument to love, to denounce, to tell the truth, but not to accuse, and not to lose tenderness." Like her, we all need to integrate being and doing, hurrying for God and waiting on God, to become authentic and attractive alternative communities which, by their very existence, present a prophetic challenge to the dominant values of a society.[37]

Second, is it adequate to describe the praxis of the witnesses in these two case studies as *prophetic* dialogue? Don't we need to add notions like "priestly compassion" and "royal dignity" to grasp what happened in these encounters? Do we risk losing the wholeness (integrity) of mission when we emphasize its contestational (or confrontational) dimension at the expense of both tenderness and dignity, by downplaying the priestly and royal dimensions in the ethos of mission?

Finally, does my choice of case studies represent a complete distortion of Christian mission in Africa, by selecting encounters laden with such deep ethnic and racial conflict? Perhaps it does. But this essay does not claim to present a complete picture of mission in Africa. By looking at two rather dramatic and unusual encounters, it does little more than experiment with the notion of "prophetic dialogue" as an interpretive lens for examining the ethos of Christian mission in Africa. It also responds to the wish expressed by Mugambi:

> If . . . Christianity helps Africans to understand the natural, social, economic and political forces that continue to dehumanize them, and if it facilitates their total liberation, then the Christian missionary enterprize of the future will be an improvement on the failures of the past.[38]

---

37. See the reflection on a prophetic "alternative community" from an African woman's perspective by A. Nasimiyu-Wasike, "Prophetic Mission of the Church: The Voices of African Women," in *Mission in African Christianity: Critical Essays in Missiology*, ed. A. Nasimiyu-Wasike and D. W. Waruta (Nairobi: Uzima Press, 1993), 179–99.

38. J. N. K. Mugambi, "Christian mission in the context of urbanization and industrialization in Africa," in *Mission in African Christianity. Critical Essays in Missiology*, ed. A. Nasimiyu-Wasike and D. W. Waruta (Nairobi: Uzima Press, 1993), 67–88.

3

Mission as New Catholicity, Afro-Westernization and Globalization

Jean Luc Enyegue, SJ

How does one describe the "New Mission" within the Roman Catholic Church in the twenty-first century? For a while, in the twentieth century, and speaking of mission in Europe, the Western world primarily saw it as a re-Christianization.[1] Since the pontificate of John Paul II, it has been called New Evangelization.[2] From the African perspective and based on recent data, the new mission within Roman Catholicism is known as *inculturation*.[3] This, I believe, is primarily a continuing *Africanization* of Christianity and mission among African peoples. For this Africanization project to be effective and remain mission-focused, it has to also be an Afro-Westernization and Afro-globalization.

---

1. H. Godin and Y. Daniel, *La France, pays de mission*? (Paris: Les Editions de l'Abeille, 1943); Paul Coulon, "De la France, pays de missionnaires à la France, pays de mission," *Histoire et Missions Chrétiennes* 9 (March 2009): 3–8.

2. Agapit J. Mroso, *The Church in Africa and the New Evangelization: A Theologico-Pastoral Study of the Orientation of John Paul II* (Roma: PUG, 1995).

3. A 2015 report from Georgetown University Center for Applied Research in the Apostolate (CARA) shows that Roman Catholicism has grown in Africa 257% from 1980, while it has decreased about 57% in the global North. The report confirms a trend within Christianity worldwide, by David Barrett. On data, see: Thomas P. Gaunt, ed., "Global Catholicism: Trends and Forecasts" (The CARA Report, June 1, 2015); Thomas P. Gaunt, "Jesuit Shift From Developed to Developing World," *CARA* 16.4 (Sping 2011); David B. Barrett, ed., *World Christian Encyclopedia: A Comparative Survey of Churches and Religions in the Modern World, AD 1900–2000* (Nairobi: Oxford University Press, 1982).

A recent book by Belgian Jesuit Léon de Saint Moulin, *Histoire des Jésuites en Afrique*, claims to narrate the history of the Jesuits in Africa not in missionary terms but, instead, "in the way Africans themselves would."[4] As he describes the distinctive feature of African Christianity in the 1970s, de Saint Moulin points primarily to Africanization, a concept that first emerged in African historiography in theological circles around the same period. A year after his *African Religion and Philosophy*,[5] John Mbiti affirmed, "Christianity has Christianized Africa, but [Africa] has not yet Africanized Christianity."[6] To Mbiti, a serious dialogue between Christianity and African religions was needed in order to avoid seeing African Christianity becoming a mere and superficial copy of Western Christianity.[7] Mbiti, in a sense, dismissed as not "really" African what had happened, up to the 1970s, in the history of Christianity in Africa. One might conclude that, within that framework, Westernization and Africanization were necessarily antithetical.

Mbiti's language was not unique to African historians or theologians, especially those who studied mission and colonialism. For if colonialism is contrary to Christian values, "colonial mission" is an oxymoron. For example, when historians like Dolores García Cantús[8] and Miquel Vilaró i Güel[9] frame the Jesuit mission in Fernando Poo (1857–1872) as a "colonial mission,"[10] they simultaneously confirm concerns raised by anthropologists like John and Jean Comaroff about the collusion between Christianity and colonization in Africa.[11]

---

4. Léon de Saint Moulin, *Histoire des Jésuites en Afrique: Du XIe siècle à nos jours* (Namur: Éd. Jésuites, 2016).

5. S. John Mbiti, *African Religions and Philosophy* (New York: Doubleday & Company, 1969).

6. S. John Mbiti, "Christianity and Traditional Religion in Africa," *International Review of Mission* 59 (1970): 430.

7. S. John Mbiti, *New Testament Eschatology in an African Background* (London: Oxford University Press, 1971), 189.

8. Dolores Garcías Cantús, *Fernando Poo: Una aventura colonial española en la África Occidental: 1778–1900* (Barcelona: Ceibas, 2006).

9. Miquel Vilaró i Güell, *El legado de los Jesuitas en Guinea* (Barcelona: Ceibas, 2010).

10. Jean Luc Enyegue, "The Jesuits in Fernando Po (1858–1872): An Incomplete Mission," in *Jesuits' Survival and Restoration* (Leiden: Koninklijke Brill, 2015), 466–86.

11. Jean and John Comaroff, "Christianity and Colonialism in South Africa," *American Ethnologist* 13.1 (February 1986): 1–22; Jean and John Comaroff, *Of Revelation and Revolution: Christianity, Colonialism, and Consciousness in South Africa*, vol. 1 (Chicago: The University of Chicago Press, 1991); Jean and John Comaroff, *Of Revelation and Revolution: The Dialectics of Modernity on a South African Frontier*, vol. 2 (Chicago: The University of Chicago Press, 1997).

They also affirm questions raised by leading West African Jesuits in the 1970s,[12] and their most recent critiques.[13]

However, analyzing the reality of missions at a micro-historical level, there seems to be parallels between the Westernization through old mission and Africanization of Christianity. The synthesized product of the missionaries' encounters with African peoples and cultures is Africanization in its own right. In mission, even when their true intent was to "Westernize," "*Catolizar e hispanizar,*"[14] in the seventeenth or the nineteenth centuries, the missionaries ended up contributing to the Africanization of the church and society. In reverse, as the first Africans who became members of religious orders or secular clergies actively tried to Africanize, especially following World War II and African independence, these Africans were simultaneously "Westernizing" and globalizing. This Westernizing development is inherently rooted in religious orders like the Jesuits, Franciscans, and White Fathers. It is inherent not only in the nature of their institution (Roman-centered, local and global altogether),[15] but also in the nature of inter-cultural encounters of most evangelizing projects and their final outcomes.

Highlighting the interconnectedness between Westernization and Africanization in mission is important not only because of the southward shift of world Christianity,[16] thanks to the translatability of missionary Christianity.[17]

---

12. Fabien Eboussi Boulaga, "La Dé-Mission," *Spiritus* 56 (Mai-Aout 1974): 276–87; Fabien Eboussi Boulaga, *Christianity Without Fetishes. An African Critique and Recapture of Christianity*, trans. Robert R. Barr (New York: Maryknoll, 1984); P. Meinrad Hebga, *Emancipation d'Eglises Sous-Tutelle: Essai sur l'ère post-missionnaire* (Paris: Présence Africaine, 1976); P. Meinrad Hebga, *Personalité Africaine et Catholicisme* (Paris: Présence Africaine, 1963).

13. Ludovic Lado, *Catholic Pentecostalism and the Paradoxes of Africanization* (Leiden: Brill, 2009).

14. Jerónimo M. Usera y Alarcon, *Memoria de la isla de Fernando Poo* (Madrid: T. Aguado, 1848); Jose Irisarri, *Misión de Fernando Poo, 1859* (Barcelona: Ceibas, 1998).

15. Thomas Banchoff and José Casanova, "Introduction: The Jesuits and Globalization," in *The Jesuits and Globalization. Historical Legacies and Contemporary Challenges* (Washington, DC: Georgetown University Press, 2016), 1–26.

16. Dana L. Robert, "Shifting Southward: Global Christianity Since 1945," *International Bulletin of Missionary Research*, April 2000, 50–58.

17. Sanneh, *Disciples of All Nations Pillars of World Christianity*; Lamin Sanneh, *West African Christianity. The Religious Impact* (London: C. Hurst, 1983); Lamin O. Sanneh, *Translating the Message: The Missionary Impact on Culture* (Maryknoll: Orbis Books, 1989); Sanneh and Carpenter, *The Changing Face of Christianity: Africa, the West, and the World*; Lamin O. Sanneh, *Encountering the West: Christianity and the Global Cultural Process: The African Dimension*, Christianity and the Global Cultural Process (Maryknoll: Orbis Books, 1993).

It is also because, within the "next Christendom,"[18] there exists non-Western mission to the West, leading to a *southernization* of Christianity in the global North. What mission historians like Dana Robert, Lamin Sanneh, or Philip Jenkins have successfully defended is the departure from the paradigm of cultural imperialism advanced by some historians and anthropologists,[19] and their essentialism. Not only do Sanneh, Jenkins, and Robert acknowledge the translatability and inter-culturality of the Christian message and its agents; they also assert African agency in the process of evangelization. Avoiding the temptation of cultural essentialism applies to both the old and the new mission.

Africanizing Christianity today means avoiding African cultural essentialism. It requires a response to the upcoming European minority within Roman Catholicism in a way that makes them feel at home, and remaining mindful of the global appeal of this New Catholicity. The New Catholicity in a globalized world cannot repeat the mistakes of the old. Black cannot simply become the new White as it deploys worldwide. The mere succession of the White by the Black in politics has shown its limits, for it to be repeated again and again in the church. Neither can the Black become so dark that it becomes inaccessible to the curious White, Red or Yellow. Pushing the metaphor further, such a prospect would make Black unbearable even for Black people themselves who, obviously, are more chocolate than black. Of course, white or black, chocolate primarily tastes chocolate. Therefore, in analyzing Catholic missions in Africa, one must acknowledge the colonial context of the birth of those missions and their many abuses. But Christianity has a core interest in distancing itself from the concept of *colonial mission*, while challenging it and what it represents. This is not to attempt a denial or revision of history. Instead, the very use of *colonial mission* perpetuates the mindset that gave birth to it among African theologians. It keeps African Christianity trapped in a bygone era. The corollary is that African Christianity is forced to continually defend its past. This became a distraction from proclaiming the good news, liberating a global world full of challenges and its new forms of colonialism.

---

18. Philip Jenkins 1952-, *The Next Christendom: The Coming of Global Christianity* (Oxford: Oxford University Press, 2002); Philip Jenkins, *The New Faces of Christianity: Believing the Bible in the Global South* (Oxford/New York: Oxford University Press, 2006).

19. Comaroff, *Of Revelation and Revolution: Christianity, Colonialism, and Consciousness in South Africa*; Comaroff, *Of Revelation and Revolution: The Dialectics of Modernity on a South African Frontier*; Comaroff, "Christianity and Colonialism in South Africa." André Droogers, "The Africanization of Christianity, An Anthropologist's View," *Missiology: An International Review* 5.4 (1977): 443–56.

In fact, from the historical perspective, and at a micro level, while some of the old missions were initially conceived and directed by a colonial government, historians like Elisabeth A. Foster,[20] Charlotte Walker-Saïd,[21] or Alice Conklin[22] have shown that state and church relationships never reached the level of total collusion. The liminal spaces between the colonial and the evangelizing projects, it appears, were key for African agency and self-realization, that is, in one word, *Africanization*. It first happened as a Western-Africanization in the old mission and, as the church in Africa becomes more African, it should evolve and become an Afro-Westernization, an Afro-Indianization, and an Afro-globalization.

"Afro" as Africanization: The Historical Meaning of a Concept

Theologians and philosophers have debated the concept of "Africanization" in the twentieth century. Steve Kaplan contends that Africanization often refers to other concepts such as incarnation, contextualization, or adaptation.[23] According to Kaplan, in its final stage, Africanization "entails the introduction of African concepts into the body of *normative* Christianity."[24] Concretely stated, Africanization is the deepening of the Christian faith in Africa, beyond mere adaptation and the materialism of missionary Christianity.

According to Laennec Hurbon, to Africanize Christianity implies going beyond the set of formal structures that were characteristic of missionary

---

20. Elizabeth Foster, "A Mission in Transition: Monsignor Joseph Faye and the Decolonization of the Catholic Church In Senegal," in *In God's Empire: French Missionaries and the Modern World* (New York: Oxford University Press, 2012), 257–77; Elizabeth Foster, "Theologies of Colonization: The Catholic Church and the Future of the French Empire in the 1950s," *The Journal of African History* 87.2 (2015): 281–315; Elizabeth Foster, "Entirely Christian and Entirely African: Catholic African Students in France in the Era of Independence," *The Journal of African History* 56.2 (2015): 239–59; Elizabeth A. Foster, *Faith in Empire : Religion, Politics, and Colonial Rule in French Senegal, 1880–1940* (Stanford: Stanford University Press, 2013); Elizabeth Ann Foster, *African Catholic: Decolonization and the Transformation of the Church* (Cambridge: Harvard University Press, 2019).

21. Charlotte Walker-Saïd, "Christian Social Movements in Cameroon at the End of Empire: Transnational Solidarities and the Communion of the World Church," in *Relocating World Christianity: Interdisciplinary Studies in Universal and Local Expressions of Christianity* (Leiden: Brill, 2017), 189–212; Charlotte Walker-Saïd, *Faith, Power and Family. Christianity and Social Change in French Cameroon*, Religion in Transforming Africa (Woodbridge: James Currey, 2018).

22. Alice L. Conklin, *A Mission to Civilize: The Republican Idea of Empire in France and West Africa, 1895–1930* (Stanford: Stanford University Press, 1997).

23. Steven Kaplan, "The Africanization of Missionary Christianity: History and Typology," *Journal of Religion in Africa* 16.3 (1986): 166.

24. Kaplan, "Africanization of Missionary Christianity," 180.

Christianity, consisting of schools, orphanages, churches, rituals, a moral code, and so on.[25] Robert Roelandt, while associating mission with colonialism and its abuses, also acknowledged the existence of a local church that, by 1959, had already reached its own maturity.[26] There were no more frontiers in mission, Roelandt said, and time had come to adjust to the call for adaptation and vernacularization from the Popes (from Benedict XV to Pius XII) and missiologists like Pierre Charles.[27] Roelandt, however, did not go as far as to suggest the end of the mission.[28] Even in places where the local church was already built, he concluded, missionary zeal was still needed "to train and form a Christian society in which the Church can grow and develop its salvific activity."[29]

In 1968, the Kenyan theologian, M. D. Odinga, called for the end of the mission, while urging the Western church to accept the principle of reciprocity by allowing Africans to be missionaries in the West.[30] His call came twenty years after some Francophone Africans, like the Catholic priest Pascal Idohou of Dahomey, had expressed their doubt about the increased indigenization of the Congolese sacred music, denouncing its embryonic and primitive nature.[31] Others pushed back against Idohou,[32] and anticipated the list of Africans calling for the *moratorium* to grow. These African theologians either defended a Western approach to African cultures, or they reacted to it within the same Western framework that had trained them. The concept of *négritude* was unique in the sense that it viewed the African primarily as the Black Man or Woman everywhere questing for the betterment of his or her life, and with

---

25. Laennec Hubron, "Les missions chrétiennes comme problème politique," *Revue du Clergé Africain* 4–5 (July 1972): 421.

26. Robert Roelandt, "A la source de l'action missionnaire," *Revue du Clergé Africain* 14 (July 1959): 338–47.

27. Benedict XV Pope, "Maximum Illud. De Fide Catholica per Orbem Terrarum Propaganda," *AAS* 11 (November 30, 1919): 440–55; Pius XI Pope, "Rerum Ecclesiae," *AAS* 18 (February 28, 1926): 65–83; Pope Pius XII, "Fidei Donum: Encyclical on the African Missions," *The Pope Speaks* 4, no. 3 (Winter 1957): 295–312.

28. Robert Roelandt, "L'évolution de l'action missionnaire dans l'Eglise Catholique," *Revue du Clergé Africain* 14 (Mai 1959): 252.

29. Roelandt, 255.

30. M. D. Odinga, "Decolonizing the Church in East Africa," *East Africa Journal* 4.4 (1967): 11–15.

31. Pascal Idohou, "Musique indigène et musique sacrée," *Revue du Clergé Africain* 3 (1948): 209–12.

32. Van de Casteele, "Musique indigène, musique religieuse," *Revue du Clergé Africain* 3 (September 1948): 392–96. Ignace Faly, "Musique indigène, musique religieuse," *Revue du Clergé Africain* 4 (January 1949): 34–37.

it, that of the whole humanity, in the intersection of Soweto, the suburbs of Paris and London, Rio de Janeiro, Chicago, Kinshasa, Douala, or Lagos.

The break between Africanization and Westernization was clearly and explicitly articulated by the early defenders of the *moratorium*. They believed that for the church in Africa truly to become African, Western mission agents and funds had to be suspended, until both sides rethink their relationship and respective identities.[33] A few years after the initial call for the *moratorium*, in 1972, Armand Duval called for a renewed focus on "Africanization." After the enthusiasm of the early years of the mission, Duval admitted, the focus on the administration of the sacraments was detrimental to "real Africanization,"[34] which included the reform of religious life in a way that responds to local needs. The promotion of the laity was its second feature, in continuity with liturgical reforms that were already being implemented. Quoting Raguin's *L'indigénisation de l'Eglise*, Duval further explained his position: "To be Catholic in that context means to Africanize, that is, to become 'particular' (*particulariser*), while, at the same time, helping African people to participate intensely to the universal thinking and culture."[35] Moreover, Christianity should produce an authentic African spirituality and theology "*adapted* and perfectly Christian, for each [African] cultural unit," so as to make African "paganism" or "animism"[36] an integral part of salvation history.[37]

Elaborating upon the concept of mission in 1978, Isidore de Souza talked about the changing world in which former mission territories would become providers of missionaries.[38] Among the challenges facing the new churches are the structures they inherited from the West, their cost, and sustainability.[39] The *moratorium*, he argued, intended to address that challenge, a solution

---

33. John G. Gatu, *Joyfully Christian and Truly African* (Nairobi: Acton Publishers, 2006); John G. Gatu, *Fane into Flame. Rev. Dr. John G. Gatu, an Autobiography* (Nairobi: Moran Publishers, 2016).

34. Armand Duval, "Jalons pour une réflecion sur l'adaption," *Revue du Clergé Africain* XXVII (November 1972): 607.

35. Duval, "Jalons pour une réflecion sur l'adaption," 616.

36. See Agbonkhianmeghe E. Orobator, *Religion and Faith in Africa: Confessions of an Animist* (New York: Orbis Books, 2018).

37. Duval, "Jalons Pour Une Réflecion Sur l'adaption," 623.

38. Isidore de Souza, "Respect des peuples et leurs valeurs. La mission aujourd'hui pour demain," *Telema* 45 (March 1986): 31–50. From the same author: Isidore de Souza, "Pouvons-nous rester Africains tout en étant membre d'une religion importée?," *Telema* 4 (Avril 1974): 23–33; Isidore de Souza, "Et si l'Afrique évangélisait à son tour l'Europe?," *Telema* 15 (March 1978): 13–26.

39. de Souza, "Respect des peuples et leurs valeurs. La mission aujourd'hui pour demain," 37.

he deemed "hasty."⁴⁰ The reason for the urgency was that some Western missionaries felt threatened by the rise of an African church and sought to maintain the *status quo* at any cost.⁴¹ Others had retreated from long-term planning, paralyzed by the uncertainty about their future.⁴² However, Dubois concluded, "the colonial era is well gone, when Europeans were all powerful and controlled the economy, the politics, the human and spiritual training of the clergy. Africanization has become an unquestionable principle today."⁴³ A certain kind of mission, said Patrick Kalilombe, was *révolue*.⁴⁴ And instead of becoming "dé-missionnaires," Western missionaries should evolve.

Mejía's use of "dé-missionnaire" was not accidental. He was, in fact, reacting to Eboussi Boulaga's *dé-mission*,⁴⁵ while defending a more *realistic* approach of the mission adopted in 1974 by the 44th International and Ecumenical Missiological Week of Namur (44e Semaine Internationale et Oecuménique de Missiologie, Namur 1974). Eboussi, Meinrad-Pierre Hebga, and Engelbert Mveng presented an African response to missionary Christianity, drawing both from the *moratorium* and from theologies of liberation.⁴⁶ Following Mejía, African bishops addressed the missionaries directly. In their letters, they acknowledged the historical role the missionaries had played in building the African church.⁴⁷ The bishops also remained realistic in their appreciation of the context, echoing Pope Pius XII and the changes in the church at the time.⁴⁸

---

40. de Souza, "Respect des peoples," 37.
41. Jules Dubois, "Echos et nouvelles," *Telema* 1, no. 75 (Avril 1975): 1.
42. Rodrigo Mejía, "Missionnaires ou démissionnaires?," *Telema* 2.75 (Juillet 1975): 73–76.
43. Jules Dubois, "Echos et nouvelles," *Telema* 1.75 (Avril 1975): 81.
44. Patrick Kalilombe, "Un Certain Type de Mission Est Révolu," *Telema* 2.75 (Décembre 1975): 75–84.
45. Eboussi Boulaga, "La Dé-Mission."
46. Engelbert Mveng, *L'art d'Afrique Noire : Liturgie cosmique et langage religieux* (Tours, 1964); Engelbert Mveng, "De la sous-mission à la succession," in *Civilisation Noire et Eglise Catholique* (Paris: Présence Africaine, 1978), 267–76; Engelbert Mveng, *Théologie, libération et cultures africaines: Dialogue sur l'anthropologie négro-africaine* (Yaoundé: Clé, 1996); Engelbert Mveng and A. Hastings, "Church and State in Concert for Liberation and Salvation," *Mission Studies* 2.1 (1985): 33–38; Engelbert Mveng, *L'Afrique dans l'Eglise : Paroles d'un croyant* (Paris: L'Harmattan, 1986).
47. Evêques Africains, "Message des Évêques aux missionnaires," *Telema* 2.75 (1975): 77.
48. "Exhortation de Pie XII au clergé indigène (28 Juin 1948)," *Revue du Clergé Africain*, 1948, 372–79. "Paroles de Pie XII sur l'adaptation: Du zèle des instituts religieux aux temps nouveaux," *Revue du Clergé Africain*, 1951, 278–80. "Lien entre le but dernier des missions et la création du clergé indigène exposé dans l'encyclique 'Evangelii Praeconnes,'" *Revue du Clergé Africain*, 1948, 345–47. "Les missionnaires étrangers 'troupes auxiliaires' de l'Evêque local," *Revue du Clergé Africain*, 1948, 347. Pope Pie XII, "L'encyclique 'Fidei Donum' (21 Avril 1957) sur la situation des missions notamment en Afrique," *Revue du Clergé Africain*, 1957, 321–37.

Some stressed that the continent still needed foreign missionaries. Others, like the Congolese, went further by defining the new role of Western missionaries as "collaborateurs avertis" (informed collaborators), invited to "assimilate" and "integrate" the reality of a "particular church" in which they were serving.[49] Missionaries, to summarize the Congolese bishops, had to Africanize. They, nevertheless, remained Europeans as they Africanized.

Contemporary Implications

Fifty years have passed since the Moratorium. European missionaries are not flocking anymore to the continent. Africans migrating from the continent are still crossing the Sahara, the Indian and Atlantic Oceans. Facing failed politics and economics at home, they seek economic opportunity for themselves and their families overseas. Can the African response rooted in traditional African cultures be adequate in the current situation of material need, duplicity, diversity, and hybridity? The tragedy we see of crossing the Sahara and the oceans certainly shines a light on the current reality of the world of scandalous disparities. These disparities ought to be the anthropological foundation of an African liberation theology, together with its global roots and implications. This very tragedy proves the urgent need for a new global humanism, based on a belief that one race cannot be whole if all races are not whole, a basic statement at the core theologies of liberation and religious reforms.

Africans should evolve, as they build their indigenous Christianity in a global world that needs them as evangelizers. For if Africans are becoming evangelizers everywhere, they should remain mindful of the catholicity of inculturation. Africans rejected missionary Christianity for not being Christian enough because they believed that Europeans did not become African enough in the old mission, its strategies, and theologies (inculturation). Africans should not therefore repeat the same mistake and expect different results as they become missionaries in Europe or America. They should, beyond the initial cultural clash, be Europeans with Europeans while in Europe. At the very least, they should let Europeans and Americans be authentically Christians in their own lands and within their cultural context. The challenge for Africans seems an easy task when given a chance; because their own hybridity resulting from the old mission whose language they still speak when they profess the same creed.

---

49. Evêques Zaïrois, "Les Évêques Zaïrois aux missionnaires," *Telema* 2.75 (1975): 78.

Afro-Westernization is the condition by which the African church will survive in the hybridity of its origin and the global world which it is supposed to evangelize. Africans should, as the Rwandan Jesuit philosopher, Théoneste Nkeramihigo, suggests, resist the temptation of cultural angelism and docetism. Such a temptation would, in fact, be ignorant of the complex historical data and contingency.[50] To Nkeramihigo, the ongoing debate over inculturation, like the one on Africanization in the 1970s, is often guided by negativity, a desire to de-Westernize at any cost. Westernization, he reminded his readers, remains a *fait accompli*. Any attempt to roll it back completely would be contrary not only to the incarnational and, therefore, historical nature of Christianity. It would also be turning a blind eye to the dynamic nature of culture itself.[51] Africans cannot simply turn inward without admitting self-defeat; in effect that their culture is not strong and flexible enough to evolve in the global competition of ideas and values and survive. Confronting outside cultures and ideas is the necessary challenge African worldviews need to move away from their "villagizing" inclinations.[52]

Through this reorientation, Nkeramihigo concludes, African peoples come to the realization of a historical fact; their encounter with foreign cultures has changed them forever; reconciling themselves to this reality is the ultimate goal of inculturation. This Afro-Westernization and Afro-globalization is an asset for Africans as they take the central stage in the global church. Promoting it also means avoiding the twofold temptation; that of "acculturation," the illusion that the new African identity can be constructed solely from the imported culture; and that of tribalism and nationalism, the belief that the new identity can ignore the imported culture.[53] Nkeramihigo's solution is a new anthropological Christology that would liberate a space allowing the people to adjust to this tension in reality, while realizing their respective potential.

---

50. Théoneste Nkeramihigo, "Inculturation du Christianisme," *Telema* 4.77 (October 1977): 19. The author does not use the concept of "africanization" in his article. I use them side-by-side in order to stress the similarity of both processes.

51. In 1977, André Droogers, another theologian held the same position, debunking what he saw as triple fallacies of "generalization," "reconstruction," and "idealization." Droogers, instead, defended "spontaneous Africanization": "'the Christian message for the most part was smothered in the embrace of African religion [and] one may even wonder whether Africanization has not been stronger than Christianization (...) In any attempt to Africanize Christianity and the church in Africa, primary attention should be given to local situations" (Droogers, "The Africanization of Christianity, An Anthropologist's View," 453–54).

52. By villagization, Ogbu Kalu understands the transfer of the traditional mindset to the modern state and church. It can, for example, take the form of big-men's rule. Ogbu Kalu, *African Christianity: An African Story* (Trenton: Africa World Press, 2007).

53. Nkeramihigo, "Inculturation Du Christianisme," 20.

If Westernization is a historical fact, then the making of the new Catholicity from Africa cannot be left solely to a very remote past, or to a *clair-obscur* future. This African identity is already in the making as the process of Westernization is embraced, resisted or assimilated. In that sense, as far as history is concerned, Westernization itself is Africanization, and vice versa. Not admitting that fact would imply the same angelism and historical docetism which Nkeramihigo warns against. Afro-globalization might be the ideal aspiration for African intellectuals, who as Ludovic Lado would say, should not to be "torn between Westernization and Africanization."[54]

---

54. Lado, *Catholic Pentecostalism and the Paradoxes of Africanization*, 225.

4

In the Power of the Spirit

Towards a Pentecostal Theoretical Framework for Missiology in Africa

J. Kwabena Asamoah-Gyadu

This chapter examines the importance of pneumatic Christianity[1] as missional movements within the African context. We consider how these movements have inspired growth and dynamism in the church in Africa and what the implications of this development are for understanding mission today. Pentecostalism, the most globalized form of pneumatic Christianity, belongs to the larger Protestant family, and it shares the traditional evangelical theological emphases on the authority of the Bible, the centrality of the cross, regeneration as the way to Christian salvation, and a call to holiness as the outflow of a new relationship with Christ. In addition to these theological themes, Pentecostal and charismatic movements became the "third force" of world Christianity from the beginning of the twentieth century because of the additional emphasis placed on the experience and power of the Holy Spirit. Pentecostalism developed because historic mainline Protestantism

---

1. In this chapter, I use the expression "pneumatic Christianity" to refer any form of Christianity that values, affirms and consciously promotes the experiences of the Spirit as part of normal Christian life and worship. This allows me to bring into the discussion not only those movements that scholars writing from Western perspectives would not delineate as Pentecostal/charismatic but also the many indigenous expressions of Christianity from Africa that privilege the experiential presence of the Spirit in Christianity but do not necessarily call themselves Pentecostal.

took an intellectual and liberal attitude to the Scriptures and, in the process, not only neglected the experiential elements of Christianity but consequently reduced mission to the provision of structures that support education, medical care, and other social interventions programmes. Pentecostals, on the other hand, begin mission with reference to the power of the word and Spirit in the transformations of people and communities. In Pentecostalism then, mission is an interventionist strategy of the Holy Spirit in the execution of a christological mandate in a world that is alienated from a holy God. This understanding of mission goes against the grain of thought in Christian cultures rooted in Enlightenment thinking in which things that could not be proven by science and rationality were not taken seriously.

In the process, Christianity suffered setbacks in the West but the independent and indigenous pneumatic churches from the non-Western world continued to expand. Mission ceased to be the preserve of Western missionary activity. There is still hope for the future because even in the secularizing West, there are a number of Christian communities that have kept the spirit of experiential Christianity alive. There are dynamic renewal movements the world over, although by and large, it is in the global South and East that these have really helped to energize Christianity by giving it a fresh lease of life in the hearts and lives of people. The God of mission, Pentecostal/charismatic Christianity teaches us, moves in the power of the Holy Spirit. In Africa today, for example, even churches that trace their roots to the works of German and British missions from Bremen, Basel, or London are all turning to charismatic renewal. The argument of contemporary charismatic movements is that the absence of the dynamic presence of the Spirit from the church and its mission turns it into something other than a place to encounter God. In the early history of Pentecostalism, for example, mission was a spontaneous activity as people who encountered Spirit-baptism took off under that inspiration to evangelize other cultures. As an enthusiastic form of religion therefore, pneumatic Christianity generally promotes radical conversions, baptism of the Spirit with speaking in tongues, healing, deliverance, prophetic ministries and other such pneumatic phenomena as miracles and supernatural interventions in general.

Pentecostalism has emerged as the most exciting and dominant stream of Christianity in the twenty-first century. This is especially so in the non-Western worlds of Africa, Asia and Latin America that are now the main heartlands of world Christianity. What this means is that we cannot talk about Christian mission today without reference to these locations where the faith now lives. The discourse and strategies of Christian mission, including its study in seminaries and faculties of theology, ought to be revised to reflect the new realities of our time. These realities, this chapter submits, include not just the rise of Pentecostalism but also the fact that non-Western Christians find its affinities with local primal backgrounds welcoming. Pentecostalism is growing in Africa, for example, not simply because Africans tend to take the biblical world of Spirit/spirits seriously but also because the spirits exist within their primal imagination. It must, therefore, not surprise us that even in contexts where Christianity may be declining such as the Northern continents, Pentecostalism with its historically younger and theologically versatile progenies are leading the way in the revival of Christian presence such as through the ministries of African immigrant churches. The rise of contemporary Pentecostalism and the revival of Christianity give practical expression to the metaphor of the Spirit as blowing wind as used by Jesus Christ in his encounter with Nicodemus in John 3. Nicodemus as a Pharisee was representative of the old, static and orthodox religious order but the Spirit, as blowing wind, represented change (John 3:8).

Harvey Cox, who in the middle of the twentieth century had joined "death of God" theologians to predict the demise of religion, had, by the end of that century, revised his thesis based on the fact of the vivacious way in which Pentecostalism was unleashing a new force of life into world Christianity. In 1995, Cox wrote that "today it is secularity, not spirituality, that may be headed for extinction."[2] Indeed, I have found the subtitle of his book, *Pentecostalism and the Re-Shaping of Christianity in the 21st Century,* adequately capturing the thrust of the global religious renaissance led by Pentecostal/charismatic churches and movements in Africa. It speaks a great deal not only of the significance of Pentecostal Christianity, but also the effect that pneumatic Christianity generally is having on world Christianity. Pentecostalism, in short, has transformed not just the face of world Christianity but also the way we understand and do mission.

Pentecost and Mission as Renewal

Pentecostal revivalism, which I have identified as the most globalized form of pneumatic Christianity in the world, is driven in part by a statement made by Peter following an enquiry from the crowd on what they should do in response to the outpouring of the Holy Spirit. After hearing Peter preach so powerfully

---

2. Harvey Cox, *Fire from Heaven: The Rise of Pentecostal Spirituality and the Reshaping of Religion in the Twenty-first Century* (Reading: Addison-Wesley Publishing, 1995).

on what God has accomplished in Jesus Christ, they asked: "Brothers, what shall we do?" Peter replied:

> Repent and be baptized, every one of you in the name of Jesus Christ for the forgiveness of your sins. And you will receive the gift of the Holy Spirit. The promise is for you and your children and those who are far off – for all whom the Lord our God will call (Acts 2:38–39).

Pentecostals took this promise seriously and not only did they appropriate it to their Christian lives, they also shared its message with people outside their own geographical locations. Until the middle of the twentieth century, Pentecostalism was still a religion on the margins of world Christianity. Today, it is impossible to talk about world Christian mission without reference to Pentecostalism. That a decade ago, the John Templeton Foundation, through the University of Southern California, made available $3.5 million for researching Pentecostalism worldwide was an indication of how important this stream of Christianity had become as a world religion. In *Fire from Heaven*, Cox explains the importance of Pentecostalism in terms of its experiential orientation:

> The story of the first Pentecost has always served as an inspiration for people who are discontented with the way religion or the world in general is going. They turn to it because it is packed with promise . . . It is about the experience of God not about abstract religious ideas, and it depicts a God who does not remain aloof but reaches down through the power of the Spirit to touch human hearts, therefore . . . in our present time of social and cultural disarray . . . Pentecostalism is burgeoning everywhere in the world.[3]

Christianity is itself a world religion and discussions on its growth and dynamism in non-Western contexts cannot be divorced from developments taking place in other parts of the globe. Thus, it is not for nothing that in the twenty-first century many faculties of theology and seminaries are appointing professors of world Christianity who would help to interpret prophetically the changing face of the faith globally. The pneumatic orientation of non-Western Christianity accounts in significant measures for the growth and dynamism of the faith in these contexts. The growth of the church in Africa draws attention to the theological truth that the presence of Jesus Christ in the life of the

---

3. Harvey Cox, *Fire from Heaven*, 4–5.

church continues through the work of the Holy Spirit. Frank D. Macchia is a Pentecostal theologian with several useful books on the Holy Spirit. Against the backdrop of the fact that Acts of the Apostles is a historical account of the Holy Spirit and the great renewal that the Spirit accomplished through the early disciples, he writes that "God was so real" to the apostles that "they lived daily in the awareness of his presence and guidance" and this included God's visitations "with undeniable signs of divine favor and power."[4]

This experiential presence of the Holy Spirit, captured for us by Macchia, is a promise that has been fulfilled through Pentecost and is now being experienced by the church as an existential reality with eschatological implications. Pentecostal/charismatic Christianity is important in the understanding of Africa within the context of world Christianity and mission because most of the churches have embraced the pneumatic dimensions of the faith. Thus, David Martin, a sociologist of religion, describes "the astonishing rise of Pentecostalism and its associated penumbra of charismatic Christianity" as "the largest global shift in the religious marketplace" over the last half century.[5] Wherever it has appeared, Pentecostalism, as my main title suggests, appeals to a biblical promise at the end of the Gospel of Luke:

> I am going to send you what my Father has promised; but stay in the city until you have been clothed with power from on high. (Luke 24:49)

– and its fulfilment in the Acts of the Apostles in terms of experiential legitimacy:

> But you will receive power when the Holy Spirit comes on you; and you will be my witnesses in Jerusalem, and in all Judea and Samaria, and to the ends of the earth. (Acts 1:8)

This *clothing with power*, as Macchia explains, was a divine act not dependent on human standards of experience but on divine standards. He describes it as essentially of self-transcendence motivated by the love of God so that one feels especially inspired to give himself or herself to others in whatever gifting God has created within.[6] Being *clothed with power* means being empowered for service among God's people. The church is empowered for living witness in its community life, its inspired proclamation, and its multiple ministries in the Spirit.

---

4. Frank D. Macchia, *Baptized in the Spirit: A Global Pentecostal Theology* (Grand Rapids: Zondervan, 2006), 13.
5. David Martin, *Pentecostalism: The World their Parish* (Oxford: Blackwell, 2002), xvii.
6. Macchia, *Baptized in the Spirit*, 14.

Pentecost and the Charismatic Experience

The expression "charismatic" comes from *charismata*, meaning "gifts of grace." "Charismatic" is, thus, used to refer to "renewal prayer fellowships" and analogous movements operating within and without historic mission denominations. Their aim is the revitalization of church life through the restoration of the graces of the Spirit – *charismata pneumatika* – in its worship life (1 Corinthians 12–14). That is why I submit that Pentecostal/charismatic or pneumatic Christianity has developed as a religion with a global culture that values, affirms, and *actively* promotes the experiential presence of the Holy Spirit as part of *normal* Christian life. There are three main reasons why pneumatic Christianity has become the religion of choice in contemporary non-Western Christianity including in Africa and the African Diaspora:

1. The emphasis on personal transformation wrought by the Holy Spirit.
2. The emphasis on the experience of the Holy Spirit with specific manifestations which makes worship both a heartfelt and body-felt experience.
3. The interventionist nature of charismatic theology which is seen in healing, deliverance and prayer for breakthroughs in life.

The bottom-line in all these three factors is the critical importance of religious experience as being of both personal and corporate value for religious people. In his book, *Reinventing American Protestantism*, Donald E. Miller refers to the contemporary churches that articulate a charismatic culture as "new paradigm churches." What he means by new paradigm churches is evident in the sort of experiential religious culture that they represent:

> These new paradigm churches . . . are changing the way Christianity looks and is experienced . . . Appropriating contemporary cultural forms, these churches are creating a new genre of worship music; they are restructuring the organizational character of institutional religion; they are democratizing access to the sacred by radicalizing the Protestant principle of the priesthood of all believers.[7]

The heart of the distinctive appeal that Pentecostal/charismatic Christianity has for people "lies in its empowerment through spiritual gifts offered to all" and that can be experienced even today.[8] This is what Miller means by the

---

7. Donald E. Miller, *Reinventing American Protestantism: Christianity in the New Millennium* (Berkeley: University of California Press, 1997), 1.

8. Martin, *Pentecostalism*, 1.

democratization of access to the sacred. To that end, one could even say that Pentecostalism must be understood as an *ecclesiological experience* rather than just a denominational movement because it brings together people with shared experiences of the Holy Spirit. Thus, a major strength of charismatic renewal is its lay-orientation, which means, the Holy Spirit democratizes access to charisma and ministry comes to belong to all rather than just the ordained. The implications of the democratization of spiritual gifts are outlined by Allan H. Anderson:

> This mass involvement of the 'laity' in the Pentecostal movement was undoubtedly one of the main reasons for its success. There was no need for a theologically articulate clergy, because cerebral and clerical Christianity had, in the minds of many people, already failed them. What was needed was a demonstration of power by indigenous people to whom ordinary people could easily relate. This was the democratization of Christianity, for henceforth the mystery of the gospel would no longer be reserved for a select privileged and educated few but would be revealed to whoever was willing to receive it.[9]

Pneumatic revivals take place both inside and outside of existing churches and denominations. Thus, the Catholic philosopher and theologian, Donald L. Gelpi, also writes that "the charismatic experience finds expression in a variety of spiritual gifts which are granted by the Holy Spirit for the benefit of the entire community."[10] Pentecostal/charismatic Christians believe that "Pentecost," wherever it occurs, does so in fulfilment of the prophecy of Joel (2:28f.), and that signs and wonders must accompany the ministry of today's church as they did in the ministry of the Apostles in Acts. Pentecostals/charismatic or pneumatic Christians "like to feel that they are alert to God's signs and wonders of whatever kind, wherever they have occurred, are occurring now, and will occur in the future."[11] The bottom line is that we cannot explain the rise of Pentecostal/charismatic Christianity and its attraction for young people in particular without reference to the activity of the Holy Spirit. God's Holy

---

9. Allan H. Anderson, "Global Pentecostalism in the New Millennium," in Allan H. Anderson and Walter J. Hollenweger ed., *Pentecostals after a Century: Global Perspectives on a Movement in Transition* (Sheffield: Sheffield Academic Press, 1999), 214.

10. Donald L. Gelpi, *Pentecostalism: A Theological Viewpoint* (New York: Paulist Press, 1971), 83.

11. David B. Barrett, "Signs, Wonders, and Statistics in the World of Today," in Jan A. B. Jongeneel (ed.), *Pentecost, Mission, and Ecumenism: Essays in Intercultural Theology* (Frankfurt am Main: Peter Lang, 1992), 188.

Spirit is a Spirit of renewal (Titus 2) and so when the church becomes too bureaucratized, set in its ways and fails to confront new challenges with a more relevant message, God does raise up prophets to speak his word afresh and groups in whom his Spirit brings forth afresh his authentic fruits. Miller's words are very apt here:

> [Not] only are the new paradigm churches doing a better job of responding to the needs of their clientele than are many mainline churches, but – more important – they are successfully mediating the sacred, bringing God to people and conveying the self-transcending and life-changing core of all true religion. They offer worship in a musical idiom that connects with the experience of broad sectors of the middle class; they have jettisoned aspects of organized religion that alienate many teenagers and young adults; and they provide programming that emphasizes well-defined moral values and is not otherwise available in the culture. In short, they offer people hope and meaning that is grounded in a transcendent experience of the sacred.[12]

This is the understanding of mission within Pentecostal settings with which we must approach themes and religious practices of the pneumatic Christian new religious movements that we examine in this study. These pneumatic reforms have taken almost a century to take root in African historic mission Christianity. Adherents of charismatic renewal groups who approve the Holy Spirit-inspired experiences described above refer to it in such terms and expressions as: "refreshment of the Spirit," "charismatic renewal," "revival," "the movement of the Spirit," or "restoration of the church." On the other hand those who dislike it call it "emotionalism," "enthusiasm," or even "occult."[13] What is new in pneumatic Christianity, as Simon Tugwell and others explain of Pentecostalism, is not necessarily the occurrence of particular pneumatic phenomena but rather "the articulation and organization in corporate Church life of what has over the centuries been known only spasmodically in isolated instance."[14]

---

12. Miller, *Reinventing American Protestantism*, 3.
13. David Middlemiss, *Interpreting Charismatic Experience* (London: SCM, 1996), 1.
14. Simon Tugwell, Peter Hocken, George Every and John O. Mills, *New Heaven? New Earth? An Encounter with Pentecostalism* (Springfield: Templegate Publishers, 1976), 22.

Africa and the Renewal of Christianity as a Non-Western Religion

The accession of Christianity in Africa has coincided with the recession of the faith in the modern West for, at a time when many Western church buildings are being sold for non-Christian purposes in Europe and North America, warehouses and cinema buildings are being converted into churches in Africa. Churches of Pentecostal/charismatic persuasion are leading the way in the renewal of Christianity as a non-Western religion.[15] Africa has become a hotbed of Pentecostal/charismatic activity, and it would not be a contradiction in terms to say that although Christian evangelization took place under the activities of historic mission denominations, Pentecostalism in both its older classical and newer charismatic forms has now taken over as the representative face of Christianity in Africa. In the following quotation, John V. Taylor very aptly summarizes the role of God the Spirit in the growth of Christianity in Africa in the 1960s:

> In Africa today, it seems the incalculable Spirit has chosen to use the Independent Church Movement for another spectacular advance. This does not prove that their teaching is necessarily true, but it shows they have the raw materials out of which a missionary church is made – spontaneity, total commitment, and the primitive responses that arise from the depths of life.[16]

The type of Christianity that inspired this observation by Taylor was the one represented by the older independent indigenous churches of Africa. Their characteristics of spontaneity, total commitment and the primitive responses that arise from the depths of life have remained important parts of Pentecostal spirituality in modern Africa. Except in Southern Africa, these older African Independent Churches are no longer paradigmatic of African Christianity and I have discussed the reasons for their decline elsewhere.[17] However, their religious and theological emphases of practical salvation, charismatic renewal, innovative gender ideology, and oral and interventionist theologies, have found new leases of life among contemporary Pentecostals on the continent. Their emergence led to the renewal of Christianity in Africa and inspired the process of "pentecostalization" currently underway in contemporary African Christianity.

---

15. Kwame Bediako, *Christianity in Africa: The Renewal of a Non-Western Religion* (Edinburgh; Maryknoll: Edinburgh University Press; Orbis Books, 1995).

16. John V. Taylor, *The Go Between God: The Holy Spirit and the Christian Mission* (London: SCM, 1972), 54.

17. J. Kwabena Asamoah-Gyadu, *African Charismatics: A Study of Independent Indigenous Pentecostalism in Ghana* (Leiden: E.J. Brill, 2005).

Charismatic Renewal and the Church Today

The restoration of *charismata pneumatika* as part of normal church life can be understood theologically as "the reactivation in Christian community of levels and capacities of the human spirit that have long lain dormant in Christian life."[18] Whether we refer to them as renewal, restoration or revival movements, the single most important characteristic they share is the experience of the Holy Spirit. That is how the renewal is explained by insiders. Arnold Bittlinger accurately represents what this is about by pointing to how charismatic renewal must be understood in terms of a response to the staid, silent, orderly and overly rational approach to the faith as inherited through the Western mission enterprise of the early nineteenth century.[19] I should also point out that most of the immigrant churches emerging in Europe have a charismatic culture. The works of Gerrie ter Haar and Claudia Währisch-Oblau attest to this fact.[20] The Holy Spirit is the source of renewal, change and empowerment. Charismatic renewal movements, thus, belong to the larger pneumatic traditions which have manifested in three main forms across the world.

They are:

- New Pentecostal Churches (NPCs). Many of these have developed mega-size congregations; they are led by charismatic personalities who preach motivational messages and take very contemporary approaches to worship; they appeal greatly to upwardly mobile young Christians who are disenchanted with the denominationalism and clericalism of the past.
- Trans-denominational Pentecostal fellowships like the Full Gospel Businessmen's Fellowship International and Women's Aglow movements. These are lay movements which also encourage "responsible church membership," a policy that has helped to facilitate renewal within historic mission churches.
- Renewal movements within non-Pentecostal historic mission denominations.

One of the earliest books to be published on neo-Pentecostalism as I collectively refer to the different streams of renewal movements is Richard

---

18. Tugwell et al., *Encounter with Pentecostalism*, 22–23.
19. See Arnold Bittlinger, ed., *The Church is Charismatic* (Geneva: WCC, 1982).
20. Gerrie ter Haar, *Halfway to Paradise: African Christians in Europe* (Cardiff: Cardiff Academic Press, 1998); Claudia Währisch-Oblau, *The Missionary Self-Perception of Pentecostal/Charismatic Church Leaders from the Global South: Bringing Back the Gospel* (Leiden: E.J. Brill, 2009).

Quebedeaux's *The New Charismatics: The Origins, Development, and Significance of Neo-Pentecostalism.*[21] In that publication he defines neo-Pentecostalism as follows:

> Neo-Pentecostalism, though grounded in the same religious experience (variously interpreted), differs markedly from its classical forerunner and counterpart. In principle, Charismatic Renewal is a "trans-denominational" movement of enthusiastic Christianity that emerged and became recognizable in the "historic" denominations . . . It is theologically diverse but generally orthodox, and is unified by a common experience – the baptism of the Holy Spirit – with accompanying *charismata* . . . to be used personally and corporately in the life of the church. Evangelistic in nature, the movement is genuinely reformist in character.[22]

Classical Pentecostalism developed into denominations very quickly. The rise of neo-Pentecostalism marked the beginning of disenchantment with religious traditions and conservatism within Christianity and the erosion of denominational loyalties within people. Thus the essential nature of neo-Pentecostalism is *trans-denominational* because the experience of the Holy Spirit is understood "to transcend denominational walls, while it clarifies and underscores what is authentically Christian in each tradition without demanding structural or even doctrinal changes in any given church body."[23] In his study of charismatic renewal movements in Ghana, Cephas Omenyo points out that "whilst these groups have become catalysts for renewal in some denominations, they have also been the cause of conflict and misunderstanding in others."[24] With the gradual integration of charismatic renewal phenomena into historic mission church life, a "charismaticization" of Christianity is currently underway in African Christianity. This is evident not only in the adoption of Pentecostal/charismatic media cultures, but also in the programmes and liturgical reforms occurring in historic mission Christianity. In the words of Omenyo, "members of the various charismatic renewal groups

---

21. Richard Quebedeaux, *The New Charismatics: The Origins, Development, and Significance of Neo-Pentecostalism* (New York: Doubleday & Co., 1976).

22. Quebedeaux, *New Charismatics*, 5.

23. Quebedeaux, *New Charismatics*, 6.

24. Cephas N. Omenyo, *Pentecost Outside Pentecostalism: A Study of the Development of Charismatic Renewal in the Mainline Churches in Ghana* (Amsterdam: Boekencentrum, 2002), 7.

are determined to remain in their 'impoverished' churches and to revitalize them with the introduction of charismatic/Pentecostal spirituality."[25]

Evangelizing the Evangelized

The reference to charismatic renewal phenomena or pneumatic Christianity as belonging to the occult by its critics recalls how the Musama Disco Christo Church (MDCC) started in Ghana. The MDCC is one of the biggest and oldest African instituted churches in Ghana, which was called Gold Coast during the colonial era. Its name means "Church of the Army of the Cross of Christ." Around 1923, when a Ghanaian Methodist catechist, William Egyanka Appiah, started speaking in tongues, seeing visions, prophesying, and healing the sick through prayer, he and his sympathizers were *firmly* ordered by the Methodist Church authority to stop what was described as their "occult activities" because "the Methodists were not like that."[26] Almost a century later, most historic mission churches have started to accommodate charismatic renewal groups and phenomena within their ranks because their very survival has come to depend on how open they are to a charismatic ecclesiology and culture.

The early success of independent churches like the MDCC is seen in the fact that historic mission churches in Africa were pressured into renewal as a result of the drift of their members into Spiritual or *Aladura* ("people of prayer") churches. The panic that followed the success of these Spiritual churches is evident in the Synod Proceedings and the Conference Reports of the Presbyterian and the Methodist churches on what to do about their own Christianity. The PCG Synod was quite honest in assessment of the situation and responded by setting up a committee in 1965 to study the phenomenon of charismatic renewal and advise the church on what steps to take. The PCG Synod Committee clarified its mandate as

> an expression of the concern of the Church about the large numbers of people who leave the Presbyterian Church in order to join a Spiritual Church or to attend meetings of healers and prophets, and secondly, about groups forming themselves within the Church which often adopted similar practices usually unfamiliar to Presbyterian Church life.[27]

---

25. Omenyo, *Pentecost*, 7.
26. Christian G. Baëta, *Prophetism in Ghana* (London: SCM, 1962), 35.
27. Presbyterian Synod Report, 41.

These "practices unfamiliar to our church" referred basically to the religious features of pneumatic Christianity: speaking in tongues, healing and deliverance sessions, holding of all-night vigils characterized by loud mass extemporaneous prayers, the use of choruses (instead of hymns), prophecies, visions, revelations, and other pneumatic phenomena associated with Pentecostal/charismatic worship services. People joined the spiritual churches because these churches provided the indigenous ecclesial contexts where the pneumatic phenomena facing resistance within the PCG enjoyed freer expression.

In the words of a 1965 Presbyterian Church of Ghana Synod report: "It must be of interest to us that the Presbyterian Church of Ghana (PCG) is proportionally best represented [in the Spiritual churches] including even some Church agents."[28] One of the conclusions of the PCG Synod Committee is thus very instructive for our purposes:

> A large number of Christians join them because they are disappointed with their former churches. They complain that the worship there is dull and that there is no "spiritual power" . . . and that there is not sufficient prayer in the old churches. They therefore seek a younger, more zealous and more "spiritual" fellowship.[29]

Ironically, the Methodist Church Ghana, studying the same Spiritual and Aladura church phenomenon, also concluded in a 1968 Conference Report that the Methodists "had become the principal patrons" of these independent churches. Whether they were patronized mainly by Methodists, Roman Catholics or by Presbyterians, the bottom line was that considerable numbers of the membership of historic mission denominations maintained allegiance to their mother churches for Sundays. In the rest of the week, however, the same members went in search of Christian spirituality that made sense in a precarious African environment with its belief in malevolent forces believed to impede human health and progress. Thus, many members of the historic mission churches adopted a system of plural belonging by maintaining membership of their mother churches but worshipped with one of the many Spiritual churches around at the time.

---

28. Presbyterian Church of Ghana, *Minutes of 37th Synod Report* (29–31 August 1966), 44.
29. Presbyterian Synod Report, 42.

'No Longer Orphans': Holy Spirit and Presence of Christ

The result of these observations is that from the 1970s, charismatic renewal prayer groups started enjoying more tolerant responses from historic mission churches in which they operated. So, epistemologically, what do we learn of Pentecostalism and mission against the backdrop of these developments? Firstly, pneumatic Christianity has to do with encountering the Holy Spirit as the dynamic presence of Christ in the church. To encounter the Spirit, therefore, is to encounter Jesus Christ and this calls for what I sometimes refer to in my Pentecostal Studies lectures as a "pneumatological Christology."[30] Jesus worked as God in human form, but we work as human beings with all the accompanying limitations of the human person. No matter how much a person is filled with the Holy Spirit, he does not become divine; he or she remains human.

This is the way to understand the weaknesses, misinterpretations and misapplications of Scripture, moral failures and the like that show up in pneumatic or Pentecostal Christianity. If a human being can be so filled with the Holy Spirit of God, that by the enabling strength of the Spirit he or she can accomplish things that only God can accomplish in Christ, then that would amount to greater works. To perform greater works is to perform above human limitations – and that is possible only through the presence and empowerment of the Holy Spirit, who by the way, is the continuing *presence* of Jesus Christ among those he has called. Nevertheless, in the midst of these accomplishments we see human failures and weaknesses at work, which are indications that perfection only comes with the return of Christ.

Conclusion: Spirit Renewal and Ministry

I started the chapter on the rise of Pentecostalism not by narrating history, but by noting that the Pentecostal movement draws our attention to the importance of the ministry of the Holy Spirit in the church today. Aware that there are all sorts of criticisms against the movement but on the whole, I take a very positive view of pneumatic Christianity. The impressive congregations some of them have built, the attraction they have for our upwardly mobile youth, the kinds of media ministries they have developed, and the religious menu they

---

30. Pneumatology is the theology of the Holy Spirit while Christology is the theology of the life and work of Jesus Christ. "Pneumatological Christology," therefore, means an understanding of the work of the Holy Spirit that is informed by an appreciation of the person and work of Jesus Christ.

constantly roll out for the public tells me, that unless the older churches for example apply themselves to the task, their future would not be that bright. In conclusion, Africa has learnt a lot from European theology and Europe in turn may need to learn a few things from the types of immigrant charismatic communions working in their midst. In the words of Währishch-Oblau, instead of feeling threatened by the New Mission Churches and rejecting their criticism of "mainline" Protestantism as fundamentalist and culturally irrelevant, the Protestant churches could in grateful joy, perceive the work of the Holy Spirit outside the confines of their own organized pastoral activities, and recognize the genesis of new churches and congregations on European soil as "the grace of God."[31]

---

31. Claudia Währisch-Oblau, "We Shall be Fruitful in the Land: Pentecostal and Charismatic New Mission Churches in Europe," in André Droogers, Cornelius van der Laan and Wout van Laar (eds.), *Fruitful in this Land: Pluralism, Dialogue and Healing in Migrant Pentecostalism* (Zoetermeer: Uitgeverij Boekencentrum, 2006), 46.

5

Kenosis as Missional Strategy for a Church in Need of Conversion

Reimagining Mission in Post-Apartheid South Africa

J. Frederick Marais

> Kenosis is (thus) the *sine qua non* of both divinity and humanity, as revealed in the incarnation and cross of Christ, the one who was truly God and became truly human.[1]

I am an ordained Dutch Reformed pastor. I served in two congregations of the Dutch Reformed Church (DRC) for 15 years and for the past 18 years at Communitas[2] as a Congregational Facilitator and as Director for Training of the Western Cape Synod. Being of European descent, a Huguenot to be more specific, I have benefitted from the injustice of apartheid up until this very day. Although I, with many other White Christians of our country, confess the sins of apartheid, I do not pretend to understand the full extent of the injustice

---

1. Michael J. Gorman, *Inhabiting the Cruciform God* (Grand Rapids: Eerdmans, 2009), 36.
2. Communitas is a network of support services of the Uniting Reformed Synod of the Cape and the Dutch Reformed Synod of the Western and Southern Cape. For further information, visit www.communitas.co.za.

of the apartheid system on our fellow Black, coloured and Indian citizens.³ I accept the ongoing reality of White privilege, and seek, with many others, ways to partake in restorative justice. I believe that listening, as a counterintuitive act of de-centring, will remain part of what it means to be a South African for years and years to come. I cannot, and should not, force or colonize anyone to listen to me, but my missional vocation is continuously to try to create a space of grace through deep de-centred listening, where it becomes safe to listen to each other and where we can receive the future as it emerges.⁴ The following lines by Njabulo Ndebele give words to my understanding of calling as a White South-African living in post-apartheid: "You, all of you, have to reconcile not with me, but with the meaning of me . . . The journey to your future goes through the dot of loving me, despite myself, on the world map that lays out journeys towards all kinds of human fulfilment."⁵

David Bosch (1929–1992) was one of the most influential prophets of the Dutch Reformed Church in South Africa in the apartheid years. Globally, he is acclaimed for his contribution to missiological conversations attempting to re-imagine mission in a post-Christendom world. His ground-breaking book, *Transforming Mission*, laid the foundation for a new understanding of mission.⁶ When the book was published back in 1991, Bosch's own church, the Dutch Reformed Church (DRC), did not take part in the acclamation. However, now, in the post-apartheid era, more than 200 pioneer congregations of the Dutch Reformed Church in Southern Africa took on the challenge to journey together as partners in an attempt to embody a missional vision. Theologically, politically, and practically, they had to deal with the legacy of the apartheid theology that shaped and isolated them so deeply. The missional vision provided them with a language and practices guiding them on this journey. One of the most important lessons learned on this journey is that missional breakthroughs for these congregations only appear when power is relinquished or taken from them. In many ways, they have to be *pushed through*

---

3. For the sake of clarity, in this essay, I have opted to use apartheid-era language where necessary.

4. C. Otto Scharmer, *Theory U: Learning from the Future as It Emerges* (San Francisco: Berrett-Koehler Publishers, 2009).

5. Njabulo Ndebele, "The Cry of Winnie Mandela" cited in Antjie Krog, *Begging to Be Black* (Cape Town: Random House Struik, 2012), ix.

6. David J. Bosch, *Transforming Mission: Paradigm Shifts in Theology of Mission* (American Society of Missiology Series. Maryknoll: Orbis Books), 1991.

the pain where political and economic power is lost.[7] Being politically and socially powerless[8] creates a lot of angst and leads to the desire for isolation. In the narratives of these pioneer congregations, we found signs of a unique missional pattern that I would like to describe as a missional strategy of kenosis. Ten years after Southern African Partnership of Missional churches, SAPMC, started, in 2013, the General Synod of the DRC adopted a policy document on the mission of the church with the title: "Framework Document on the Missional Nature and Calling of the Dutch Reformed Church." On the kenotic nature of the missional church, the document states:

> The church practices a kenotic existence, emptying itself and giving itself away totally. The church moves to places and networks where it does not yet have any presence with the message of the gospel. This can take a huge toll on the church; but in our imitation of Christ, it is our solemn duty and privilege.[9]

Paralyzed by the Power Shift: A Church in Hiding

Post-Christendom has been described as an era where the churches have lost their power and have to mourn the loss of their powerful position in the past.[10] The loss of power for White congregations in Southern Africa is of a different kind and should, therefore, not be confused with that of the post-Christendom Europe or North America. The shift in power came almost overnight when political transformation took place in the mid-nineties, leading to the collapse of apartheid. The majority of the population, including most of the White population, embraced the first democratic election in 1994. None of the violence expected materialized. Worldwide, many regarded the peaceful transformation in South Africa as a miracle. The Rainbow Nation was born and the country could enjoy unity under the leadership of Nelson Mandela after the tension of the bitter conflict during the forty years of apartheid. A

---

7. Patricia Taylor-Allison and Frederick Marais, "Pushed through the Pain: The Spirit transforming churches across the world" is the title of a comparison study of congregations in South Africa and in the United States of America (*Blogs-Communitas*, 1st Sept 2008, https://communitas.co.za/push-through-the-pain/).

8. Although it is true that the Afrikaner and Afrikaner institutions like the Dutch Reformed Church lost their political and social power, economically they remain one of the most powerful groups in the country.

9. Dutch Reformed Church General Synod Report (2013), 6.

10. For instance, see Patrick Keifert, *We Are Here Now: A New Missional Era* (Eagle: Allelon Publishing, 2006).

power shift took place and gradually the White minority who were in power had to face this reality and get used to it.

The euphoria subsided as the impact of the power shift reached local communities and congregations. Few could hide from the impact on all spheres of society and, unexpectedly, communities (especially communities of faith) started to withdraw from their public roles. The White Afrikaner churches that supported apartheid went into hiding to survive the impact of this massive transformation. They could not find friends in government anymore.[11] Those prophetic anti-apartheid churches suddenly found their members and friends in positions of power in the new government.[12] As such, it became difficult for them to maintain a prophetic voice against the new injustices of post-apartheid South Africa. Both sides seemed paralyzed by the transformation so many prayed and struggled for. They found it difficult to imagine a role for the church in the new South Africa. Unfortunately, the old divisions of apartheid South Africa kept the ecumenical movement from a unified witness on issues such as justice, reconciliation and restitution.[13]

South Africa is highly acclaimed for our liberating constitution with the Bill of Rights as the cornerstone of our democracy (Assembly 1996). The missionary irony, or tragedy, was and remains, that our country is facing immense societal challenges, and it does not seem to be making progress on important fronts. Churches do not seem to know how to address these issues adequately.[14] There are many reasons for the inability of churches in South Africa to address the core issues in our society. Here, I focus on the Dutch Reformed Church and their loss of power, and the subsequent loss of their identity and understanding of mission.

The political transition of power in South Africa had a massive effect on the position and credibility of the DRC church and her congregations in the new democratic South Africa. They were publicly shamed for their moral and theological support of apartheid. They were pushed back into politically powerless positions. Although the Stellenbosch systematic theologian, Willie

---

11. F. E. Deist, in J. N. J. Kritzinger and W. A. Saayman, eds, *Mission in Creative Tension: A Dialogue with David Bosch* (Pretoria: S.A. Missiological Society, 1990), 124–39.

12. See John Allen, *Rabble-Rouser for Peace: The Authorized Biography of Desmond Tutu* (London: Rider), 2006.

13. See State Capacity Research Project, "Betrayal of the Promise: How South Africa Is Being Stolen," May 2017, https://pari.org.za/wp-content/uploads/2017/05/Betrayal-of-the-Promise-25052017.pdf.

14. Elnari Potgieter, South African Reconciliation Barometer Survey, 2019 Report (Cape Town, Institute for Justice and Reconciliation, 2019), http://www.ijr.org.za/home/wp-content/uploads/2019/12/800108-IJR-Barometer-Report-2019-final-web.pdf, 51.

Jonker, confessed the Dutch Reformed Church's sin in supporting apartheid at a conference in Rustenburg in 1990, the leadership did not participate in confessing their guilt at the hearings of the Truth and Reconciliation Commission (TRC) under the leadership of Desmond Tutu. When different synods of the church later confessed to the sin of apartheid, it was too little, too late to restore their public image. In the midst of all this turmoil on a national level, local congregations had to find a way to re-understand themselves and their mission. In a sense, the denomination and its congregations were forced into a kenotic mode by the loss of their power and this new reality was quite disorienting. In the next section, I look at the possibilities that arise when the kenotic nature of the life of Christ shapes the identity and mission of a church that lost its power.

Kenosis as a Missional Strategy

More and more, the *kenosis* of Christ is being used as an approach to facilitate our understanding of mission. In the past two decades, aware of post-Christendom reality, some missiologists, especially those in urban contexts, began to recognize the advantages of such an approach. Earlier, David Bosch connected kenosis with "his [Jesus'] identification with those on the periphery."[15] Yves Raguin observes:

> Kenosis places us in a state of receptivity. We develop an instinctive attitude of listening, trying to understand, letting ourselves be permeated with the atmosphere of our surroundings, passing beyond what is merely heard and seen to reach the personality of the people with whom we live, or those we may meet. In this way we learn to know others from within. . . . Kenosis, then, is the gateway to mutual understanding, and beyond this, to an intimate sharing that is the consummation of a relationship in union . . . . By dispossession of self we are able to absorb the amazing riches of others, the persons in themselves and as embodying a cultural tradition.[16]

In my attempt to suggest a kenotic mission theory for the DRC, I draw on the work of three New Testament scholars: Michael Gorman, Stephan Joubert

---

15. Bosch, *Transforming Mission*, 513.
16. Yves Raguin, *I Am Sending You: Spirituality of the Missioner* (Manila: East Asian Pastoral Institute, 1973), 111–12.

and Joseph Hellerman and their work on the Christ hymn in Philippians 2:5–11. Joubert, in his ethical[17] reading of Philippians 2:5–11, points to the stark difference between Paul's descriptions of the physical presence of Jesus in Philippians 2:5–11 and the bodily or anthropomorphic form of the typical Graeco-Roman deities. "Jesus deliberately chose to exchange his divine μορφή (*morphe*, meaning 'form' or 'shape') for the μορφή of a slave."[18] In doing that, Christ models a kenotic life by emptying himself voluntarily of all the privileges of his deity and associating fully with humanity's plight. This kenotic act reveals his true character, and not a temporary "strategy" that terminates with his exaltation as Lord: "The suffering Jesus on the cross is now the exalted Lord overall, but he still is who he is in terms of his character and deeds."[19] Paul models this kenotic life of Christ as "ethical exemplar" for the Philippians, and this should have "universal applicability" for the ethics of his followers.[20] Joubert laments that sadly, the vibrancy of Paul's picture of Jesus' humble character, which gave rise to this ethos among early Christians, has been ideologically forced from the centre to the periphery since the fourth century. It needs to be reclaimed by means of a new theological ethic.[21]

Hellerman follows the same line of argument but applies it to ecclesial life.[22] His study focuses on the socio-political world in the text: "It is commonly acknowledged, however, that Roman elite society was highly stratified and that this stratification was replicated in various non-elite social settings throughout the empire."[23] This would include those elite males in Roman society engaged in a quest for "the acquisition and preservation of personal and familial honour." These concerns, in turn, generated a consuming passion to identify persons publicly according to social status. Various other displays of social

---

17. Note the debate on an "ethical or soteriological" read of the Christ Hymn as explained by Floor and Viljoen. See L. Floor and Francois Viljoen, "Die Christus-Himne in Filippense: Soteriologies of Eties?" *In die Skriflig/In Luce Verbi* 36 (2002).

18. Joubert, Zimmermann and van der Watt. "The Kenotic Morphë of Christ and Character Formation in Paul's Ethical Discourse in Philippians 2:5–11," *Biblical Ethics and Application* (2017): 278.

19. Joubert, "The Kenotic Morphë," 280.

20. Joubert, "The Kenotic Morphë," 284. Joubert reminds us "Policarpus, in his *Epistula* and *Philippenses* about 60 years later, understands Christ's sacrificial life as the expected pattern of conduct for believers."

21. Joubert, "The Kenotic Morphë," 285.

22. These works of Hellerman include "The Humiliation of Christ in the Social World of Roman Philippi (Parts 1 and 2)," *Bibliotheca Sacra* 160 (July–Sept 2003): 321–36; (Oct–Dec 2003): 421–33; and *Embracing Shared Ministry: Power and Status in the Early Church and Why It Matters Today* (Grand Rapids: Kregel Academic, 2013).

23. Hellerman, "The Humiliation, Part 1," 322.

rank prevailed in the public arena and were duplicated throughout the empire, and this was done at a municipal level as well. Hellerman argues that this would also include smaller and remote cities including Philippi, especially under the reign of Augustus.[24] He continues to explore the implications of the Graeco-Roman social world for the Christian community in the "colony" of Philippi: "Perhaps more than any of Paul's converts, Christians in the Philippian church would have been under great pressure to conform in their own social relations to the marked stratification of the surrounding environment."[25] Paul, however, would resist this in his writing to the congregation. "Specifically, Paul resisted the idea that his readers should accommodate themselves to the social verticality and pride of honours that so indelibly left their mark on life in Philippi."[26] Paul would radically redefine the behaviour and attitude of the Christian community in reminding them of the voluntary humility of Jesus Christ in Philippians 2:6–11. In the same manner as Joubert, Hellerman does not focus on the ontology of the incarnation, but how the "picture of Jesus' self-humiliation would have resonated in the readers' social context," in particular reference to slavery and the cross,[27] the lowest class in their society.[28] It is clear "to ascribe to Jesus the status of a slave (Gk. *doulos*) was to assign to him a position of the greatest opprobrium in the social world of Paul's readers."[29] Slavery and the shameful death on the cross redefined shame and honour for the young Christian community: "The juxtaposition of the two ideas – *stauros* and *doulos* – served to compound the social stigma associated with both slavery and crucifixion in the ancient world and thereby to reinforce in the public arena the social hierarchy that served the interests of the dominant culture."[30]

---

24. Hellerman, "The Humiliation, Part 1," 324, 326.
25. Hellerman, "The Humiliation, Part 2," 423.
26. Hellerman, "The Humiliation, Part 2," 424.
27. Hellerman explains: "With Bartchy, wealthy freed men made much of their individual economic advantage and the esteem of their patron (ex-owner), in order to bolster their social standing. Elites, on the other hand, utilizing the natal status of the slave as the fundamental evaluative criterion, generally relegated all slaves – rich or poor, powerful or powerless – to a single class that they situated decidedly below free persons of any stripe on the social pyramid." Hellerman, "The Humiliation, Part 2," 425.
28. Hellerman, "The Humiliation, Part 2," 424.
29. Hellerman, "The Humiliation, Part 2," 427.
30. Hellerman, "The Humiliation, Part 2," 430.

Gorman views the kenotic act and attitude of Christ in Philippians 2:6–8 as "a counterintuitive narrative identity of Christ and God."[31] He identifies in verses 6–8 the following pattern:[32]

text	2:6a	2:6b	2:7–8
	Although in the form of God	Did not (exploit equality with God)	But (emptied himself . . . humbled himself)
Narrative pattern	Although	Not	But
Semantic pattern	Although (status)	Not (selfish act/ selfishness)	But (selfless act/Selflessness)
Syntactic pattern	Concessive participle	Negative verb	*alla* + (affirmed verbs)

In agreement with Joubert and Hellerman, Gorman does not regard the kenosis of Christ as a temporary phase or stage, but as a "counterintuitive narrative of identity." He, therefore, suggests that the particle *hyparchōn* must be translated causally – because – and not concessively – though or although – as most translations do.[33] The kenotic act of Christ on the cross, therefore, is a theophany.[34]

Kenosis as a Missional Strategy for the DRC

Let us return to our main question. What would a possible missional strategy look like for a church that erred by grasping power for its own benefit? It seems that Gorman's suggestion of a "counterintuitive" narrative is appropriate, and this is the challenge. As the first followers of Christ had to be warned by Paul not to align with the prescribed social need for status and honour in their society, the DRC is reminded by the same text to re-imagine themselves as a counter-culture. Of course, this will also be counterintuitive for a community who are used to being in power. The challenge goes deeper; the kenotic act of Christ is a voluntary act. He *chose* not to exploit his power by emptying himself. The proposal is that it could liberate the DRC to move from the lament of

---

31. Gorman, *Inhabiting the Cruciform God*, 25.
32. Gorman, *Inhabiting the Cruciform God*, 17.
33. Gorman, *Inhabiting the Cruciform God*, 20.
34. Gorman, *Inhabiting the Cruciform God*, 29. Also see John Lee Lounibos, *Self-emptying of Christ and the Christian: Three Essays on Kenosis* (Eugene: Wipf & Stock, 2012), 108.

their loss of political and social power, to making the counterintuitive move to choose to let go of power and privilege, for the sake of others. In the next section I will explore these possibilities further.

Ecclesial Discerning Kenotic Pattern (Habit):

I am going to apply Gorman's kenotic pattern of status – not holding on, for the sake of others – to the context of a democratic South Africa as described above. I suggest that this pattern could help as an ecclesial missional habit for the church who benefited unjustly from the apartheid regime.

Become Aware of Status

The pattern or habit starts with questions regarding status. The DRC as a faith community confesses to its status as called, gathered and blessed by the Triune God, invited to participate in God's mission. This is a typical missional identity statement. It needs to be taken out of generic abstraction to make sense in reality. We need to contextualize these claims in the context of post-apartheid South Africa. The DRC is a church that benefited from the injustice of apartheid and therefore has relatively easy access to resources. This historic privilege will follow them for decades to come. Many in and outside the DRC will contest this particular historical and contextual grounding of the confession. The contextual conversation is what is important, not the statement. It would doubtless need missional listening to understand the impact of "privilege," and the courage of truth telling. Many congregations often claim their lack of resources and influence, when often the opposite is true. For a congregation to participate in a kenotic mission, it needs an honest conversation regarding its historical, political, and social status in its community. Without doing this, they will not be able to empty themselves appropriately.

Did Not Abuse Power

The next phase of the kenotic pattern is "not holding on or exploiting 'power.'" As a missional community, the DRC could follow the *phroneo* (attitude) of Christ by not holding on or exploiting their power and privilege. *Phroneo* can also mean "to think in a specific way." In this case, the Philippians are exhorted to think the way that Jesus Christ would think. Louw and Nida also mention that *phroneo* has a relational context, meaning that in my relationship with specific people, I will have a specific *phroneo*. This is already instructive for churches. The mindset of Christ is not to be understood in abstraction, but in specific contextual relationships.

Gorman, following Hellerman describes this "downward movement as the antithesis of the alternative – selfish exploitation of status."[35] This will open up a rich but contested conversation through which the missional character of a congregation will surface further. Built into the kenotic movement is a voluntary limitation of (further) abuse of exploitation. "Not to abuse or exploit" must also be contextualized in the particularities of the relationships at hand. If a particular community becomes aware of injustice or privilege, they are encouraged to stop (not to). If, following Hellerman's argument, kenosis is to be understood as a restriction of imperial exploitation, then it could also mean a willingness to restrict oneself from harming others (further). The focus is not on "our rights and privileges" but on how we should restrict ourselves for the benefit of others. In the case of Christ's kenosis, the pattern is: Christ could abuse power, but restrained from abusing it. For a faith community such as the DRC and its colonial and political history, it is different. The DRC could and did abuse and exploit others. Phil 2:6–8 is, therefore, a call for all offenders to confess and repent of the abuse and exploitation.[36] For any church that aspires to be missional, such as the DRC, kenosis should be part of what it means to be missional. One simply cannot be missional and continue historic patterns of abuse and exploitation. Alternatively, in terms of Gorman's pattern, the kenotic movement is not from status to selfless act. The middle phase, "did not exploit," might be the twist in the missional tale.

It is important to note that the restriction from abuse of power, the *willingness* to be stripped off all power was, in the case of Christ, a voluntary act. It is something different when power is taken away from you. Kenosis is not the same as losing power. It is an intentional choice to restrain oneself from any power abuse. Churches that have lost power do not become missional instantly. In fact, if they claim their loss of power to be a missional act, they misunderstand the kenosis of Christ. Kenosis says, "I can, but will not exploit my power for my own advantage." Victimhood is not part of Paul's definition of the kenosis of Christ.

---

35. Gorman, *Inhabiting the Cruciform God*, 17.

36. The application in this article is on the DRC. The same argument would apply to gender discrimination and violence; corruption in the public and private sectors etc. In short to all that abuse power.

Did . . . Selfless Act

The last movement in the kenotic pattern is selfless act(s) of service. With this Christ completed the pattern. Christ, who was in the "form of God" (*morphe Theos*), humbled himself to the "form of a slave" (*morphe doulos*). The service act is selfless, stripped from any intention to harm or to capture, or dare we say "colonize," but to free the other to flourish. To participate in mission, the church with the same *phroneo* as Christ ought to shape their mission as selfless acts rather than imperial acts that colonize the other. Mission becomes a continuous emptying of the self in serving the world for the sake of their salvation, healing, justice, and reconciliation.

The desire of the institutional church for self-preservation by any means necessary will resist this call to selfless service at all costs. But, if the church can find the courage to accept the invitation to come and participate in what God is doing, to come and serve selflessly as Christ did, to come and empty yourself for the sake of others, not for yourself, it can be revitalized out of its paralyses. The invitation to participate with the kenotic mindset (*phroneo*) of Christ is the missional conversion that a church with colonial heritage, with tendencies of serving itself at the cost of others, has to accept. Is it different for other churches who fought against apartheid? Yes and no. The kenotic mission is a mission for all who follow Christ. There is simply no other alternative. But no, we should not use this as a call for the victims of injustice to endure more suffering. For the victims, kenosis is a word of comfort and promise. The victims could and should remind the church to comfort them with selfless acts of love and comfort, to fight for their cause selflessly. Pretorius argues convincingly that there should be empathy and patience with those who were wounded through injustice and exclusion. The internal scars or trauma of injustice, discrimination and exclusion is not to be removed by the adoption of a new constitution and economic policies.[37] The effect of injustice lingers on for a long time.

Conclusion: Kenosis Releases the Church from "Power Paralysis"

So, what happens when congregations understand their mission as a kenotic act and attitude? I will conclude by pointing to some patterns that I have experienced in my journey with congregations.

---

37. Helgard Pretorius, "Resurrecting Wounds in the After-life of Apartheid," 2018, https://www.andrewmurraysentrum.co.za/wp-content/uploads/2019/05/HELGARD-PRETORIUS-Resurrecting-Wounds.pdf.

Giving Up Control and Taking Risks into the Not-Knowing

At the "Living the Missional Calling" conference of SAPMC in Somerset-West in 2009, I described this realization with the following words: "We were all on a journey without knowing where it would lead us . . . After two years . . . the angst was mounting; we could not see results . . . (we were) hitting a wall. And, then, an unexpected turn-around happened. In desperation, the congregations and the leadership of SAPMC started to be honest about their angst and not-knowing."[38] This created a space where everybody felt free to be honest about not-knowing. When congregational leaders start to identify with the kenotic nature of Christ, they start to imagine a different style of leadership where they are not to control the affairs of their congregation, but to take risks, sometimes with the smallest of clues, into the unknown. One leader observed, "A conversation with unknown partners who listened intently to us helped us discover how God is working in and through our vulnerability."[39] Another added, "It was a turning point to realize that it is not you who take people on a journey; it is the Holy Spirit leading us when we dwell in the word and listen to each other when we gather as a faith community." In his book, *Missional Map-Making Skills in Times of Transition*, Alan Roxburgh calls this style of leadership "map-making."[40] He says, "Good map-makers do more than logically describe what is going on. They *enter into the experience of the in-between*, engaging the emotions that come with realizing that common sense is no longer common."[41]

Accepting Vulnerability

Mission was not a new concept to the DRC. We all understood that the church should reach out across its boundaries. However, most of the time mission was done from a position of power: from the haves to the have-nots. The missional vision was submissive to that, and it challenged us to follow Jesus into his vulnerability – to empty ourselves from the power that we received – is the kenotic challenge (Phil 2:6). This challenged us to plunge into relationships that are not contracted on the basis of our power and privilege. This is a serious confrontation when the church has a deep engraved culture to the enslavement

---

38. Frederick Marais, "The Emergence of Our Missional Calling in Living the Missional Calling," DVD SAPMC Conference, Helderberg Somerset-West, 11th Nov 2009.

39. Marais, "The Emergence of Our Missional Calling."

40. Alan J. Roxburgh, *Missional Map-Making: Skills for Leading in Times of Transition* (San Francisco: Jossey-Bass, 2010).

41. Emphasis mine, Roxburgh, *Missional Map-making*.

of power. It creates a culture where the church can only interact with others from a position of distance sustained through the power of resources. To be missional, we were learning, is to be vulnerable. Missional ministry is not to reach out to the needy, but to form a new community where all are in need of community. "Kenosis means powerlessness, continual purification growing from self-centeredness, growing in openness."[42]

From a Community of Hierarchy to Equality and Participation

A kenotic understanding of mission also had an almost uninhibited impact on our understanding of structure in congregations. Hellerman fittingly described how hierarchy, status, reputation, and connections were patterned in the empire.[43] The church, though, is not the empire. So, when Christians gathered to worship, to fellowship, and to meet and eat, the ruthless, divisive, and status-shaped backbone of the empire snapped. There would be no slave and no free in the church. There would be no Roman, no Greek, no Egyptian, and no barbarian. This was God's grand social experiment, and the Romans – from elites to the slaves – experienced the church as nothing short of a wild revolution of equality.[44]

Missional habits, such as *Dwelling in the Word and Dwelling in the World*, transformed our formal meetings, conferences and worship services into spaces of inclusion. In a congregation in the City Bowl of Cape Town where the hierarchy of older leaders ruled through a culture of conflict, I witnessed a dramatic change when missional habits were introduced. The hope was that these habits would cure the toxic culture of conflict, but the transformation was more dramatic. Slowly over three years, the inner structure of attention shifted away from the sins and wrongs of the other towards an appreciation of their gifts and talents. The practice of "affirmation" at first was impossible and ended in just more negative energy of ongoing accusations. Over and over the practice of affirmation was exercised until it became a habit. This inner shift in the attention of the listening eventually broke down the closed system of a small group of dominating leaders excluding others. The congregation was surprised that after three years of practicing these missional habits, more and

---

42. Nagabal Szabolcs, "The Ministry of Reconciliation through Kenosis," *Mozaik* 1.1, (2003): 10.

43. Hellerman, "The Humiliation."

44. Scot McKnight, *A Fellowship of Differents: Showing the World God's Design for Life Together* (Grand Rapids: Zondervan, 2014), Kindle Edition, Location 89.

more strangers in the city started to find a home in this congregation. The habits of listening and affirmation transformed them. In listening to others, they started to practise kenosis in their relationships toward strangers. By listening and not only speaking to strangers, they experienced hospitality and homecoming. Contrary to their fear, practising the missional pattern of kenosis was not an act of ecclesial suicide, but an act of liberation, as Paul promised the first congregation in Europe a long time ago.

6

Catalytic Church Mission and Peacebuilding in Africa

A Review of the Church's Prophetic Role in Socio-Political Change

Elias O. Opongo, SJ

What is the mission of the church in Africa today as far as peacebuilding and reconciliation is concerned? There are three ways of answering this question. One is to consider the existing types of conflict and disharmonies that threaten human dignity. These types of conflict include violent aggression, inter-ethnic and inter-religious conflicts, political violence, and religious extremism. A second way is to examine the structures of violence that largely contribute to systematic marginalization of parts of the population in a country. Two examples of these structures are unemployment, especially among the youth, and inequitable distribution of national resources. A third way is to study the dynamics of power behind the above forms of violence and examine how the church has responded or ought to respond as part of its mission of building the kingdom of God on earth and acting as a catalyst for socio-political change in Africa.

The church's mission in peacebuilding is subject to a continuing dual tension. On the one hand, it prioritizes proclamation of the gospel. On the other hand, it considers service to God's people through improving life conditions, and constant advocacy for justice and peace. There ought to be caution in accommodating the two sides of this healthy tension. Any kind of dichotomy is inimical and fails to bring the full realization of the kingdom of God to God's people. This is what one can refer to as mission in praxis. The promotion of peace and social justice in Africa has its roots in the Second Vatican Council which emphasized "the duty of the Church in the promotion of justice and peace in all spheres of human society with the light and leaven of the Gospel."[1] This explains why scholars are of the opinion that "there can be no social transformation or any missional praxis for human and cultural development embraced by African Christians and Africans in general without well-ordered, peaceful and reconciled communities."[2] The praxis approach ensures that the good news of the gospel becomes a reality in people's lives.[3] The existential mission of the church today demands that there be a clear commitment of the church in realizing God's kingdom on earth, mainly through three different but interrelated aspects of mission – proclamation of the gospel, provision of social-economic needs of the population, and peacebuilding and reconciliation. Our discussion here will primarily focus on peacebuilding and reconciliation and be concerned with Africa as far as factors that diminish and threaten human dignity.

The Church's Mission in Peacebuilding

The word "mission" has had different connotations in Africa. Right from the beginning of evangelization, those who brought the word to the continent were referred to as missionaries. Writing in 1926 about mission in Africa, Edwin Smith stated that:

> The year 1415 marked a new era in the history of Africa. For it was then that the Portuguese, by the capture of Ceuta on the Barbary coast, began the process which has continued to our own day, moved less by the love of exploration than by a desire for gold and ivory and slaves and zeal for converting the heathen,

---

1. Polycarp Pengo, *The Church in Africa: Mission and Challenges* (Vietcatholic.net 2011).

2. Stan Chu Ilo, "*Africae Munus* and the Challenges of a Transformative Missional Theological Praxis in Africa's Social Context," *Transformation* 31.2 (2014): 124.

3. Emmanuel Katongole, "The Gospel as Politics in Africa," *Theological Studies* 77.3 (2016): 713.

the Portuguese thereafter began to sail their caravels southwards along the western coast of Africa.[4]

The above statement is loaded with a number of realities that Africa had to endure in the process of receiving the word of God. Indeed, the primary evangelization to Africa was a mixed bag of exploitation, unidirectional trade and slavery. In fact, early missionaries suppressed African traditional religions and certain cultural practices that were meaningful to the African society but deemed unreligious by the colonial church. In other words, the word of God came violently to Africa. As such, the word "mission" had to undergo transformation for it to become and remain relevant to the African reality. Gradually the church was seen as providing both the proclamation of the gospel and basic social services like hospitals, schools and churches as places for worship.

There has been a consistent growth in the number of Christians in Africa. According to the Pew Research Center, the number of Christians in Africa has been growing and by 2050 four in ten Christians will be in Africa and the number will rise from 517 million in 2010 to 1.1 billion in 2050.[5] For African theologians like Stan Chu Ilo,

> . . . the momentum of African Christian expansion reflects Africa's unique map of the universe and the social, cultic, cultural, religious, and spiritual priorities and aspirations of African people. They also present opportunities for the renewal of World Christianity through the trends in African Christianity which reflect African types and models of Christianity.[6]

Despite the tremendous growth of the church in Africa, the church encounters challenges such as conflicts, injustice, violence, inter-ethnic and religious discrimination and marginalization. In spite of this the church has played an important role in the promotion of education and health in the continent through the construction of hospitals, health centres, dispensaries, hospices, and clinics as well as socio-cultural centres and schools. The mission for peacebuilding and reconciliation often takes place among broken

---

4. Edwin W. Smith, *The Christian Mission in Africa: A Study on the Work of the International Conference at Le Zoute, Belgium, September 14th to 21st, 1926* (London: The International Missionary Council, 1926), 2.

5. Joseph Lie, "Global Christianity – A Report on the Size and Distribution of the World's Christian Population," Pew Research Centre, 19th Dec 2011, http://www.pewforum.org/2011/12/19/global-christianity-exec/.

6. Ilo, "*Africae Munus*," 118–19.

relationships, where the society at micro and macro levels faces violence, discrimination, hatred, marginalization, racism, ethnic conflict or religious segregation or hatred. These situations call for urgent response from the church with the commitment to drawing humanity together in order to preserve the image of God. Such a mission of the church is transformative given that it aims to deconstruct perceptions of division and marginalization, and create new experiences of reconciliation.

Ilo argues that:

> ... a transformative missional theology in Africa which places emphasis on reconciliation must be both Trinitarian and Afrocentric. It must conceive reconciliation as the work of God and pastorally and practically work towards making it possible for God's grace to be felt in those places where there is need for healing.[7]

Addressing the culture of violence and historical injustice that different countries have faced in Africa is fundamental. Victims of violence in Rwanda, Kenya, Sierra Leone, Angola, DRC, Burundi, South Sudan among others, have a right to justice even as the church works towards reconciliation. Perpetrators of violence have to be held accountable. The church has an important role to play in promoting a culture of peace based on accountability, tolerance and respect of human rights, mainly geared towards socio-political change. According to Appleby, shaping the culture of peace "means the striving to create a culture of nonviolence, peace and justice, a society for which human dignity and human rights are sacrosanct written both in law and in human hearts."[8] The responsibility therefore falls on the church to promote justice and peace for the people through inclusive initiatives that involve all Africans.

Contextual Analysis of the African Continent

In the African context where there is ethnic diversity within each nation-state, social conflict easily emerges. Such conflicts surface as a result of competition for natural resources, systemic economic, social and political marginalization of certain groups within the country, human rights abuses, and indiscriminate violent action against specific sectors of the society. The conflicts can turn into

---

7. Ilo, "*Africae Munus*," 124.

8. Scott Appleby, "Building Sustainable Peace: The Roles of Local and Transnational Religious Actors," in *Religious Pluralism, Globalization, and World Politics*, ed. T. Banchoff (New York: Oxford University Press, 2008), 2.

rebellion, riots, revolutions, civil disobedience, demonstrations, marches, racial and religious violence.[9] Rudolf Rummel argues that in the twentieth century most civilian deaths were carried out by governments, in what he refers to as *democide*.[10] These deaths were largely through political violence, state terror, and extrajudicial killings. Democide was carried out by the political leadership's desire to impose its laws, rules and regulations on the population and enforce them through ruthless and violent application of force, often military. In such situations, the state uses instruments of violence, subdues the will of the citizens, and instrumentalizes fear as a strategy for governance.

In Uganda, extreme political violence in Idi Amin's regime (1971–1979) led to the deaths of more than 300,000 people. In Ethiopia the government unleashed violence against civilians in what came to be known as the "Red Terror." The Red Terror took place between 1974 and 1978 following the Derg regime's ascendancy to power in 1974 through a bloodless coup against Emperor Haile Selassie. The violent conflict between Renamo and Frelimo (1976–1992) in Mozambique led to the deaths of thousands of civilians. In Sierra Leone the rebel group Revolutionary United Front (RUF) and Sierra Leone government forces (1991–2002) meted out brutal violence against civilians maiming and killing many. More than 70,000 people were killed, and 2.6 million people have been displaced. Similarly, in Rwanda in 1994, state sponsored genocide killed more than 800,000.

In South Sudan thousands of people died since the eruption of violence in the youngest nation in Africa, with more than one million people displaced as refugees into the neighbouring countries. The Central Africa Republic has been locked in internecine and vicious conflict that has led to many deaths. The pseudo-religious conflict between Muslims' Seleka militia and Anti-Balaka militia of Christian and traditional religious affiliates has protracted instability within the country, making the country ungovernable. In DRC multiple rebel groups are responsible for death of close to five million people. The capacity to contain violence is weak and is exacerbated by a lack of political will to bring peace. Joseph Kabila initially refused to step down despite coming to the end of his mandate. Kabila later left office following the election of Felix Tshikedi in December 2018. Kenya, Uganda, Zimbabwe and Ivory Coast have also experienced election-related violence. There are other low intensity conflicts in Burundi, Togo, Mozambique, Ethiopia, Madagascar, Nigeria, among others.

---

9. Steenkamp Chrissie, "Violence and Social Conflict," in *The Oxford International Encyclopaedia of Peace*, ed. N. J. Young (2010): 4:318.

10. R. J. Rummel, *Death by Government* (New Brunswick: Transaction Publishers, 1994).

In Cameroon, the Anglophone minority have been demonstrating against the marginalization of the Anglophones by the government of Paul Biya. Idris Deby of Chad has postponed elections claiming lack of sufficient funds to conduct the elections. Deby won the elections when they were eventually conducted in April 2021. Deby died shortly thereafter from battlefield injuries. Yoweri Museveni in Uganda has changed the term and age limit in the constitution to allow him to stay in power indefinitely. Robert Mugabe of Zimbabwe was forced out of office in November 2017 by the military after 38 years in power. In early 2018 after allegations of corruption and abuse of office, the Africa National Congress (ANC) unseated Jacob Zuma from presidential office in South Africa.

Prophetic Role of the Church in Socio-Political Change

These diverse incidences of violence and political agitation demonstrate that multiple political instabilities on the continent add to the crises of leadership, poor economic and social infrastructure as well as chronic unemployment. The church has played an important role in fostering peace, both at the grassroots and top leadership levels, standing out as the conscience of the society. For example, in 1980, just after Zimbabwe's independence, the Catholic Bishops stated that:

> In a plural society like Zimbabwe, it is important to have a clear view of the relationship between the church and the state. The church is not identified with any political community, nor is she bound to any political system. Rather her function is to be the moral conscience of the nation, the sign and safeguard of the supreme value of the human person.[11]

The role of the church as an impartial advocate and arbitrator is fundamental to creating consciousness within the society to respect and protect human dignity as well as safeguard the common good of the society. The church, while responsible for the care of souls through proclamation of the word of God and provision of social services, has the responsibility to speak up against

---

11. *Welcome Zimbabwe: A Statement of the Roman Catholic Bishops of Zimbabwe* (17th April, 1980), quoted in Oscar Wermter, "The Role of the Church(es) in the Promotion of the Rule of Law and Democracy in Zimbabwe," in *Assessing Progress in the Implementation of Zimbabwe's New Constitution: National, Regional and Global Perspectives*, eds. Alexander D. Berndt, Oliver Christian Ruppel, and Kathrin Maria Scherr (Baden-Baden: Nomos, 2017), 139.

injustices, oppression and marginalization of people, as well as social, political and economic structures that threaten the wellbeing of human persons.

Among Catholics, many episcopal conferences used pastoral letters to advocate for social change, speak out against violation of human rights, and defending political freedom, economic and social rights as well as citizen participation in democratic processes.[12] The bishops of the Great Lakes region, for example, in speaking against genocide, reiterated that: "The protection of people from genocide ensures that the human person is not subjected to the immense suffering and trauma that accompany an experience of genocide."[13] The Great Lakes bishops, in an effort to address these conflicts, formed a regional consultation body of bishops from northern Uganda and eastern DRC to deliberate, strategize and identify the best pastoral approach to addressing protracted conflicts in the region. To a great extent these efforts have not been successful due to the complexity of the regional conflict and the difficult political terrain that created suspicion and enmity between the regional states. In West Africa, responding to the killings carried out by the Fulani herdsmen, especially in Benue State in Nigeria, the Anglican bishops issued a statement which read in part that:

> The bishops observed that as a result of the continuous inaction of the Government, people are beginning to suspect that there is complicity of the Federal Government in these despicable acts. We, therefore, call on the Federal Government, as a matter of urgency to address these ugly trends and ensure that the culprits are brought to justice.[14]

The African Catholic bishops under the Symposium of Episcopal Conferences of Africa and Madagascar (SECAM), issued a pastoral letter entitled "Governance, Common Good and Democratic Transitions in Africa," which stated that:

> The Church . . . has been at the heart of all efforts towards better governance. In many countries, during the delicate democratic transitional period of the 1990s, the Church played a clearly

---

12. Terence A. McGoldrick, "Episcopal Conferences Worldwide and Catholic Social Thought, in Theory and Praxis: An Update," *Theological Studies* 75.2 (2014): 376–403.

13. AMECEA Documentation Service, "Message of the Bishops of the Great Lakes Region of Africa" No. 465 (February 15, 1997).

14. Anglican Communication News Service, "Nigerian bishops speak out against increasing attacks by Fulani herdsmen," 23 January 2018, http://www.anglicannews.org/news/2018/01/nigerian-bishops-speak-out-against-increasing-attacks-by-fulani-herdsmen.aspx.

visible role of support. Five out of the eight National Transitional Conferences that were organized during this epoch were chaired by Catholic Bishops. This intervention by the Church helped, in many cases, to ensure peaceful democratic transitional processes with a lot of success, through inclusive consultations and dialogue. Many Christians in some volatile situations helped in bringing about peace and reconciliation. The Church has to take her responsibilities in the socio-political domain. She has to be fully involved in the in-depth transformation of our society.[15]

The church's prophetic role, as noted above, has been underscored by its interventions for political change at national level in the DRC, Congo-Brazzaville, Guinea-Conakry, Mozambique, and South Africa. In Zimbabwe the church courageously spoke against the oppressive regime of Robert Mugabe. In 2016, a group of church leaders challenged the president in an open letter stating:

> We, the undersigned church-based organizations, noting the deteriorating political situation in the country, worried about continued curtailing of people's freedoms by your government, concerned about the socio-economic crisis that has reached levels that threaten survival of the helpless masses and ultimately peace of the nation, disturbed by the increasingly restive populace and the brutal show of force by state machinery, do call upon you, Mr President, to:
> - Humbly admit before God and the Zimbabwean populace that the country is in a dire situation that requires an extraordinary collective response to rescue it from a total collapse that may trigger a regrettable spontaneous civil unrest.
> - Open up for national dialogue in the light of the above.
> - Stop unleashing terror on citizens for expressing genuine grievances.

---

15. SECAM, *Governance, Common Good and Democratic Transitions in Africa* (Accra: SECAM, 2013).

If you fail to address these issues by September 28, we will be forced to exercise our democratic right to petition Parliament to impeach you.[16]

In South Africa and Mozambique, the church was instrumental in spearheading reconciliation processes. The church in South Africa joined hands with other religions in fight against apartheid. With the end of apartheid in 1994, the church was asked to play another important role of reconciling the whole nation though a truth commission. Thus, the seventeen-member Truth and Reconciliation Commission (TRC) was formed headed by the Nobel laureate, Desmond Tutu. They were given two years to "hold hearings on allegations of human rights abuses committed from March 1, 1960, through December 6, 1993."[17] While the TRC did not achieve full reconciliation for South Africa, it brought forward many elements of the hidden truth that the majority of South Africans were never aware of. The big challenge today for the church and other actors in South Africa is to respond pastorally and socio-politically to unemployment, insecurity, marginalization of the majority of the population, land distribution and related inequalities, as well as often tense inter-racial and ethnic relations.

The bishops of Malawi, in their 1992 pastoral letter, strongly spoke against dictatorship of the then president, Kamuzu Banda. The pastoral letter led to a sudden turn of events and the government succumbed to pressure and allowed multiparty politics which expanded democratic space. At the same time the letter led to mass arrests, threats to the lives of the bishops and control of any public demonstrations. However, both local and international pressure led to eventual call for democratic elections in which Banda was defeated in 1994.[18]

In Kenya, the inter-religious initiative in the late 1990s known as the "Ufungamano Initiative" was meant to counter the government's capture of the constitutional review process. The initiative's momentum grew, eventually forcing the government to agree to a more inclusive process. Subsequently, more than ten years later the country promulgated a new constitution in 2010.

---

16. Zimbabwean church leaders, "Stop Police Brutality: Open letter to the President of the Republic of Zimbabwe, His Excellency R. G. Mugabe," Mike Campbell Foundation, 23rd Sept 2016, http://www.mikecampbellfoundationresources.com/page/stop-police-brutality.

17. Lynn S. Graybill, "South Africa's Truth and Reconciliation Commission: Ethical and Theological Perspectives," in *Ethics and International Affairs*, ed. J. H. Rosenthal (Georgetown: Georgetown University Press, 1999), 372.

18. AMECEA Documentation Service, "Message of the Bishops of the Great Lakes Region of Africa" No. 465 (February 15th 1997), reproduced in *SEDOS Bulletin* 29.5 (May 1997).

In Burkina Faso, the Catholic bishops in 2015 spoke against the coup d'état by the military against the transitional government formed after the removal of former president Blaise Compaoré.[19] The bishops embarked on a programme aimed at training identified youth leaders, lawyers and educators in peacebuilding, human rights, nonviolence and citizen participation in democracy in all the dioceses and arch-dioceses in the country.[20] Resource-oriented conflict is yet another concern for the church in Africa.

Historically, there have been conflicts related to competition for resources in Sierra Leone, Angola and more recently in DRC, among others. The Catholic Social Teaching stipulates that the environment and natural resources belong to all humanity. Natural resources are a gift from God which must be evenly shared among all human beings including future generations. This is why the Catholic Synod Fathers at the Second Special Assembly for Africa expressed "strong concern and sadness at the senseless destruction of natural resources as well as degradation and abuse due to human actions borne out of greed for profit both by local Africa leaders and in complicity with foreign interests,"[21] which is already unsustainable and should be curtailed. Pope Francis warned in his Encyclical *Laudato Si* that: "If present trends continue, this century may well witness extraordinary climate change and an unprecedented destruction of ecosystems, with serious consequences for all of us."[22] The church is therefore charged with the responsibility of creating awareness and educating the people on environmental challenges, lobbying governments to adopt and implement policies that are environmentally friendly and geared towards development of renewable sources of energy and conscientization on the importance of planting trees. The church also demands that "Mining Law and Licences of the extractive and mining industries be revised and formulated in such a way that they protect local peoples' interests and rights, and protect the environment."[23] This is particularly important given the resurgence of major extractive industries in Africa and the lack of stringent measures in place to

---

19. Catholic News Service, "Burkina Faso Bishops Call for Fresh Elections, Denounce Military Coup," 22 September 2015, https://www.catholicregister.org/home/international/item/20928-burkina-faso-bishops-call-for-elections-denounce-military-coup.

20. Catholic News Service, "Burkina Faso Bishops."

21. Pengo, *The Church in Africa*, http://www.theologia.va/content/cultura/es/plenarie/2008-dal-secolarismo-alla-secolarita/talks/paper9.html..

22. Francis, *Laudato Si* (Vatican City: The Vatican, 2015).

23. Pengo, *The Church in Africa*, http://www.theologia.va/content/cultura/es/plenarie/2008-dal-secolarismo-alla-secolarita/talks/paper9.html

ensure communities benefit from the proceeds while at the same time the environment is protected.

Another area of concern for the church in Africa is the issue of migration. There is large movement of populations within Africa, mainly due to protracted conflict, political persecution and search for economic opportunities. Unfortunately, migration often renders affected populations susceptible to exploitation for cheap labour, human trafficking, sexual abuse, imprisonment, violence and even deaths. At the Second African Synod Pope Benedict XVI in his Exhortation, *Africae Munus*, elaborates that: "The human conscience can only respond with indignation to these situations. Migration inside and outside the continent thus becomes a complex drama which seriously affects Africa's human capital, leading to the destabilization or destruction of families."[24] The sudden influx of populations following conflict has rendered some host countries vulnerable to insecurity, environmental constraints and political instability. According to the UNHCR, Africa hosts 26% of world refugees, with more than 18 million people displaced, mainly from Central Africa Republic, Somalia, South Sudan and Burundi.[25] There is, however, need to review the manner in which refugee hosting has been carried out on the continent. Moving more towards integration than encampment would be an effective way in realizing a sustainable approach to Africa's refugee crisis. The tradition has been to confine refugees to the camps and supply humanitarian aid, whereas refugees can also be integrated into the local population and be encouraged to farm or work and provide for their basic needs. Hence, the church needs to advocate even more for an approach to refugees that treats them with greater dignity.

Further still, the church in Africa is also faced with the challenge of addressing the dignity of women and youth. Given the traditional values of many African societies, women have in most cases been treated as second-class citizens, and denied basic rights that should give them equitable opportunities in life. The church has taken measures towards the "restoration of the dignity of the women in Africa"[26] by educating women, creating empowerment and advocacy programmes as well as income generating programmes for marginalized women. Women are also vulnerable to human trafficking, and

---

24. Benedict XVI, *Africae Munus*, no. 84, The Holy See website, 19th Nov 2011, http://w2.vatican .va/content/benedict-xvi/en/apost_exhortations/documents/hf_ben-xvi_exh_20111119_africae-munus.html#Chapter_I.

25. United Nations High Commission for Refugees (UNHCR), "Africa," accessed 23rd Feb 2021, http://www.uhcr.org/africa.html.

26. Pengo, *The Church in Africa*.

in response, the church has come up with projects to rescue women from trafficking and create awareness on potential predators. Pope Benedict XVI in his exhortation to the Second African Synod stated that:

> Giving women opportunities to make their voice heard and to express their talents through initiatives which reinforce their worth, their self-esteem and their uniqueness would enable them to occupy a place in society equal to that of men – without confusing or conflating the specific character of each – since both men and women are the "image" of the Creator (cf. *Gen* 1:27).[27]

The growing number of youth unemployment in the continent, human trafficking, child labour, recruitment into the armed militia and gangs, as well as drug trafficking are equally issues of urgent concern. According to the Africa Development Bank: "Of Africa's nearly 420 million youth aged 15–35, one-third are unemployed and discouraged, another third are vulnerably employed, and only one in six is in wage employment. Youth face roughly double the unemployment rate of adults, with significant variation by country."[28] The Catholic Church in Africa has taken measures towards empowering youth with the necessary information they need for their growth. It uses World Youth Day to empower youth through reflection, study and prayer. Pope John Paul II for example, in *Ecclesia in Africa* stated that "we know very well that youth are not only the present but above all the future of humanity. It is, thus, necessary to help young people to overcome the obstacles thwarting their development: illiteracy, idleness, anger, drugs."[29] The future of Africa is in securing the needs of the youth and ensuring that there are sustainable economic, political and social structures to guarantee their education, employment and well-being.

Conclusion

The church's task in peacebuilding is daunting particularly given that it entails diverse and fundamental components of human existence. As noted above, the church has played a vital role in responding to enabling conditions that generate conflicts and diminish human dignity. The church created social safety nets aimed at restoring the lost or damaged dignity and safeguarding

---

27. Benedict, *Africae Munus*, no. 57.

28. Africa Development Bank Group, "Jobs for Youth in Africa: Catalysing Youth Opportunity Across Africa," March 2016, https://www.afdb.org/fileadmin/uploads/afdb/Images/high_5s/Job_youth_Africa_Job_youth_Africa.pdf.

29. John Paul II, *Ecclesia in Africa* (Yaounde: Libreria Editrice Vaticana, 1995), no. 93.

the common good. To a large extent the church does not have answers to political challenges but her presence and solidarity with the suffering masses is crucial in catalysing social, economic, and socio-political change. The church in Africa must thus strive to remain apolitical and work in collaboration with civil societies to bring about the effective change in society. Pope Benedict XVI emphasizes that "while a distinction must be made between the role of pastors and that of the lay faithful, the church's mission is not political in nature. Her task is to open the world to the religious sense by proclaiming Christ."[30] The church must take it upon itself to reshape the culture of violence and impunity into one of accountability.

The church has been able to provide emotional as well as spiritual support to communities affected by war. The church's peacebuilding initiatives have facilitated the process of dialogue, mediation, and reconciliation.[31] Hence, the church ought to continue building a culture of non-violence that seeks alternatives to extreme forms of violence. The Gandhi Peace Foundation, the International Fellowship of Reconciliation, Nonviolent Peace Force and Nonviolence International all provide training in nonviolent action in different parts of the world. Militarization of conflicts and peace have not shown any substantial success in many conflicts that our world has known. The church's mission for peace and reconciliation therefore remains fundamental as an alternative response to human situations of conflict with love, trust-building, healing, forgiveness and reconciliation.

For the African church, peacebuilding is not an addendum in her commitment to mission, it is part and parcel of *missio Dei* and so is expressed in multiple activities aimed at building the Kingdom of God here on earth. This peacebuilding mission is founded on the greatest commandment of love for God and neighbour, worked out by enhancing social cohesion through planting seeds of love, tolerance, understanding, empathy, care for the poor and marginalized. It also includes the care of the environment, promotion of rights and duties, dialogue and mediation, forgiveness and reconciliation. All of the above are part of the larger mission of transforming our world and allowing humanity to live life to the full. In order to achieve this, the church needs to be the moral voice that draws social and political leaders to work towards promoting and protecting human dignity, common good, active

---

30. Benedict, *Africae Munus*, no. 23.
31. Tsjeard Bouta, Ayse Kadayifci-Orellana and Mohammed Abu-Nimer, *Faith-Based Peace Building: Mapping and Analysis of Christian, Muslim and Multi-Faith Actors* (Hague/Washington DC: Clingendael/Salam Institute for Peace and Justice, 2005), 1–152.

citizen participation in social organization and integral development focused on improving the quality of life.

7

Mission and Development

Rowanne Sarojini Marie

The aim of this chapter is to reflect on the symbiotic relationship between mission and development in the changing context of Africa. Through the lenses of a People Centred Development Model (PCD),[1] it seeks to explore the paradigm shifts in development discourse, and examines missional responses in the wake of such changing contexts. Developmental changes in the modern world – issues such as information explosion, the environment and climate change, a new political landscape, and a greater awareness of gender issues – can no longer lean on the backdrop of colonial means and methods. These means and methods, to an extent, repressed the process of development. Such changes therefore need to go beyond the provision of charity to the poor to rising up against the structural injustices that plague the most vulnerable of our communities. In the developing context of Africa, such notable changes have great impact on the church, which in turn calls for a re-visioning of mission methods and practices.

Mission and Development: A Symbiotic Relationship

Mission and development share a symbiotic relationship. Mission's mandate is *development*, and equally development initiatives and interventions are missional in nature. This was modelled through the life and times of Jesus and should continue to shape and inform the church's mandate. On the occasion of his inaugural sermon, Jesus selected this text: "The Spirit of the Lord is upon me because He has anointed me to *preach the gospel* to the *poor*; He has

---

1. McGlory Speckman, *A Biblical Vision of Africa's Development* (Pietermaritzburg: Cluster Publications, 2007), 24–46.

sent me to heal the broken hearted, to preach deliverance to the captives, and recovering of sight to the blind, to set at liberty them that are bruised."[2] It is in texts such as these that we recognize an interconnectedness between the intended purposes of mission and development.

Emanating from the character of Christ, the church by its very nature is missional. Its missional character makes it God's instrument to transform humans into what God intended for them. The church is therefore beckoned to respond to the realities in society. It is, thus, *called out of* the world and *sent* back into that same world to manifest the reign of God on earth. Its outreach should address both spiritual and physical needs of the community. At the heart of the missional nature of the church, we discover the God of the Bible as a God of development, a God who is concerned about the poor, weak, vulnerable, isolated and powerless.

The concepts of "mission" and "development" are addressed from a wide range of theological perspectives and worldviews. When one considers the term "mission," one cannot help but turn to the work of David Bosch, who was an influential missiologist and theologian best known for his book *Transforming Mission: Paradigm Shifts in Theology of Mission*.[3] It is noted that other chapters of this book will give more attention to the work of Bosch, but for the purpose of this chapter, it is necessary that we briefly distinguish between *mission*, referring primarily to *missio Dei* (God's mission) and *missions* (the *missiones ecclesiae*: the missionary ventures of the church). *Missio Dei* reflects the nature and activity of God's involvement in and with the world, pronouncing the *good news* that God is a God for people, and that the church is a privileged participant in such activity. Missions, then, refer to particular forms of participation in *missio Dei*, subject to specific times, places and needs.[4] Importantly, Bosch submits that the mission of the church needs to be constantly renewed and re-conceived.[5] Not only is the church's concern linked with conversion, church growth, and the reign of God, but it is also intrinsically involved in economy, society and politics.

The term "development" can be complex, ambiguous and multifaceted, with various sub-divisions such as human (personal), social, political and

---

2. See Luke 4:18, where Jesus reiterates the words of the prophet Isaiah 61:1–2 (NRSV).

3. David Bosch, *Transforming Mission: Paradigm Shifts in the Theology of Mission* (Maryknoll: Orbis Books, 1991).

4. Bosch, *Transforming Mission*, 10.

5. Bosch, *Transforming Mission*, 519.

economic.⁶ Writing from an African perspective, McGlory Speckman helps us to streamline the sub-divisions into two focal points namely, People-Centred Development (PCD) and Growth-Centred Development (GCD). PCD is the process which places people at the centre of development and is concerned with human development.⁷ It focuses on the people's needs and interests, regardless of their background, education and socio-economic status and looks at ways in which people can be developed in terms of skills, resources and education, in order to help them to live an improved quality of life. GCD, on the other hand, focuses mainly on economic growth. Although society needs economic growth, in some cases this happens at the cost of the poor and vulnerable people of society – a situation where the rich become richer at the expense of the poor. True development requires people to have the power to influence the decisions that affect their lives. This is called genuine community participation. The participation of people in development plays a critical role because it creates empowerment – and without participation, empowerment is not possible. For participation to be meaningful, people must feel empowered in different ways, for example, political, economic, social and institutional. PCD goes hand in hand with empowerment and participation, enabling people to influence the process of development and, thus, determine their own needs. The relationship between the social, political and economic goals is fully recognized by human development or people-centred development.

A contemporary African understanding of development draws on seminal theorists such as Ronald Sider,⁸ David Korten,⁹ and Amartya Sen.¹⁰ Each of them offers us working definitions and helpful frameworks. While all these scholars wrote from a Western perspective, their formative works in the area of development theory have become the bedrock upon which African scholars are building. For example, Amartya Sen introduced the concept of "development as freedom" which is also the title of his book on the subject. His overall argument asserts that true freedom must include the freedom to access

---

6. Stan Burkey, *People First: A Guide to Self-reliant Participatory Rural Development* (London: Zed Books, 1993).

7. Speckman, *A Biblical Vision*, 24.

8. See Ronald J. Sider, *Rich Christians in an Age of Hunger: A Biblical Study* (Downers Grove: InterVarsity Press, 1977). Ron Sider is the founder of Evangelicals and Social Action and has authored many other publications on the church and social action.

9. See David C. Korten, *When Corporations Rule the World*. 2nd ed. (Bloomfield: Kumarian Press, 2001).

10. Amartya Sen, *Development as Freedom* (New York: Knopf, 1999). Sen is an Indian economist noted for his contributions to welfare economics and social choice theory and for his interest in society's poorest members.

social services such as healthcare, sanitation and nutrition, just as much as it considers economic and social freedom. He adds that the freedom-centred perspective has a universal similarity and shares a common concern with an improved quality of life, which becomes fundamental to the purpose and function of development. Korten also underpins his concept of development as an improved quality of life, stating that development is "a process by which the members of a community increase their personal and institutional capacities to mobilize and manage resources to produce sustainable and justly distributed improvements in the quality of life, as perceived and felt by the people themselves."[11]

Notwithstanding these various descriptions, contradictions, and challenges, what becomes clear is the synergetic relationship between mission and development, with both sharing the common space of *good news to the poor*, including an engagement with the diverse issues to which the poor of society are most vulnerable. Christian mission thus becomes a vital means of making positive contributions to the achievement of development objectives and goals, and vice versa. Hence, mission is understood to include God's movement to the world and the church as an instrument of that mission. To participate in mission is to take part in the movement of God's love toward people. Mission, therefore, can no longer be seen merely as the practical extension of the church. It has to be understood fundamentally as a *representation of God* by God's people in the world. The people-centred development is one of the vehicles that fulfils the mission mandate of the church.

Mission in a Transforming and Developing Context

We live in a dynamic context where change is inevitable. It is the age of information explosion, post-modernity, post-Eurocentrism, post-colonialism, post-imperialism, post-socialism and post-industrialism. It is an age of globalization marked by borderlessness. It is also a time of severe climate change plus a new awareness of the place of women in society.[12] Such changes are noted in all spheres of everyday life such as political, social, environmental, cultural, economic, religion and education. Even more, African societies reveal a dichotomous structure consisting of both "Third World" and "First

---

11. David Korten, *Getting into the 21st Century* (Bloomfield: Kumarian Press, 1990), 67.

12. Harold Le Roux, *The Church and Mission* (Pietermaritzburg: Cluster Publications, 2011), 15.

World" dimensions.[13] One cannot undertake the development process without analysing the changing social structures.

In *When Corporations Rule the World*,[14] David Korten argues that in such changing contexts, communities face a number of concerns and challenges. He broadly classifies this as the threefold global crises of poverty, social disintegration, and ecological degradation, which are symptomatic of our institutions and values malfunctioning. He suggests that "the more we focus our attention directly on the symptoms rather than on transforming the institutions and values that cause them, the more certain we can be that the crisis will deepen for the lack of appropriate action."[15] Hence, within such rapidly changing contexts, responses to poverty should therefore not be limited to and focused on almsgiving and charity, which Korten, in his popular framework of the four generations of development, refers to as "relief and welfare."[16] Korten quotes Wayne Ellwood who states: "If you see a baby drowning, you jump in to save it; and if you see a second and a third, you do the same. Soon you are so busy saving drowning babies, you never look up to see that there is someone there throwing babies into the river."[17] Korten notes that "relief and welfare" interventions provided by missionaries and churches, as essential as they may have been, generally offered immediate and temporary help, in most cases addressing the symptoms of underdevelopment and not of development itself.[18] Christianity is said to have begun by preaching and practising the "gospel of love and charity" which included almsgiving and care for widows, orphans, slaves, travellers, the sick, the imprisoned and the poor, all driven by love, mercy and compassion.[19] Such good works and acts of charity continued to permeate through the work of various mission endeavours since the early church. Pillay points out that the missionaries, especially those of the nineteenth century, are to be commended for sowing the seed from which Christianity grew in the twentieth century. They did extensive evangelistic work and built churches, schools, and hospitals. Not only were these important aspects of their ministries at that time, but were also

---

13. Roswith Gerloff, *Mission is Crossing Frontiers* (Pietermaritzburg:Cluster Publications, 2003), 210.
14. Korten, *When Corporations Rule the World*.
15. Korten, *Getting into the 21st Century*, 114.
16. Korten, *Getting into the 21st Century*, 113.
17. Korten, *Getting into the 21st Century*, 113.
18. Korten, *Getting into the 21st Century*, 118.
19. Adolf Von Harnack, *The Mission and Expansion of Christianity in the First Three Centuries* (Harper: New York, 1967), 147–98.

foundations for subsequent developments.[20] The Christian church has always been involved in the transformation of society, particularly as it relates to the poor and oppressed, as an imperative of its missional responsibility. However, in a changing context, such missional responses need to move beyond the "relief and welfare" types of interventions. The paradigm shifts of mission in a developing context create an awareness that society is not static but is a dynamic entity. Society is subject to constant and incessant change, most of which is slow but can sometimes become rapid and sudden. This necessitates an evolution of our methods of mission and development.

Beyond Relief and Welfare: A Matter of Justice

In this rapidly changing context, our understanding of poverty needs to be re-examined to move us beyond hand-outs and charity. The phenomenon of poverty can be classified into two categories. The first is *absolute poverty*, and it happens where incomes are so low that even a minimum standard of nutrition, shelter, and personal necessities cannot be maintained. In other words, absolute poverty means that the individual is so poor that his/her next meal may mean the difference between life and death. The second is *relative poverty* and this is an expression of the poverty of one entity in relation to another. This concept of relative poverty refers to people whose basic needs are met but still experience some levels of disadvantage. In society, we are often confronted with *case poverty*, which refers to individuals or individual families who experience poverty (be it absolute or relative), and *community poverty* which manifests itself where almost everyone in a community is poor.[21] Poverty inevitably is an issue of justice, and needs to be approached as such. Alan Boesak singles out the Belhar Confession (1986) where it states: "in a world filled with injustice and enmity, God in a special way is the God of the destitute, the poor and the wronged . . . the church as God's possession is called to stand where God stands, namely against injustice and with the wronged."[22]

The New Testament records a dynamic story that was narrated by Jesus. This is the story of "The Rich Man and Lazarus," recorded in Luke 16:19–31 –

---

20. Jerry Pillay, "The Church as a Transformation and Change Agent," *Herv. Teol. Stud.* 73.3 (2017): 2.

21. Frik De Beer, *An Introduction to Development Studies* (Oxford University Press: New York, 2000), 2.

22. See Alan Boesak, *The Tenderness of Conscience – African Renaissance and the Spirituality of Politics* (Stellenbosch: Sun Press, 2005).

and like many of Jesus' parables, it was a story about justice. Jesus used it to reveal a profound truth that God expects us to use our influence and resources to challenge the status quo and stand in the gap for those who are suffering. The two characters in the story are a wealthy man and a beggar which illustrates great disparity between the rich and the poor, the *haves* and the *have-nots*. It represents a warning anecdote about the dark consequences of failing to deconstruct the systems of vast social and economic disparity that hold our world hostage. The rich man was a bystander to Lazarus's poverty and did not see it as his problem to solve. The Christian church regularly represents the rich man – the wealthy, the privileged, the powerful, and the educated, who often fail to see the *Lazaruses* in our world. To do justice in our community and world means going into our world to reform, restore, repair, rebuild and redeem the brokenness we see all around us. Justice is about reconciling broken relationships between God and humanity, as well as between the exploiter and exploited, rich and poor, Black and White, male and female, the powerful and the weak.

Ann-Cathrin Jarl, for example, constructs a theory of justice by building on narratives of injustice that both expand and improve our understanding of justice.[23] For us to fully understand the concept of justice and see its connectedness to lived experiences, Jarl is mindful of the need to address and understand injustice. "Telling stories about injustice is a way to improve knowledge about what justice may require."[24] She goes on to highlight the five 'faces' of oppression and domination which she sees as a method of identification of injustices, namely, the exploitation of the power of work, cultural marginalization, powerlessness, cultural imperialism and, finally, violence directed against women.[25] Jarl does not see the value in the telling of stories when there is nothing learned about injustice from them. Justice is not just a state of affairs but a continuous effort and attempt to overcome injustice. Therefore, narratives such as Lazarus and the rich man must compel us to revisit our notions of the poor and the oppressed. For example, if we were to compare and contrast the person of Lazarus with such changing context, this could be depicted as such:

---

23. Ann-Cathrin Jarl, *In Justice: Women and Global Economics* (Minneapolis: Augsburg Fortress, 2003), 100.
24. Jarl, *In Justice*, 87.
25. Jarl, *In Justice*, 87.

Lazarus *Then*	Lazarus *Now*
Represents an individual; seen as a person	Represents the classes and masses
Abandoned by the selfishness of the rich In other words, he was left poor	Exploited at the profit of the ruling class In other words, he was made poor
Asking for charity	Demanding justice

A post-colonial reading of such narratives provides a framework and point of orientation for the story of the community of the poor, and becomes an intentional attempt to overcome the dualism that exists between colonial thinking and lived experiences. The praxis of mission is *life*, and its context means the *real life* situation.[26] Context analysis thus becomes an imperative in understanding, interpreting and serving communities effectively. The reading of such narratives in a colonial missional approach would have responded by handing out charity to the poor and oppressed, rather than challenging the causes of their oppression and poverty. European missionaries in Southern Africa during the nineteenth and twentieth centuries played a strangely ambiguous role, where on the one hand, they appeared compelled by a strong desire to genuinely serve humanity and bring about material and social changes which would improve its quality of life. On the other hand, they were consumed by moral self-righteousness which led them to pass hasty and uninformed judgments upon indigenous mores, norms and values they were scarcely equipped to understand. Seeking to bring changes to the patterns of living, the emphasis of missionaries in Southern Africa was on "uncompromizing and moral Christian behaviour."[27] They targeted issues such as beer drinking, initiation, *lobola* (the cultural practice of paying brideprice before marriage), polygamy and what they perceived to be ancestral worship. They gave little or no attention to the systemic and structural causes of poverty, oppression and marginalization. Missionaries seldom interrogated reasons for the Lazarus of today being made poor.

On the contrary, studies reveal that missionaries themselves could have contributed, either directly or indirectly, to the impoverished and disadvantaged conditions that many indigenous Africans found themselves in. For example, during the second half of the nineteenth century, trade was a factor used to create European dominance over Africans. Mission stations

---

26. Bongani Mazibuko in Gerloff, *Mission is Crossing Frontiers*, 208.

27. Franco Frescura, "A Case of Hopeless Failure: The Role of Missionaries in the Transformation of Southern Africa's Indigenous Architecture," *Journal of the Study of Religion* 28.2 (2015): 1.

became trade centres and because of the inroads that missionaries made into local communities, they were seen as important conduits by the traders for the purpose of access, control, trade, and political networks.[28] The export economy established by Europeans meant that Africans extracted raw materials while Europeans returned manufactured goods. This trade advantaged Europeans at the expense of the indigenous populations. Worse still, missionaries also insisted that their converts adopt their lifestyles, wearing European clothes and living in European-style houses, which yet again offered a potential market for European manufactured goods.[29] Early missionaries who arrived in the Cape Colony, for example, carried "beads as well as Bibles" to their mission stations outside the colony.[30] The mix of commercial activities with their religious duties, to engage in evangelism on the one hand and trade on the other, became a means to support themselves and their families to supplement the meagre material and monetary assistance they received from their societies. Thus, the introduction of European goods by missionaries among African societies created a growing dependency on European material goods. Such encounters and more reveal that whilst the Lazarus of the Bible was left poor by the selfishness of an elite rich man, the Lazarus of today, who is representative of the masses, was made poor under the tyranny of a ruling class, and to an extent, in the guise of "mission," creating dependence which offered little or nothing to the quality of life.

The African continent is scourged with poverty and inequality since the gap between the poorest and the richest in Africa is also one of the widest in the world.[31] Unemployment and underemployment continue to contribute to the vicious cycle of poverty. But Africa needs to be propelled to move beyond relief and welfare. As we observe significant paradigm shifts, mission strategies need to advance trajectories of justice in addressing the global phenomenon of poverty and not remain on the path of relief and welfare. Missionary practice, theological discourse, and ecclesial self-understanding must become part of our mission imperative where the poor are empowered to be agents of their own

---

28. See Fidelis Nkomazana, "Missionary Colonial Mentality and the Expansion of Christianity in Bechuanaland Protectorate, 1800 to 1900," *Journal of the Study of Religion* 29.2 (2016).

29. Nkomazana, "Missionary Colonial Mentality."

30. See Roger Beck, "Bibles and Beads: Missionaries as Traders in Southern Africa," *Journal of African History* 30 (1989): 211–25.

31. "Decent Work for Africa's Development: Signs of Hope," *World of Work Magazine* 49, Dec 2003: 4–10, https://www.ilo.org/wcmsp5/groups/public/---dgreports/---dcomm/documents/publication/dwcms_080606.pdf.

development instead of remaining caught in the web of dependency. Mission methods, therefore, need to engage tools of empowerment and capacity building in communities.

Mission that Empowers

Development is about empowering people to become agents of their own change. Empowerment is fundamental to development as it equips people with the authority or power to achieve certain tasks or overcome particular challenges. Without a sense of power, communities cannot meaningfully improve their situations. It is only with this sense of empowerment that poverty-stricken communities can claim a voice in seeking help and improvement.[32] Acknowledging that a better situation is possible can influence a community to change. Empowerment is, therefore, necessary to help people in developing areas to conquer their powerlessness by re-instituting personal and community power. Empowerment comes in the form of democracy, equity, capacity building and participation. People's participation in development implies empowerment and vice versa. Genuine community participation means that people must have the power to influence the decisions that affect their lives. Without empowerment, participation becomes ineffective. All the different aspects of empowerment, such as political, economic and institutional, must be present for participation to be meaningful. It entails a change of mind-set or of opinions one holds concerning oneself or a phenomenon. Eradicating poverty necessitates initiating processes that empower people to change their mind-sets, gain knowledge, discover themselves and take charge of their own life. The twin processes of empowerment and participation constitute the basis of a people-centred form of development.

Mission by its very nature is intended to be people-centred. The expansion of the missionary movement into Africa was partly a result of a growing conception of European Christianity's responsibility for the regeneration of African peoples. In addition, humanitarian awareness and conscience played a vital role in stimulating European interest in Africa and gave an impetus to their mission work. For all the ills that were happening in Africa, Christianity was considered to be the answer, and a key to civilization and eventually colonization of the continent (which was seen as the only "remedy"). Viera Pawliková-Vilhanová contends that some missionaries believed that their converts could become genuine Christians only if they became Europeanized

---

32. Robert Chambers, *Putting the Last First* (Routledge: Abingdon, 1983), 131–37.

and were therefore attempting to "produce Black Europeans."[33] Mission schools were often boarding schools because missionaries believed that new converts would more easily give up all or most of their traditions when they were far-removed from the traditional cultural influences of their homes. Missionary school systems promoted Western values and desires and, thus, often led to missionaries being viewed with distrust. Practices that sought to Europeanize Africans were condemned as activity that inadvertently damaged communities where missionary methods were culturally insensitive, patronizing, or disrespectful.

This condemnation is strongly evident in a Catholic document, *Dignitatis Humanae*, which argues that each person should be allowed to seek religious truth freely and that the coercive methods of the missionaries should always be avoided, "especially when dealing with poor or uneducated people."[34] The aim of missionary schools was to ultimately use the platform of *education* to *Christianize and civilize the heathen* – the heathen referring to indigenous Africans of non-European descendent.[35] Here in South Africa, inasmuch as missionary education was strongly aimed at promoting a colonial agenda, it was also supplementing the South Africa state's legislation such as the Groups Areas Act of 1950 to ensure the continuance of White dominance.[36] In fact, records show that in South Africa, for example, the Cape Governor subsidized missionary schools and institutions so that they may provide industrial training and elementary education that accorded with the labouring role given to Black youth in the colonial economy, with no encouragement towards critical thinking, originality, and creativity. Consequently, learners in this system were taught how to be honest and committed domestics, servants, and helpers when they entered the labour market.[37] One such school, for example, was the St Theresa Catholic Missions school established in 1916 in the old Transvaal province. Its aims and objectives were to train Black Africans in industrial

---

33. Viera Pawliková-Vilhanová, "Christian Missions in Africa and Their Role in the Transformation of African Societies," *Asian and African Studies* 16.2 (Nov 2007): 249–60, https://www.sav.sk/journals/uploads/102313498_Vilhanov.pdf.

34. Paul VI, *Dignitatis Humanae*, The Holy See website, 7th Dec 1965, http://www.vatican.va/archive/hist_councils/ii_vatican_council/documents/vat-ii_decl_19651207_dignitatis-humanae_en.html.

35. See Lazarus Lebeloane, "Missionaries and Mission Schools," *Studia Historiae Ecclesiasticae* 32.1 (May 2006): 103.

36. Lebeloane, "Missionaries and Mission Schools," 103.

37. Lebeloane, "Missionaries and Mission Schools," 103.

and domestic work.³⁸ Traditional mission practices are said to have created dependency on the mission field. This is a serious matter of stifling people through practices that keep them immature and helpless. Rick Wood asserts:

> The sad reality of missions' history is that we have often created dependency by staying too long and doing too much for people rather than equipping them to make disciples one generation after another and trusting the Holy Spirit to lead them to maturity as they obey the Word. We should never do for others what they can and should do for themselves. This is how you keep dependency from developing in every area of life and ministry.³⁹

Wood cautions that the abundance of outside funds robs the local people of the initiative to support their own outreach and to discover that they have the ability and privilege of developing the local resources they need to support their own work. As such, foreign funds, as helpful as they may be, can never be a substitute for the devoted, passionate involvement of committed local people using locally developed resources to improve the quality of life. Recurrently, when missionaries move from being advocates to becoming innovators, it is then that the dependency syndrome takes hold. Such a syndrome could be avoided if missionaries limit themselves to being advocates, permitting locals the privilege of being the innovators.

Conclusion

The emergence of a new generation of Christian missionaries is surfacing. It is a generation who are resisting the taboo of the so-called *White saviour complex*, which depicts the mentality of relatively rich Westerners who set off to "save" people of colour in poorer countries.⁴⁰ Colonial approaches to mission work, to an extent, created what development practitioners term as "dependency." A re-visioning of mission must primarily be seen through the lens of social justice and advocacy, with proselytizing as a secondary condition. Nyerere asserts that "human dignity is not dependent on the kindness of others . . . It can, in fact, be destroyed by kindness which emanates from an action of charity."⁴¹ Mission

---

38. Lebeloane, "Missionaries and Mission Schools," 104.

39. Rick Woods, "Dependency: the Crippler of People and Movements," *Mission Frontiers* (Sept–Oct 2016), https://www.missionfrontiers.org/issue/article/dependency.

40. Woods, *Slaying the Dependency Dragon*.

41. Julius Nyerere, *Man and Development* (London: Oxford University Press, 1974), 113.

endeavours that create dependency and remain at the superficial level of relief, welfare, and charity, are disempowering and despotic, leaving people entangled in a cycle of depravation. It is people who remain at the crux of mission and development. When mission initiatives are done in ways that give rise to *self-leading*, *self-proliferating*, and *self-supporting* structures, devoid of dependency and enslavement to a colonial minority, it can be called *development*.

8

African Charismatic Movements and Urban Missiology

Ignatius Wilhelm (Naas) Ferreira and Joseph Bosco Bangura

The scope of this chapter is threefold. First, after giving an overview of contemporary Pentecostal and charismatic missiology, we trace the rapid urbanization and social change taking place in Africa. Using examples drawn from post-war Sierra Leone, we discuss some lesser known problems arising from cities that make life a dystopia for many. Second, we review the attempts of African charismatics to engage with and leverage the challenges posed by the urbanization and cultural displacement on Africa's youthful urban followers. And third, we outline key convictions that are constitutive of African charismatic urban missiology. Our goal is to frame the outlines of an African charismatic urban missiology that reflects the public's concerns about urbanization and calls charismatics to move away from centripetal to centrifugal missions as it engages the metropolis in ways that bear witness to the reign of God in Africa. We start with a premise that African charismatic urban mission remains an unexplored area of research in the budding field of African Pentecostalism, and to begin to contribute to this research, this chapter applies three methodological approaches. First, we review existing literature on Pentecostal and charismatic missiology in order to ascertain the gaps that prevent a proper framing of an African charismatic urban missiology. Second, we draw from years of involvement in Pentecostal/charismatic churches and pastoral ministry in Sierra Leone where we tracked down the charismatic reaction to urbanization. Third, through our teaching and research at North-West University in South Africa, we were challenged by students from Francophone and Anglophone Africa to reflect on what the rise of charismatic movements means for urban missions in Africa.

Charismatic spirituality is arguably the most noticeable form of Christianity in Africa with followers of newer charismatic and Pentecostal movements accounting for the most vibrant Christians on the continent.[1] Africa's new Christianity arose from the 1970s and 80s revival meetings of university student ministries.[2] After their founding, the movements went on to develop into independent churches and ministries outside classical Pentecostalism or historic missionary and mainline denominations.[3] This new church development in Africa has been variously described as charismatic, neo-charismatic and neo-Pentecostal churches.[4] Our use of African charismatic movements in this chapter refers to all these new expressions of African Christianity. Among the many defining theological characteristics, African charismatics are known to emphasize divine healing, miracles, demons and exorcism, dreams and their interpretation, prophecy, prosperity, anointing with olive oil and distinguishing between spirits.[5] Many of these charismatic churches have a large following among the young, educated urban élite who feel that this version of Christian spirituality connects directly with their existential needs.[6]

The urban context, in which they were founded, prepared African charismatics not only to face life in the city, but also prepared them for the woes that blight African cities. African charismatics, who represent the growing urban élite and socioeconomically empowered middle class, are thinking afresh about ways with which to reach their cities and bring about revival on the African continent. Spurred by the looming end of all things – *eschaton* – charismatics argue that city dwellers are to be evangelized and rescued from the potential secularity that Africa's rapid urbanization brings to its cities.[7]

---

1. Kenneth Hylson-Smith, *To the Ends of the Earth: The Globalization of Christianity* (London: Paternoster, 2007), 139.

2. Matthews Ojo, *The End-time Army: Charismatic Movements in Modern Nigeria* (Trenton: Africa World Press, 2006), xvii.

3. Peter Hocken, *The Challenges of the Pentecostal, Charismatic and Messianic Jewish Movements: Tensions of the Spirit* (Farnham, England: Ashgate, 2009), 29.

4. Allan Anderson, *African Reformation: African Initiated Christianity in the Twentieth Century* (Trenton: Africa World Press, 2001), 15–20.

5. For a discussion of the theologies of contemporary African Pentecostal and charismatic movements, see J. Kwabena Asamoah-Gyadu, *Contemporary Pentecostal Christianity: Interpretations from an African Context* (Eugene, Oregon: Wipf & Stock Publishers, 2013); Clifton Clarke, ed. *Pentecostal Theology in Africa* (Eugene, Oregon: Pickwick Publishers, 2014).

6. Allan H. Anderson, *An Introduction to Pentecostalism: Global Charismatic Christianity*, 2nd ed. (Cambridge: Cambridge University Press, 2014), 132.

7. Benno van den Toren, "Secularisation in Africa: A Challenge for the Churches," *African Journal of Evangelical Theology* 22.2 (2010): 17–18.

Inspired by Jeremiah's prophecy that calls on exiles to pray for the city,[8] African charismatics find a direct and unquestionable call to urban missions. Jeremiah's imagery of an exiled community and the challenges of city life suggest to African charismatics they must seek the peace and prosperity of the city because theirs inseparably depends upon the peace of the city. The African city is, in most cases, the light for the entire nation (Matt 5:14) and a place where young adults, unreached peoples, rich business executives and the poor live.[9] Many charismatics consider themselves as watchmen who have been posted to spiritually guard the city (Ezek 3:17), proclaiming the gospel to the city and denouncing the sinful, impure, shameful and deceitful acts that are committed in it (Rev 21:27). Resistant cities are under the consequences of God's wrath (Gen 18), while those that respond with a sense of deep contrition are saved (John 3:16). In their view, this interest in the prosperity, welfare, moral and spiritual purity of the city coheres with God's plan for the future of Africa's expanding cities. As the affluence of a city's inhabitants grow, it is all the more important that they get the chance to hear the Christian gospel.

Overview of Pentecostal and Charismatic Missiology

Pentecostalism by its very nature is distinctively missional.[10] Pentecostals have always been engaged in global missions where they risked their lives,[11] and planted "Bible-believing" churches. Today contemporary charismatic theology understands mission to have originated in the compassionate heart of God, and is communicated to the church through the Holy Spirit.[12] However, academic interest in the missiological permutations of global Pentecostalism were significantly bolstered after the publication of *Called and Empowered: Global Mission in Pentecostal Perspective*.[13] Until the appearance of this publication, prophetic voices mainly spoke for and gave prescriptions about

---

8. Jeremiah 29:7.

9. Tim Keller, "What is God's Global Urban Mission?," in *Christ Our Reconciler: Gospel, Church, World*, ed. J. E. M. Cameron (Nottingham: Inter-Varsity Press, 2012), 119–20.

10. See J. M. Penney, *The Missionary Emphasis of Lukan Missiology* (Sheffield: Sheffield Academic Press, 1997).

11. Allan Anderson, "The Vision of the Apostolic Faith: Early Pentecostalism and World Mission," *Swedish Missiological Themes* 97.3 (2009): 295.

12. Andrew Lord, *Spirit-shaped Mission: A Holistic Charismatic Missiology* (Bletchley: Paternoster, 2005), 28.

13. Murry W. Dempster, Byron D. Klaus and Douglas Petersen, *Called & Empowered: Global Mission in Pentecostal Perspective* (Peabody: Hendrickson, 1991).

the missiological trajectory of contemporary Pentecostal and charismatic movements, particularly those from Christianity's new hotspots in the global South. Written by a younger generation of Pentecostal scholars, *Called and Empowered* outlines biblical, theological, strategic and cultural undercurrents that lie at the heart of Pentecostal missiology. This work inspired other treatises that stress a conglomeration of pneumatological theology and the urgency of the *eschaton* as features that characterize Pentecostal missiology.

Judging from earlier efforts taken to document Pentecostal missiology, Veli-Matti Kärkkäinen observes that eschatological fervour and the crucial role of the Holy Spirit are the pulling factors that explain Pentecostalism's continued engagement with mission work.[14] Having argued for the need for scholars to progress beyond these currents, Kärkkäinen goes on to highlight four interlocking threads around which Western Pentecostal and charismatic missiology revolves: Jesus Christ and the full gospel; the Holy Spirit and empowerment; salvation and the vision of holism; and church and the spirit of *koinonia*. These, he admits, are not to be conceived as representing a full-scale Pentecostal theology of missions but are only a representation of its theological intuitions.[15] Pursuing a different thread of reflection, Korean missiologists Wonsuk and Julie Ma call for a pneumatologically enhanced creation theology that embraces both the Old and the New Testaments in the present discourse of Pentecostal and charismatic missiology. Such a theology, they argue, takes a biblically wholistic view of God's revelation, with which to enter into dialogue and engage the many contextual issues affecting Korean Pentecostal and charismatic theology of missions.[16] Allan Anderson integrates Christocentric and pneumatological perspectives in his explanation of the global Pentecostal and charismatic missiological praxis. Using this two-pronged approach, Anderson avers further that "Pentecostal and charismatic movements . . . proclaim and celebrate a salvation (or "healing") that encompasses all of life's experiences and afflictions." This admission allows him to argue that Pentecostals and charismatics are of the opinion that the preaching of the word in evangelism must be accompanied by the outworking of signs and wonders. Divine healing in particular is an indispensable part of the movement's overall

---

14. Veli-Matti Käkkäinen, "Pentecostal Mission and Encounter with Religions," in *The Cambridge Companion to Pentecostalism*, ed. Cecil M. Robeck Jr. and Amos Young (Cambridge: Cambridge University Press, 2014), 295.

15. Veli-Matti Käkkäinen, "Pentecostal Mission and Encounter with Religions," 298–302.

16. Wonsuk Ma and Julie Ma, *Mission in the Spirit: Towards a Pentecostal/Charismatic Missiology* (Oxford: Regnum International, 2010).

evangelistic strategy.[17] It is this ability to address practical needs that affect the lives of people in their immediate context that enables Pentecostal and charismatic missiology to attain a contextually relevant character. The fact that Pentecostal and charismatic missiology promises and delivers on healing has become a major attraction for more people to the movements.

Although these factors still motivate Pentecostal missiology, it must be pointed out that the prevailing socioeconomic and political contexts in the global South have significantly changed. Pentecostal and charismatic groups now have to adapt to changing social contexts foisted upon people by expanding or contracting economies, political instability, democratic and social development.[18] Nations in sub-Saharan Africa are in the process of modernizing infrastructure as citizens open up to the ever-increasing influence of globalization. The end of apartheid in South Africa led to the rise of a new social class whose economic positioning is beginning to impact public governance. Buffeted by these changes, Pentecostals and charismatics have redefined traditional African cultures, demonizing elements that contradict Scripture and taking onboard aspects that are biblically and progressively modern.[19] From a cultural anthropology perspective, this self-conscious Pentecostal vision of modernity places the faith at the centre of the agenda of the global religious market,[20] so that Pentecostalism is able to apprehend religion as a cultural resource that enables practitioners to engage the world.[21] African Pentecostals and charismatics are engaging culture nationally and are meeting the needs and aspirations of the marginalized in ways that mainline Protestantism has failed.[22] Further, African Pentecostals and charismatics are also engaged in global missions, planting churches across the African continent and among the African Diaspora.[23] The African Pentecostal and

---

17. Allan Anderson, *An Introduction to Pentecostalism*, 212.

18. See Bryan Born, "Promise of Power: How New Pentecostals respond to the rapid social change in Botswana," *Missionalia: Southern African Journal of Mission Studies* 35.3 (2009): 43–66.

19. Ruth Marshall, *Political Spiritualities: The Pentecostal Revolution in Nigeria* (Chicago: The University of Chicago Press, 2009).

20. André Droogers, "The Cultural Dimension of Pentecostalism," in *The Cambridge Companion to Pentecostalism*, ed. Cecil M. Robeck Jr. and Amos Young (Cambridge: Cambridge University Press, 2014), 197.

21. David Martin, *Pentecostalism: The World, Their Parish* (Oxford: Blackwell Publishers, 2002).

22. Alistair E. McGrath, *The Future of Christianity* (Oxford: Blackwell Publishers, 2002), 109.

23. For useful literature see Afe Adogame and Cordula Weissköppel, *Religion in the Context of African Migration* (Bayreuth: Eckhard Breitinger, 2005).

charismatic commitment to global missions seems to be driven by the belief that Western Europe has drifted away from the very faith it once brought to Africa. As such Europe needs to be reconverted to Christianity and Bible-believing churches planted throughout the highly secularized continent of Europe.[24] This reverse flow of African Pentecostal and charismatic missionaries is slowly reshaping the religious landscape of the Northern Hemisphere.[25] While African Pentecostal and charismatic missiology tries to be global, it has not lost sight of its local attraction. African Pentecostals and charismatics are acutely aware of the local context where their ministries are based. Accordingly, they have adopted modes of expression that make sense to people in their given socioeconomic and cultural context. This, as Andrew Walls reminds us, is precisely what is to be expected from the southern hemisphere where the growth of Christianity has been most pronounced.[26] The theology it produces answers deeply felt cultural questions. It promises hope amidst the competing socioeconomic challenges of its members. Pentecostalism's ability to mediate direct and immediate experience of God and its use of language and form of communication which enables it to bridge cultural gaps has further broadened the gains of the movement.[27] African Pentecostal and charismatic churches are expanding their ministry base in the metropolis.

Charismatic Metropolitan Missions in Africa

A closer look at the ecclesial dynamics of African charismatics would indicate traits that are helpful in constructing the movement's urban missiology. First, to understand charismatic urban missiology, we need to begin with a reconsideration of the movement's view on health, wealth, and human wellbeing. Although the charismatic teaching on health, wealth, and power are perhaps the most notorious of its theological underpinnings,[28] few efforts have been taken to understand the missiological motifs of these doctrines. For many urban youths, the promise of success in the city is still a distant dream because they continue to struggle to make a living amidst the buzz of life. They lack money to pay for basic social services such as education, healthcare, or housing. Food

---

24. Alistair McGrath, *The Future of Christianity*, 25.

25. Ogbu Kalu, *African Pentecostalism*, 271–91.

26. Andrew Walls, *The Missionary Movement in Christian History: Studies in the Transmission of Faith* (Maryknoll/Edinburgh: Orbis Books, 1996), 9–10.

27. Alistair McGrath, *The Future of Christianity*, 108–9.

28. See for instance, Andreas Heuser, editor, *Pastures of Plenty: Tracing Religio-scapes of Prosperity Gospel in Africa and Beyond* (New York: Peter Lang Edition, 2015).

is in short supply. These woes make city life a nightmare for many. Some begin to question what is amiss that they have not made it even when they are now living in the city. Charismatics take these questions and the social context of the urban population seriously. Charismatics address their message of deliverance, success and power to the many social issues that city life and urbanization present. The charismatic faithful hear from their preachers that good health and material abundance are suggestive of God's blessings upon one's life. Ill health, misfortune and bad luck are believed to be caused by demons who are out to destroy human life. As a safety net against these diabolical forces, the believer needs to present themselves at those churches where they can obtain spiritual healing, deliverance and exorcism.[29] Preachers who teach such messages model a life that mirrors the success of these doctrines. The youth who are overwhelmed by urbanization find that charismatic theologies project a sympathetic approach to their plight and offer solutions that cushion the effects of transition from rural life to urban societies.[30] Consequently, because charismatic doctrines promise hope in the face of the stultifying circumstances of urban life, many are drawn to the movement.

Second, rural-to-urban migration often leads to cultural displacement and alienation for those who immigrate to cities. The new immigrant suddenly realizes the cultural values that once engendered meaning for life and promoted community cohesion are threatened by impersonal city life. Without this cultural grid upon which the events of life are adjudged, the urban settler's daily life becomes cumbersome. Because charismatics were exposed to this context, they present themselves as people who are able to help urban dwellers regain their sense of self-worth they lost through migration to the city. Sunday and midweek services become events where Christian cohesion is developed with brothers and sisters in Christ. The sense of community that churches provide compensates for the cultural loss and traditional displacement they now experience. The church becomes the new arena for imbibing a form of Christian cultural cohesion which helps young people deal with the multifaceted challenges of urban life. Support systems that lend a helping hand in time of need (such as during childbirth, marriage or death) have also been created within the movement.[31] The Bishops and their spouses become the new parents

---

29. Dena Freeman, ed., *Pentecostalism and Development: Churches, NGO's and Social Change in Africa* (Basingstoke: Palgrave Macmillan, 2012), 13.

30. Allan Anderson, *An Introduction to Pentecostalism*, 220–21.

31. See Irene John, "Charismatics and Community," in *A Reader in African Christian Theology*, ed. John Parratt (London: SPCK, 1997), 135–36.

who provide some sort of parental counsel and pastoral support, accompanying the urban élite through critical moments of their lives. Born again colleagues become real brothers and sisters. A kind of fellowship develops within the movement which helps in the rediscovery of human dignity which they believe has been recreated in Christ (2 Cor 5:17). The spirit of *koinonia* that develops within the church[32] allows urban youth to experience oneness and solidarity that transcends ethnicity and social status. The fullness of life in Christ they share replaces kinship ties they once had but have lost through migration.

Third, charismatics are beginning to be politically active and to set up business enterprises across the cities of West Africa. In spite of the apolitical posture that had been characteristic of earlier forms of Pentecostalism in Africa, today's charismatics are politically active.[33] In fact, charismatics claim to have a vision for public governance that is radically different from what existed before their formation. Charismatics see themselves as transformed individuals who have a moral responsibility to change society through involvement in focussed activities that promote genuine business, economic development, and facilitates political reform. Although they acknowledge that sociological tools are necessary to succeed in the public sphere, however Christians who are politically active affirm that spiritual warfare is a central component of their daily routine.[34] Therefore, when charismatics acquire business deals and contracts, or get into elected positions, they bring their faith convictions to bear directly upon these life situations. They allow their faith to influence the decisions they make in public service.

Political and economic involvement is driven by the charismatic belief that God is personally involved in the affairs of everyday life.[35] Charismatics understand that "God is not a vague and distant figure but a reality to be encountered."[36] For charismatics, this understanding makes it customary to seek God's involvement through prayer and fasting before undertaking any venture. From their reading of Scripture, charismatics find that Jesus was not only familiar with the marketplace but also recruited his disciples from there, (Mark 6:3). The apostle Paul (Acts 9:1–16) and many other early Christians (Acts 9:36–43; 10:1;

---

32. See Veli-Matti Käkkäinen, "Pentecostal Mission and Encounter with Religions," 301–2.

33. See John F. McCauley, "Pentecostals and Politics: Redefining big man rule in Africa," in *Pentecostalism in Africa: Presence and Impact of Pneumatic Christianity in Postcolonial Societies*, ed. Martin Lindhardt (Boston: Brill, 2014).

34. Ed Silvoso, *Anointed For Business* (Ventura, California: Regal, 2002), 20.

35. Dena Freeman, *Pentecostalism and Development*, 19.

36. Clark H. Pinnock, "Church in the Power of the Holy Spirit: The Promise of Pentecostal Ecclesiology," *Journal of Pentecostal Theology* 14.2 (2006): 158.

20:33–35) who had supported his ministry were actively involved in shaping the politics of their day. To them, national politics cannot be left in the hands of unbelievers. Nations who do so run the risk of bringing untold suffering upon its citizenry (Job 34:30; Prov 11:10; 28:12; 29:2). Therefore, because of the command to do business until Jesus returns (Luke 19:13), charismatics have set up private universities in Ghana and Nigeria.[37] Their establishment provided relief for countries in dire need of quality tertiary education. The media has also been an area of interest where charismatics have also been involved. Christian radio and television stations such as *Believers Broadcasting Network* and *Destiny Television* have been set up in Sierra Leone. Small scale businesses with names such as "Anointed Hands Hair Saloon," "El Shaddai Fast Foods," and "My God is Able Cold Store" have also been set up.[38] Through these activities, charismatics intend to reach out to urban dwellers.

Fourth, the mediatization of the charismatic faith and use of advanced marketing strategies also disclose elements of Africa's charismatic urban missions. Charismatic movements have tapped into the exponential growth and use of mobile information technologies, particularly social media. To accelerate its outreach programmes among the urban élite, the movement now operates private radio and television stations where they broadcast live worship services. These services are also streamed live online for the benefit of the African Diaspora living overseas. The media departments of charismatic churches produce and sell consecrated religious products such as handkerchiefs, DVDs, miracle calendars and books. The churches are present online, where they have live discussion forums. English is the language of worship, counselling and administration. The leaders preach using tablet computers and their sermons are projected using software programmes such as PowerPoint and Open Song. Their leaders have a large following on social media websites where they advertise upcoming events, post devotional material and express messages of good will to members who are celebrating special life events. This ability to be attentive and responsive to the needs of its affluent urban élite members must not be seen as a move toward secularization, but a re-adaptation towards a religiously oriented modernity.

And fifth, as the grip of secularization looms over cities, charismatics appear to be mediating a resurgence of camp meetings, conferences, and

---

37. Paul Gifford, "A View from Ghana's New Christianity," in *The Changing Face of Christianity: Africa, the West and the World*, ed. Lamin Sanneh and Joel Carpenter (New York: Oxford University Press, 2005), 93.

38. Allan Anderson, *An Introduction to Pentecostalism*, 132.

seminars that were pivotal to their formation. These events, usually convened around catchy theme statements, are meant to embolden the spiritual life of followers. These events require collaboration with international evangelists. Because they are carried out during annual conventions, the churches organize elaborate services of consecration for its founders whose titles changed from General Overseers to Bishops, or Apostles. Others use this occasion to ordain and commission new church workers or dedicate their newly built auditoriums. Further, such occasions are used to publicly recognize the achievements of leading charismatics who serve in important political, civil or public sector positions. The pageantry that accompanies these occasions aims to raise the public profiles, the international images, and the national standing of the church. Crusades, fire conferences, camp meetings and seminars are intended to empower church members for success in specific areas of life. The high point of such occasion comes when healing, deliverance and miracles are performed by the college of prelates. The involvement of foreign bishops is meant to confirm their calling to foreign missions. The church also benefits reciprocally, because the founders get invited to serve as guest preachers in foreign countries.

It does appear from the foregone exploration, that contemporary African charismatic urban missiology appears to act in a functional and contextual way. This approach assures the wellbeing of its members. The movement's Christian fidelity develops in its members a sense of positive self-esteem that is crucial for planning, decision-making and creativity.[39] For this reason the churches continue to attract huge numbers of the urban élite. The movement's welcoming and enabling environment helps the urban youth cope with the challenging realities of life in the city. By its display of characteristics that encompass practical relevance to the daily problems of life, charismatics may be facilitating a contextual ministry that responds to the needs and aspirations of its youthful urban members.

Conclusion

The trajectory of African charismatic metropolitan missions outlined above leaves a number of outstanding issues. First, African charismatics tend to display centripetal rather than centrifugal urban missionary impulses that support the movement's centralized leadership structure. The central church

---

39. D. J. Louw, "The Merging of Globalization with the Notion of an African Renaissance: A Practical Theological and Pastoral Assessment," in *African Theology Today*, ed. Emmanuel Katongole (Scranton: University of Scranton Press, 2002), 235–36.

where the bishops, founders, general overseers and their spouses are based, is the place where church members are to assemble to receive spiritual power. Such power puts them on the path to prosperity and professional excellence. It is the founder's charisma that becomes the selling point for missions, miracles, and healing. The posters and evangelistic materials bear the image of the founder, with clear emphasis placed on his or her central gift. One would therefore argue that the purpose of this focus on the leader is to embolden the centre where the movement's monarchical leadership is based. This propensity for remaining centripetal rather than centrifugal seems to have compromized their urban missionary involvement.[40] In order to widen the scope of the revival mediated by charismatic churches, it must ensure that its commitment to missions affect all segments of the society, not just the urban élite who are able to financially support the movements.

Second, the emphasis on success makes charismatic urban mission somewhat oblivious to the systemic issues of poverty, deprivation, and corruption in Africa's cities. In a context of poverty, where traditional beliefs play an important role, it is easy to argue, as charismatics have done, that demonic forces are responsible for poverty, war, and human suffering. African charismatics believe that deep-seated spiritual and demonic forces can frustrate well-intentioned community development plans and eventually destroy countries.[41] Pentecostalism incorporates a holistic ontology that fits well with the lived experiences of many Africans and accords with most traditional African ontologies.[42] Although as a continent Africa is endowed with many natural and mineral resources,[43] many see this very wealth as the primary cause for the protracted conflicts and the terrible state of underdevelopment many of these African countries are living under. Charismatics note that the loans and structural adjustment programmes of international financial institutions (IFIs) of the 1980s and early 90s compounded the situation. The loans and the dubious conditions under

---

40. See Christopher J. H. Wright, *The Mission of God: Unlocking the Bible's Grand Narrative* (Downers Grove: InterVarsity Press, 2006), 523–30.

41. See Irene John, "Charismatics and Community," 131; Mark Shaw, *The Kingdom of God in Africa: A Short History of African Christianity* (Grand Rapids: Baker, 1996), 265–66; Christina Maria Breman, *The Association of Evangelicals in Africa: Its History, Organization, Members, Projects, External Relations, and Message* (Zoetermeer: Boekencentrum, 1996), 194.

42. Dena Freeman, *Pentecostalism and Development*, 22.

43. Sierra Leone for instance is rich in natural mineral resources, including diamonds, gold, bauxite, rutile, iron ore, among others. The mismanagement of proceeds from the extraction of these mineral resources was blamed for the continuous underdevelopment of Sierra Leone. See Extractive Industries Transparency Initiative, "Extractive Industries – Sierra Leone" accessed 10 December 2014, https://eiti.org/SierraLeone.

which they were given to African political leaders of the day imposed harsh and insensitive policies that exacerbated further the misery of Africa.[44] Even though it is easy to use culture to explain poverty, charismatics still struggle to present solid biblical theology for continuing its teaching on success. Even their use of Jeremiah 29:7 leaves much to be desired because the movement's biblical interpretation fails to account for sin as the cause of Israel's exile. The urban youth are in cities not because of sin but because they are in search of better opportunities in life. This struggle clearly puts the hermeneutical apparatus adopted in support of success and prosperity theologies on a shaky ground. The charismatic approach selectively uses biblical texts that only support the position that God always desires to bless his people. This selective interpretation of Scripture represents not only the basic problem of prosperity teachings but also a recipe for building a biblically groundless Christianity that may not stand the test of time.[45] Charismatics may still need to explain why the urban élite fail to prosper even after they exercise faith, sow a seed and are anointed.

Third, charismatic urban missiology is also susceptible to the risk that people may be only attracted to the churches because of the hope of healing, miracles, and deliverance from demonic possession. Even though the Bible talks about spiritual warfare (Eph 6:12), however, it would be wrong to argue that there is always a spiritual cause for every problem in life. Human problems are also caused by the physical causes. Furthermore, living out the believer's victory in Christ can help in spiritual warfare. It might be argued that if charismatics were to use their position in Christ, their involvement in healing, deliverance and spiritual warfare would be far more biblically grounded.[46] Where this to happen, it will produce Christians who are not only up against principalities and powers, but know that the cross represents the decisive victory they need to prevail in spiritual warfare. Until these issues are addressed, African charismatic urban missiology will still be framed in disproportionate outlines and threads.

---

44. See Ruth Marshall, "Power in the Name of Jesus," *Review of African Political Economy* 52 (1991): 25.

45. See Gordon Fee, *The Disease of the Health and Wealth Gospels* (Costa Mesa: Word for Today, 1979), 3.

46. See Timothy Warner, *Spiritual Warfare: Victory over the Powers of this Dark World* (Wheaton: Crossway Books, 1991), 55, 58–59.

9

Neo-Prophetism and Rebranding of *Missio Dei* in African Christianity

Chammah J. Kaunda

This chapter employs the *missio Dei* constructionist turn to postulate that the neo-prophetism that we see rising in Africa is a socially-constructed phenomenon that depends on belief systems and moral imaginations of particular social-cultural contexts. The chapter explores two case studies of prophets within Southern African to demonstrate how both the ideas of *missio Dei* and *neo-prophetism* are socially constructed. It argues that in seeking to leverage material resources, these prophets have taken advantage of the African worldview (with its orientation toward supernatural explanation of reality) as means to attaining material ends. I argue here that these prophets synthesize the traditional worldview and emerging elements from vagaries of the present to provide ways of dealing with the moral and existential challenges that result from neo-colonialism.

The Rise of Neo-Prophetic Movements

I define a neo-prophetic Christian ministry as one whose prophetic imagination is enabled by the prophetic traditions of the African religious heritage but is not limited to pre-Christian or contemporary capitalist worldview. Prophets in these neo-prophetic movements utilize traditional African prophetic imagination as resources to facilitate self-construction, self-identity awareness and prophetic actions. These neo-prophetic ministries cannot be understood only from within the discourses and structures of traditional African notions of prophet. They must be seen in the multiple ways they interpret and/or misinterpret various systems they borrow from global cultures, especially American Pentecostalism, biblical traditions, and African traditional notion of the prophet. Neo-prophetic ministries take advantage of the collective consciousness and worldviews within a particular society.

The rise of neo-prophetic movements in African Pentecostalism is fast becoming a major focus of academic discussion. In the two decades since 2000, a significant body of literature has emerged across disciplines about the cultural, religious, social, political, and economic implications of this radical Christianity.[1] These movements have profoundly affected every aspect of Sub-Saharan African societies. They have, in some nations, attempted to reshape both their nation's history and identity. The movements could be described as another stage of African search for spiritual power and identity in Africa.[2] They demonstrate a paradigm shift from the other African Pentecostal-type trends in that they manifest their own distinct ethos, mission, style, and emphasis that is different from other African Pentecostal movements and, as such, can be studied as a sub-discipline of African Pentecostal studies.[3] They have synthesized elements and approaches of African prophetic traditions, the African Initiated Churches (AICs), classical Pentecostalism and neo-Pentecostalism.[4] The key distinctive feature in this synthesis is the way neo-

---

1. Jane E. Soothill, *Gender, Social Change and Spiritual Power: Charismatic Christianity in Ghana* (Leiden and Boston: Brill, 2007); Samuel Zalanga, "Religion, Economic Development, and Cultural Change: The Contradictory Role of Pentecostal Christianity in Sub-Saharan Africa," *Journal of Third World Studies* 27.1 (2010): 43–62; Dena Freeman, ed., *Pentecostalism and Development: Churches, NGOs, and Social Change in Africa* (Basingstoke: Palgrave Macmillan, 2012); Amos Yong and Katherine Attanasi, eds., *Pentecostalism and Prosperity: The Socioeconomics of the Global Charismatic Movement* (New York: Palgrave Macmillan, 2012), 35–59; David M. Gordon, *Invisible Agents: Spirits in a Central African History* (Athens: Ohio University Press, 2012); Nimi Wariboko, *Nigerian Pentecostalism* (Rochester: University of Rochester Press, 2014); Chammah J. Kaunda, "Neo-Prophetism, Gender and 'Anointed Condoms': Towards a *Missio Spiritus* of Just-Sex in the African Context of HIV and AIDS," *Alternation* 23.2 (2016): 64–88; Vinson Synan, Amos Yong, and J. Kwabena Asamoah-Gyadu, eds., *Global Renewal Christianity: Spirit Empowered Movements Past, Present and Future* (Florida: Charisma House, 2016).

2. Ogbu Kalu, *African Pentecostalism: An Introduction* (Oxford: OUP, 2008), 4.

3. Paul Gifford, *Ghana's New Christianity: Pentecostalism in a Globalising African Economy* (Bloomington: Indiana University Press, 2004); Cephas N. Omenyo, "Man of God prophesy unto me: The prophetic phenomenon in African Christianity," *Studies in World Christianity* 17.1 (2011): 30–49; Opoku Onyinah, "Deliverance as a way of confronting witchcraft in modern Africa: Ghana as a case history," *Asian Journal of Pentecostal Studies* 5.1 (2002a): 107–34.

4. Cephas N. Omenyo and Abamfo O. Atiemo. "Claiming religious space: The case of neo-prophetism in Ghana," *The Ghana Bulletin of Theology* 1.1 (2006): 55–68; Emmanuel Kingsley Larbi, "The nature of continuity and discontinuity of Ghanaian Pentecostal concept of salvation

prophetic movements have rebranded their missiology, utilizing traditional African spiritual resources as dominant missio-ideological imaginations. Their embedding into this worldview has attracted thousands of people searching for explanations to the causes of their various mishaps and about their destiny.[5] Scholars like Opoku Onyinah argue that the prophet models of these movements thrive on the belief that the prophet can predict and/or explain hidden events and sources of evil frustrating human existence.[6]

Missio-Dei-Constructionist Turn

Missiology, in a nutshell, is a systematic study of how local churches in specific sociocultural, religious, economic and political contexts participate in the mission of God in the world. This is in keeping with the former Archbishop of Canterbury Rowan Williams' argument, "It is not the church of God that has a mission. It is the God of mission that has a church."[7] The churches all over the world affirm that "God is at work in the world to redeem creation, and God invites us to participate in this mission."[8] As David Bosch rightly defines, "mission is quite simply, the participation of Christians in the liberating mission of Jesus wagering on a future that verifiable experience seems to belie. It is the good news of God's love, incarnated in the witness of community, for the sake of the world."[9] The liberation and the form of participation in mission remain the responsibility of each Christian community. This means that participation and interpretation of God's mission is never neutral. Williams acknowledges,

---

in African cosmology," *Asian Journal of Pentecostal Studies* 5.1 (2002): 87–106; J. Kwabena Asamoah-Gyadu, "Mission to 'set the captives free': Healing, deliverance, and generational curses in Ghanaian Pentecostalism," *International Review of Mission* 93.370–371 (2004): 389–406; Martin Lindhardt, "Pentecostalism and the Encounter with Traditional Religion in Tanzania: Combat, Congruence and Confusion," *PentecoStudies* 16.1 (2017): 35–58.

    5. Omenyo and Arthur, "The Bible says!" 50–51.

    6. Joseph Quayesi-Amakye, "The problematic of exorcism and spiritual warfare: a dialogue with Apostle Dr. Opoku Onyinah," *Journal of the European Pentecostal Theological Association* 37.1 (2017): 68–79.

    7. The often quoted statement has been attributed to either Rowan Williams, former Archbishop of Canterbury, or Jürgen Moltmann, cited in Mission and Public Affairs Council (Church of England), *Mission-shaped Church: Church Planting and Fresh Expressions of Church in a Changing Context* (London: Church House Publishing, 2004); Alan J. Roxburgh and M. Scott Boren, *Introducing the Missional Church: What It Is, Why It Matters, How to Become One* (Grand Rapids: Baker Books, 2009), 20; Roger Standing, *As A Fire By Burning: Mission as the Life of the Local Congregation* (London: SCM, 2013).

    8. Roxburgh and Boren, *Introducing the Missional Church*, 20.

    9. David J. Bosch, *Transforming Mission: Paradigm Shifts in Theology of Mission* (Maryknoll: Orbis Books, 1991), 519.

> If "church" is what happens when people encounter the risen Jesus and commit themselves to sustaining and deepening that encounter in their encounter with each other, there is plenty of theological room for diversity of rhythm and style, so long as we have ways of identifying the same living Christ at the heart of every expression of Christian life in common. This immediately raises large questions about how different churches keep in contact and learn from each other, and about the kinds of leadership we need for this to happen.[10]

Thus, missiology investigates how various Christian communities interpret, respond to, and engage in the *missio Dei* in their particular contexts. The notion of *missio Dei* constructionist category is found in contemporary missiological studies where some scholars explicitly employ the term "social construction" to describe mission.[11] For example, some researchers studying paradigm shifts in mission from New Testament times to postmodern argue that mission has always demanded a new approach in each new context.[12] Mission is, therefore, a dynamic process that occurs through social and environmental interactions, and emphasizes that God's redemptive work happens within socially constructed human contexts. The mission of God is an ongoing dynamic redemptive process which the church contextualizes through participation as it challenges dominant characterization or construction of the world. Missiological analysis within a *missio Dei* constructionist turn takes a critical stance towards missional approaches that do not promote the fullness of life for all. The measure of life-giving participation in the mission of God is whether it promotes abundant life for all, whether it is sustained by just and equitable social actions, and whether it emerges from the margins.[13] This implicitly suggests that not all participations in the mission of God are sanctioned by God. Authentic participation in the mission of God is a selfless response to actualize within society that fullness of life intrinsic within God's own life

---

10. Rowan Williams, foreword to *Mission-shaped Church* by Mission and Public Affairs Council, vii.

11. John C. Sivalon, *God's Mission and Postmodern Culture: The Gift of Uncertainty* (Maryknoll: Orbis, 2012); Gerhard Lohfink, *Jesus and Community: The Social Dimension of Christian Faith* (Philadelphia: Fortress, 1984).

12. Bosch, *Transforming Mission*; Wilbert R. Shenk, *Changing Frontiers in Mission* (Maryknoll: Orbis, 1999).

13. Jooseop Keum, ed., *Together towards Life: Mission and Evangelism in Changing Landscapes* (Geneva: WCC Publications, 2013).

and being.[14] A clear understanding of human existential struggles within a sociocultural context is at the centre of missional participation. This requires an understanding of how historical socio-cultural contexts shape the way in which mission is defined and how it is practiced. Thus, *missio Dei* constructionism is significant because it helps us unravel how dominant ideologies within particular contexts shape the mission of God and orient the approach of the church. These dominant ideologies in the context have potential to legitimate a particular approach to mission, an approach that may promote interests of the powerful and rich at the expense of others. Understanding this potential pitfall can help the church eschew the dominant ideologies so that it adopts a biblically-informed missional praxis. This is also helpful in finding alternative ways of critiquing the manifestations of the dominant worldviews that shape our sense of mission as we seek the fullness of life for all. Authentic mission in this contemporary age of secularism, materialism, neoliberal capitalism and religio-political exploitation and oppression is at the margins because "transformation never genuinely happens at the centre but at the margins where the reality of people seeking fullness of life becomes a new creative core."[15]

Emergent Prophetic Missional Praxis in Southern Africa

Missiology in general does not seek to engage God as its direct object of analysis, but the missional praxis of the church. Missional praxis, understood in this sense, is observable and testable using tools from social sciences. For Johannes Van der Ven, only the reception, responding and the reaction of the believers concerning the divine mission in the world can be the object of missiological analysis.[16] This is because the reception and understanding of the mission of God in the world is expressed through the experiences of the community of faith. In other words, the way the community of believers embody the mission of God in the world is informed by the experiences which are shaped by their cultural context. The section demonstrates from two case studies of the neo-prophets how a *missio Dei* constructionist framework functions.

---

14. D. Stephen Long, *The Goodness of God: Theology, the Church, and Social Order* (Grand Rapids: Brazos Press, 2001).

15. Chammah J. Kaunda and Roderick R. Hewitt, "Together towards Life: Reconceptualising Missio-Formation in Changing Landscape of World Christianity," *Pharos Journal of Theology* 96 (2015): 11.

16. Johannes Van der Ven, "Empirical Methodology in Practical Theology: Why and How?" *Practical Theology in South Africa* 9.1 (1994): 29–44.

Case One: Shepherd Bushiri

Shepherd Bushiri, who calls himself the 'Major One,' is a Malawian self-proclaimed prophet, founder and general overseer of Enlightened Christian Gathering Church (ECG) in Tswane, South Africa, and the Shepherd Bushiri Ministries International (that has branches in several countries around the world). He calls himself "Major One" because he believes he operates in the line of the Major Prophets of the Old Testament. He established the ministry in 2010 in Malawi and relocated to South Africa in 2012. The church claims to have grown to nearly 35,000 members in a space of eight months. Bushiri also runs a Christian television station called The Prophetic Channel which claims to be viewed by millions across the world. Bushiri is listed among the top 10 richest Pentecostal leaders in the world.

Bushiri was raised in a rural Presbyterian Church in Malawi. He claims that his birth was so mysterious that, when he was born, his mother named him "Shepherd," in recognition of the Lord's presence and protection during delivery.[17] He also claims to have had a direct divine encounter while he was a young boy in which he was taken to heaven and saw Jesus. God told him that, "I am the Lord who has called you. I am the only One who can deliver mankind. Go and tell the people to serve Me."[18] This encounter forms the foundational narrative of his ministry. The ECG mission statement describes it as "a modern congregation of Christ-centered believers celebrating God through the prophetic, healing and deliverance ministries."[19] Bushiri perceives himself as a modern prophet, offering an alternative to Old Testament prophetic traditions. He emphasizes that "generally, most people within the church think of the Old Testament when they look for their template of what a prophetic person should be like. Major One embodies what a modern prophet of the Most High should be."[20] Thus, Bushiri does not define himself in the order of Old Testament prophets. He rather defines himself as a pioneer of the new template of prophetism. He describes his ministry as an outworking of the Book of Acts

---

17. "About Prophet Shepherd Bushiri," Enlightened Christian Gathering Church (ECG), accessed 16 February 2018, http://ecgghana.org/about.php.

18. Roland A. Y. Holou, a Bushiri enthusiast has given a detailed discussion of Bushiri's history, tracing his narrative from his birth to 2016. See his "Prophet Shepherd Bushiri (Major 1) – Diaspora of Malawi (Africa) in South Africa," accessed 17 August 2016, http://africandiasporaleaders.com/prophet-shepherd-bushiri-major-1/. The article also appears as book chapter by the same author. See Roland A. Y. Holou, *The Most Influential Contemporary African Diaspora Leaders* (Bloomington: Author House, 2016).

19. See "About Us - ECG Church," accessed June 21, 2021, https://ecgchurchnyc.org/explore/#explore-belief-sec.

20. Bushiri, "Celebrating the Works of God."

in modern African society. He believes this is demonstrated in his emphasis on miraculous healings and prophetic utterances. He believes his ministry responds to the world by setting "the captives free from the oppression and the bondage of the devil."[21] Bushiri sees himself as a spiritual son[22] of a Zimbabwean multimillionaire prophet, Uebert Angel. Angel himself is a spiritual son of a Ghanaian prophet, Victor Kusi Boateng, of the Power Chapel Worldwide in Kumasi. Boateng is a spiritual son of Archbishop Nicholas Duncan-Williams, the General Overseer of the Christian Action Faith Ministries in Accra, which has more than 20,000 members and more than 250 branch churches located in Africa, North America and Europe. Duncan-Williams is a chairman of the National Association of Charismatic and Christian Churches in Ghana. He is named by the *New African* magazine as one of the one hundred most influential Africans in the cultural and religious category. Bushiri is known for an extravagant, consumerist, and materialistic lifestyle. He celebrates his birthdays with presidential convoys – luxurious cars, designer suits and international singers delivering musical performances.[23] In some African nations, he has received high-level security and a welcome befitting political leaders.[24] Bushiri projects himself as a modern prophet with a special call to produce millionaires among his congregants. Thus, he prays for people to get "miracle money." He sells "Lion of Judah Anointing Oil," claiming that the oil can cure every sickness including mental illnesses, HIV and AIDS. It also claimed he can resurrect the dead and kills witches who trouble his clients. His approach appeals to an African worldview and synthesizes it with both biblical ideas and neoliberal capitalism to produce what he describes as a modern prophet. To his followers, Bushiri is an embodiment of a traditional African prophet in modern society, a representation of all that the followers seek to achieve and become.

---

21. ECG, "Ministries," accessed 16 February 2018, http://www.ecgministries.org.

22. This language of spiritual lineage or parentage is common among African Pentecostals. It speaks of mentorship and relationship between spiritual mentors and their protégés in charismatic terms, where the spiritual parent determines the spiritual child's access to the anointing and gifts of the Spirit.

23. Bushiri, "Prophet Shepherd Bushiri Celebrates Birthday in Grand Style (Feb 20, 2016) #Part 1," accessed 16 February 2018, https://www.youtube.com/watch?v=A5q96wwKxxk.

24. Shepherd Bushiri Ministries Media Department, "Major 1 as a Nation Builder: A Prophet to the Nations," accessed 16 February 2018, http://major1.online/nation-builder/.

Case Two: Emmanuel Makandiwa

Makandiwa is another case of a self-proclaimed prophet situated within the African traditional prophetic imagination. Makandiwa was born and raised in rural Zimbabwe. His parents were devoted leaders in the Apostolic Faith Mission Church (AFM). Makandiwa claims that during the time he worked on his father's farm, he had recurring supernatural encounters. He heard God telling him how he would be used of God in pastoral ministry. He asserts that one afternoon, while caught in a supernatural vision, the shade that he was sleeping under caught fire. But the fire did not burn the shade despite having wooden planks. As the people present rushed to quench the fire with buckets of water, they were amazed to find him still sleeping and to emerge without a single burn. He claims that from that day on, the supernatural manifestations increased, which caused him to heed to the call of God to become a full-time minister.[25] He travelled to Ghana to meet Victor Kusi Boateng, Bushiri's spiritual grandfather, who agreed to take him on as a spiritual son and advised him on how to plant his own church. When he returned to Zimbabwe, he assumed the title of a "prophet" and went on to establish the United Family Interdenominational Ministries in 2008. The church has a membership of over 70,000. He has branch churches in Zimbabwe and South Africa.[26] His followers describe him as a personification of God's love. His ministry is characterized by prophesy and supernatural manifestations of the power of God through healing, miracles and deliverances. He claims to perform miracles ranging from "manhood enlargement" to changing "people's HIV statuses" as well as causing the birth of a healthy baby from a three-day-long pregnancy, and he also sells his own miracle-working anointing oil which has divine power for "economic advancement."[27] Makandiwa, like Bushiri, reconstructs African traditional prophetic worldview within modern capitalist thought. The African traditional prophetic phenomenon of Makandiwa is framed within neoliberal capitalism. He has lucrative businesses and there are rumours that Makandiwa purchased a gold mine from a Chinese firm, Ming-Chang, at

---

25. Peter Nyoni, "Who is Prophet Emmanuel Makandiwa?" accessed 16 Feb. 18, www.zimdiaspora.com.

26. "Emmanuel and Ruth Makandiwa," United Family International Church, http://www.ufiministries.org/index.php.

27. Pauline Mateveke, Clemenciana Mukenge and Nehemiah Chivandikwa, "Media Representation of Prophet Emmanuel Makandiwa: A Comparative Study of The Herald and News Day (2012)," in *Prophets, Profits and the Bible in Zimbabwe: Festschrift for Aynos Masotcha Moyo*, edited by Ezra Chitando, Masiiwa Ragies Gunda and Joachim Kügler (Bamberg: University of Bamberg Press, 2013), 263–80.

US$1.3 million, and for this reason, he is named as one of the fifty richest individuals in Zimbabwe with stock in blue-chip companies as well as prime real estate, especially in Harare.[28] He owns a multi-million dollar property. He is named as one of the most influential leaders by the Zimbabwe Institute of Management (ZIM). The *New African* magazine has named him one of a hundred most influential African leaders in the cultural and religious category alongside his spiritual grandfather, Duncan-Williams, and the famous South African Anglican Archbishop Emeritus, Desmond Tutu.[29] In 2016, Makandiwa launched "Brand Makandiwa" as a celebration of his achievements through various products released on the market, such as books and branded wares. Makandiwa runs a broadcasting network called Christ TV, which he launched in 2014. This channel is broadcast throughout Sub-Saharan Africa and some parts of Europe.[30] Makandiwa, like Bushiri, is also engaged in humanitarian projects, politics and international prophetic ministry. He was reported to have high regard for Robert Mugabe and it is believed he contributed to the construction of an orphanage run by Grace Mugabe, the first lady.[31]

Africanness or Hybridity

The two case studies show that the relevance of neo-prophetic ministry in the African context is grounded in recognition of the traditional African thinking embedded in conservative Christianity. For instance, the concept of a spiritual lineage is significant in African neo-prophetic imaginations. At a congregational level, this refers to members of the church claiming to be sons and daughters of the senior leader. In this system of thought, the members' spirituality derives from that of the senior leader or prophet. This forms a parent-child relationship in which the members understand themselves to be living under the spiritual protection of their prophet. Their success and achievements in their secular endeavors are defined as a result of their association with the prophet. Therefore, for the spiritual covering to remain effective, they share their material success with the prophet. However, this *modus operandi* is also upheld within neo-prophetic ministries. The prophetic ministry is believed to

---

28. "Top 50 richest people in Zimbabwe," Nehanda Radio, accessed 16 February 2018, http://nehandaradio.com/2015/05/24/top-50-richest-people-in-zimbabwe/.

29. Mateveke *et al.*, "Media Representation of Prophet Emmanuel Makandiwa," 263–80.

30. "UFIC launches TV channel," *The Herald*, 1st Nov. 2013, accessed 16 Feb. 2018, https://www.herald.co.zw/ufic-launches-tv-channel/.

31. "Emmanuel Makandiwa," accessed 16 Feb. 2018, https://www.pindula.co.zw/Emmanuel_Makandiwa.

be organized in rank system defined by the degree of spiritual authority, roles and responsibilities within the spiritual hierarchy. The more one is perceived to know about spiritual mysteries, the more powerful the individual is seen to be. This power is used to confront more powerful demonic forces than those which can be overcome by prophets in lower ranks. This constitutes a form of prophetic succession in which one prophet transmits spiritual authority to other prophets. The junior prophets in turn seek to achieve a high level of spiritual power or to become more successful than their fathers. However, each junior prophet has also an obligation to give material gifts to the spiritual father. This phenomenon needs to be analyzed more adequately within African parent-child oriented spirituality.

Theorizing Neo-Prophetism as Socially Situated

In what ways do the two case studies show neo-prophetic *missio Dei* as socially constructed? It is difficult to understand contemporary *missio Dei* within neo-prophetic ministries without recognizing the culturally constructed systems of identity, power, and mission. The power of the prophet is entrenched within the identity that a specific religious community ascribes to them. This is based on the cultural construction of the prophetic identity. These two case studies show that for a prophet to be accepted, he must exhibit some specific characteristics with which that particular society is familiar. Every prophet seeks first to meet specific criteria unconsciously set within the particular cultural context in order then to be socially accepted. The prophets position themselves within culturally accepted prophetic traditions whose content they utilize in their own efforts to garner support and influence. In traditional African consciousness, the prophet's power is located in metaphysical dimensions. The prophet is more than a mere human being. He has spiritual power to explain the ultimate cause – the original cause and source of the misfortune. The prophet's credentials are mystical and are derived from God and confirmed through apparent displays of supernatural abilities. The prophets' interactions with the common people are guided by culturally defined beliefs and practices expressed in spiritual conversations that involve delivering divinely directed messages, discerning spiritual forces at work and prescribing the solution.

Bushiri and Makandiwa use supernatural encounters within birth and burning bush narratives to legitimate their prophetic ministry. These narratives are imbued with power dynamics. They show how these prophets have secret access to the metaphysical power which gives them hidden knowledge known only by the worshipper. By claiming their words as supernatural utterances, the prophets disempower worshippers. They hinder them from questioning the revealed knowledge so that they unquestioningly receive it with reverence as divine revelation. Thus, Bushiri and Makandiwa achieve their divine mission by positioning themselves as mystical and powerful. They claim to promote the well-being of spiritual seekers or potentially destroy them if they fail to recognize the authority of the prophet. They take their place as new African healer-prophets[32] with "all consonant with the world-affirming and pragmatic orientation of traditional religious beliefs and practices."[33] They claim to meet African human needs through spiritual resources offered by the power of the Holy Spirit in the name of Jesus. They conceive the power of the Holy Spirit as a contextual resource for liberating the African continent from demonic forces which manifest through poverty, sickness, and political instability. The notion of spiritual power appears to provide an avenue for reinterpreting traditional concepts of misfortune in modern Africa. Some argue that neo-prophets have failed to transform the African spirit world beyond African primal religion, rather continuity has been maintained beneath a "Christian" guise.[34] However, the prophetic ministry is not a monolithic and closed system, rather a dynamic and fluid system which largely borrows, shapes, negotiates, and interprets other traditions, especially Western Pentecostalism and African indigenous religions. The prophets are not only borrowing from and being shaped by other traditions but have sought to utilize traditional ideas such as witchcraft to engage material ideas within contemporary capitalist ideologies. Witchcraft is one of the intangible African spiritual concepts that are used to market prophetic powers which are geared towards "the neoliberal ideals of privatization and corporatization applied increasingly to all spheres of human

---

32. Cephas N. Omenyo and Wonderful Adjei Arthur, "The Bible says! Neo-prophetic hermeneutics in Africa," *Studies in World Christianity* 19.1 (2013): 50–70; Paul Gifford, "The Primal Pentecostal Imagination: Variants, Origins and Importance," *Suomen Antropologi* 34.2 (2009): 44–52; Ezra Chitando, Masiiwa Ragies Gunda, Joachim Kügler eds., *Prophets, Profits and the Bible in Zimbabwe: Festschrift for Aynos Masotcha Moyo* (Bamberg: University of Bamberg, 2014); Barbara Bompani and Caroline Valois eds., *Christian Citizens and the Moral Regeneration of the African State* (London and New York: Routledge, 2018).

33. Rosalind I. J. Hackett, *Religion in Calabar: The Religious Life and History of a Nigerian Town* (Berlin: Water de Gruyter, 1998), 164.

34. Paul Gifford, *Christianity, Development and Modernity in Africa* (London: Hurst and Company, 2015); Anthony O. Balcomb, "Theology, the Enchanted Universe, and Development: Reflections around a Zambian Case Study in the light of Charles Taylor's "A Secular Age," *Scriptura* 112.1 (2013): 1–12; Abraham Akrong, "Neo-Witchcraft Mentality in Popular Christianity," *Research Review New Series*, 16.1 (2000): 1–12.

life."³⁵ The neo-prophets position themselves as engaged in cosmic battles on behalf of their members against witches, wizards, enchantments, divinations and sorcery. These elements of evil are critical factors in spiritual warfare which only the prophets have the secrets to overcome. This mystically oriented discourse on evil has found a fertile ground in neoliberal contexts with its emphasis on the marketing of spiritual products.³⁶ Thus, many neo-prophets prefer an individualistic, liberalized approach to ministry which gives exclusive power to personalization of spirituality and ministry. Contrary to traditional notions of prophetic traditions which received impetus and accountability from the community's ancestral traditions, neo-prophetic movements function within neoliberalism. The neo-prophets "live by the generalized principle of competition in all social spheres of life," reducing their religious communities to private businesses and adherents to clients.³⁷

Bushiri's and Makandiwa's neo-prophetic movements link spirituality to contemporary lifestyle and wellbeing products which unconsciously promote a neoliberal agenda. The neo-prophets constantly reimagine and reinvent themselves by seeking new ways for asserting and exerting their power using all available resources within their reach. These include political associations, public exhibition of wealth, investing in businesses, involvement in humanitarian projects and threatening to harm those who oppose them. Thus, the neo-prophets do not position themselves as participating in the mission of God. They consider themselves the media through which God fulfils the mission in the world. They are the embodiment of God's mission.

Conclusion

This chapter has argued that the phenomenon of neo-prophetism (that shapes the neo-prophetic movement in Africa today) is socially constructed and that it depends on the traditional African worldview both for its functionality and sustainability. By the means of two case studies of self-proclaimed prophets,

---

35. Jeremy Carrette and Richard King, *Selling Spirituality: The Silent Takeover of Religion* (London and New York: Routledge, 2005), 2.

36. Asonzeh Ukah has described in details how spiritual products are branded as advertised to spiritual consumers. See Asonzeh Ukah, "Roadside Pentecostalism: Religious Advertising in Nigeria and the Marketing of Charisma," *Critical Interventions: Journal of African Art History and Visual Culture* 2 (2008): 125–41; Asonzeh Ukah, "Branding God: Advertising and the Pentecostal Industry in Nigeria," *LIWURAM: Journal of the Humanities* 13 (2006): 83–106.

37. Keri Day, *Religious Resistance to Neoliberalism: Womanist and Black Feminist Perspectives* (New York: Palgrave Macmillan, 2016), 4.

Shepherd Bushiri and Emmanuel Makandiwa, the chapter has shown how the prophetic gifts are utilized to leverage material resources by taking advantage of the African orientation towards a supernatural explanation of reality and supernatural desire for healing. This African worldview provides the context for people like Bushiri and Makandiwa to take advantage of the people's need for divine interventions—something that is normal in the African traditional religious system—for their own material well-being. How do we make theological sense of this? First, we do well to continue believing that God provides for humanity. One of God's names in the Scriptures is Jehovah Jireh, which means "God will provide." We may need to place our trust more in God than in the prophets. It is God who provides, not the prophets. Second, we must also learn that some who claim to be prophets are out to cheat God's people of their blessings. The Bible encourages us to discern all Spirits (1 John 4:1–6). Spiritual power can easily be corrupted. The performing of miracles is not a sign that it is the Spirit of God at work. In addition, we ought not let the suspicious works of some prophetic leaders make us dismiss all of God's prophetic work among us. Third, we can learn from African religion where it is normal for people to bring gifts to their charismatic leaders who must use such gifts for the good of the community and never accumulate wealth for themselves. Whatever is given to them for spiritual purposes can only be used as intended. When such rules are broken, they face harsh consequences. It is for this reason that some of the most charismatic leaders live and die poor. Within the Christian faith, we see some wisdom in the faith communities who refuse to accumulate riches. Finally, this discussion of neo-prophetism and the prosperity gospel in Africa has shown that this is a topic that needs further research. We will understand African Christianity better when we have a fair knowledge of what drives movements like this, especially in a continent like Africa.

10

Contextualized Missions and Theological Education in the Global South

A Case Study from East Africa

Peter Maribei and Kyama Mugambi

This chapter examines Mavuno Church's Transformation Loop, an ecclesiologically-driven, non-formal model of theological education that emerged from the Mavuno family of churches in Nairobi, Kenya. We, both authors of this chapter, have served within Mavuno Church in various leadership capacities since its inception in 2005. First-hand experiences of Transformation Loop inform the insights provided in this chapter. The advanced theological education from seminaries based in Africa provides the foundation for the authors' emic reflections. We begin by giving a brief history of Mavuno Church to offer a context for how the Transformation Loop emerged as a model of theological education. Then we examine the various elements of the Transformation Loop in relation to missions. We end by discussing the implications of the Transformation Loop model for theological education and the place of formal theological institutions.

Why Informal Theological Education?

Christian populations proliferating in Africa in the last few decades have generated an interest in the contributions that the African church might make to the future of World Christianity and mission. According to a demographic study conducted by the Pew Center in 2010, one in four Christians in the world was living in sub-Saharan Africa.[1] Christians now constitute one half of the continent's population, accounting for 618 million of the 1.3 billion Christians in Africa.[2] Lamin Sanneh and Andrew Walls argued that the reason for vibrant Christian expression in Africa lies in the infinite translatability of the gospel. This translatability of the gospel facilitates its transmission into new cultures and contexts.[3] The entry of the gospel in Africa's diverse cultures begins as a process by which recipients *own* its message, and eventually become its transmitters.[4] In this way, mission is an indispensable part of the Christian experience. We take the term "missionary" in both its broad and narrow senses. In the broad sense, the missionary is the messenger of the gospel who announces reconciliation between Christ and the world, human cultures, sectors of society, as well as local and international arenas. In other words, "All Christian witness is, therefore, missionary, in so far as it relates to the human condition."[5] Social and institutional transformation falls in this broader sense of mission. In the narrow sense, we understand mission to be about communicating the gospel to people within and beyond the sphere of the communicator. Evangelism, international missions, cross-cultural mission, missions by the African Diaspora and other categorizations fall within this narrow definition. With due respect to the broad definition above, we believe that the celebrated growth of Christianity on African soil is largely the result of indigenous efforts emerging within this narrower sense of mission.

In the past, the present and foreseeable future, the church in Africa remains the primary agent of growth for Christianity as well as the primary sending

---

1. Skirbekk, Stonawski and Goujon, "Global Christianity: A Report on the Size and Distribution of the World's Christian Population," Pew Research Center, December, 2011, doi: 10.13140/2.1.5098.1761, 53.

2. Johnson, Zurlo, Hickman and Crossing, "Status of Global Christianity 2015, in the Context of 1900 to 2050."

3. Andrew Walls, *The Missionary Movement in Christian History: Studies in the Transmission of Faith* (Maryknoll: Orbis Books, 1996), 25; Lamin Sanneh, *Translating the Message: The Missionary Impact on Culture*, 2nd ed. (Maryknoll: Orbis Books, 2009).

4. Walls, *The Missionary Movement*, 25.

5. Kyama Mugambi, "Mission is Not Western: Kenyan Perspectives on Identity, Church Planting, Social Transformation, and Bold Mission Initiatives," *Anvil: Journal of Theology and Mission* 34.1 (2018): 12–20.

agency for missionaries.[6] It follows that the training of leaders is indispensable to meet the mission needs of this growing church. The form and structures that have traditionally been used to develop leaders came from missionary initiatives. The initial foundational framework for this training strategy was the formal theological institution.[7] Over time, this paradigm has proved inadequate for various reasons. First, it depends on a large and often unsustainable financial outlay for physical infrastructure, personnel, and operations.[8] For much of its history, with few exceptions, theological institutions in Africa have largely depended on the generosity of the Western church.[9] Second, theological curricula in these institutions are often not contextualized for the African continent. The study material is largely drawn from Western institutions and scholarship. It often does not reflect the local concerns or attempt to address African challenges. Third, in a rapidly post-denominational environment, the old models served clergy within strictly defined ecclesiastical borders.[10] The church in many places in Africa functions across denominational lines. Earlier models of theological education do not make adequate provision for this in their curricula. Relevant models of theological education will be an antidote to the challenges facing African Christianity, such as the shift in worldviews, socio-political and economic pressures, globalization, and religious pluralism.[11] Paradigms of theological education must include the laity, the youth and adults to be relevant to present missiological needs. Contextualization of theological education is a current discussion even in the West from where many increasingly outdated models emanated. Alternative paradigms to formal

---

6. Mugambi, "Mission is Not Western."

7. Wanjiru M. Gitau, "Revitalization of Christianity in Nairobi: The Mavuno Church," in *African Urban Christian Identity: Emerging Patterns*, ed. J. Steven O'Malley and Philomena Njeri Mwaura (Nairobi, Kenya: Action Publishers, 2016), 56–81.

8. Emmanuel Bellon, "Theological Education in Africa: Business or Mission?" *Insights Journal* 2.2 (2017): 21–33.

9. Bellon, "Theological Education in Africa," 21–22.

10. Grant LeMarquand and Joseph D. Galgalo, eds., *Theological Education in Contemporary Africa* (Eldoret, Kenya: Zapf Chancery Publishers Africa, 2004), 16–17; J. Kwabena Asamoah-Gyadu, *Contemporary Pentecostal Christianity: Interpretations from an African Context* (Oxford, England: Regnum Books International, 2013), 148; Desta Heliso, "Africa and Christian Theological Education," in *Preparing Saints for the Africa God Wants*, ed. Aiah Foday-Khabenje, James Nkansah-Obrempong, John Jusu and Ted Barnett (Nairobi, Kenya: Association of African Evangelicals, 2016), http://aeaafrica.org/wp-content/uploads/2018/02/AEA-Jubilee-A5-Booklet.pdf; John Elias, "Models of Theological Education for the Laity," *Journal of Adult Theological Education* 3.2 (2006): 179–93.

11. Chammah J. Kaunda, "Checking Out the Future: A Perspective from African Theological Education," *International Review of Mission* 105.1 (2016), 114.

theological education are emerging among some American evangelical circles. One example is the church-based theological training movement or C-BTE which attempts to build a culturally relevant model in the postmodern and technologically oriented Western society.[12] Reed calls this model of theological education an ecclesiologically-driven, non-formal model. For Reed, the term "non-formal" refers to "an ordered, systematic educational process that lies outside the formal education system."[13] It does not rely on professors, curriculum, libraries, grades, degrees, and accrediting associations.[14] Reed goes on to suggest that formal theological education institutions are inadequate to transmit the "entire constellation of beliefs, values, techniques . . . contained in the biblical truths, images, and models to be imitated throughout the Scriptures."[15] To the contrary, local churches are capable of developing the theological education that can drive the agendas they choose to prioritize.

Mavuno Chapel and the Transformation Loop

Mavuno Church is a non-denominational evangelical congregation whose headquarters is in Nairobi, Kenya. The church began in September 2005 as a plant of the Nairobi Chapel, another older non-denominational congregation that started in 1952. The British settlers who did not fit in with the Anglican church to which many of their compatriots paid homage, began a church that had no strong clergy-laity divisions.[16] The legacy was based on the Plymouth Brethren, a movement of small congregations made up of an educated elite and did not have ordained clergy. By 2005, Nairobi Chapel had grown to 2,000 adults. Mission through church planting became the focus of the congregation's activities. Mavuno was one of five churches planted in August 2005 within Nairobi. It situated itself strategically in a middle-class residential area in the southern part of Nairobi. From early on, it targeted young, urban, educated Kenyans in their twenties and thirties as this generation was sceptical of spiritual authority and considered the long-standing denominations irrelevant to their lives.

---

12. Jeff Reed, "Church-Based Ministry Training Which Is Truly Church Based," Paper Presented at the 30th ACCESS Annual Conference, Moody Bible Institute (January, 2001), 3. https://silo.tips/download/church-based-ministry-training-which-is-truly-church-based.

13. Reed, "Church-Based Ministry Training," 3.

14. Reed, "Church-Based Ministry Training," 3.

15. Reed, "Church-Based Ministry Training," 2.

16. "Our Beginnings," Nairobi Chapel, accessed August 8, 2020, https://nairobichapel.net/about-us/beginnings/.

The vision of Mavuno Church is to "plant a culture-defining church in all the capital cities of Africa and the gateway cities of the world by 2035."[17] Since its inception, it has planted churches in the capital cities of seven other African countries as well as in Berlin, Germany.[18] Through its partnerships and outreach, it has also influenced other churches such as Mariners Church.[19] Another growing network of churches called the Rooted Network has adopted aspects of this model.[20] Muriithi Wanjau, the senior pastor, and his team formulated a catchy mission statement, "Turning Ordinary People Into Fearless Influencers Of Society," to broadly outline the missional thrust of the community.[21] Until today, the church sees the scope of its mission not only as evangelizing and doing outreach, but also transforming other sectors of society including media and the arts, business and the economy, family and education, politics and governance, and health and the environment.[22] The breaking down of culture into spheres of influence is not new or particularly unique. A similar perspective known as the "seven mountains of culture" dates back to the 1980s.[23] What is unique about Mavuno is the concrete link between its holistic mission and a viable discipleship strategy with which to engage it. To facilitate this, Mavuno developed a discipleship strategy known as the Transformation Loop (T-Loop). It is a holistic model that not only develops ministers for the church, but also mobilizes the whole community to take the whole gospel to the whole world.

---

17. "Our Vision," Mavuno Church, accessed August 8, 2020, https://www.mavunochurch.org/our-vision-2/.

18. These are Uganda, Rwanda, Burundi, Ethiopia, Zambia, Malawi and Democratic Republic of Congo.

19. Mariners Church is a mega-church in the United States.

20. "Rooted," Rooted Network, accessed March 28, 2017, https://www.experiencerooted.com/.

21. "Our Vision," Mavuno Church.

22. "Our Vision," Mavuno Church.

23. The seven sectors described by churches and evangelistic organizations sought to organize mission activities around concrete points of focus. This is not dissimilar to socio-economic theory which has, for a long time, formulated approaches that study the public, private, non-profit and, more recently, community sectors. Loren Cunningham, *Making Jesus Lord: The Dynamic Power of Laying down Your Rights* (Washington, DC: YWAM Publishing, 2001), 134; "Putting Faith into Action," Live with Purpose Church, accessed July 17, 2018, https://www.livewithpurposechurch.org/about/seven-mountains.

The Transformation Loop as Non-formal Theological Education

The Transformation Loop is a discipleship tool made up of a series of progressive steps that a person undergoes in the course of their life-long discipleship journey. It presumes that discipleship is not merely a one-time event of coming to faith in Christ but a "lifelong process along a series of observable transitions or rites of passage."[24] As such, it acknowledges that everyone is at some point on this journey. Subsequently, spiritual maturity is understood to be a state of commitment to the process rather than an end-product. It was also designed to help people find and move towards their next step whether it be establishing a personal relationship with Christ or growing towards maturity in Christ. It has, thus, inspired leaders and members to engage in activities which have influenced different sectors of society including the entertainment industry, poverty alleviation, and education for the disenfranchised. These initiatives are celebrated annually in each of Mavuno's congregations.[25] Overall, the Transformation Loop is a form of non-formal theological education that reorients a person's life from being self-centred to being missional. It takes people on a four-stage journey of discipleship, and each stage facilitates discipleship in a different environment. It begins in society with outreach activities to *complacent* people who are not yet committed to Christ and his church. Through environments, relationships, and experiences individuals progress through a series of stages – from the *complacent* Christian to one who *consumes* Christian content, from the *consumer* of Christian content to a *connected* member of a community, from the *connected* member to one who is *committed* to mission, and from one who is *committed* to mission to one who is *compelled* to go out to transform society. Through this process of transformation they join God in God's mission to reconcile everything to himself. Let us look at each stage in turn.

Stage 1: From Complacent *to* Consumer

From surveys, observation and experience, Mavuno Church leaders identified many of their potential congregation members as apathetic and disinterested

---

24. Wanjiru Gitau, "Focusing Scholarly Discourse on Megachurches: The Evangelical Revitalization Movements' Theory in a Case Study of Mavuno Church" (PhD Diss., Africa International University, 2015), 172.

25. Each congregation hosts events in November to highlight and celebrate members and their initiatives influencing society. For example, the church has celebrated Richard Njau and his "Clean the Airwaves" media campaign, and Daisy Waimiri with her *Maono* micro-finance initiative for women groups in rural and peri-urban areas.

in church even though they were mostly young adults who had prior church experience and had stopped participating because they felt that church was irrelevant and boring. As a result of their exposure to relativistic and postmodern societies through media, formal education, travel, among many things, they had come to question the exclusive claims of the gospel and ended up perceiving the church as old-fashioned and Christians to be too restrictive to enjoy the pleasures of life. Of course, these observations are not unique to Mavuno Church. Other scholars have made similar observations.[26] Chammah Kaunda, for instance, notes that the rapid spread of postmodernism is influencing young Africans' social imagination, cultural sensitivity and awareness, political-economic consciousness, identity construction, educational approaches, and communication.[27] The result is a growing scepticism of authorities such as those in churches. Consequently, younger generations are searching for new African communities that celebrate diversity, complexity, richness, ambiguity, emergent identities, and new socio-cultural life.

Mavuno Church crafts mission activities that reach into the society, seeking out these potential converts. One of the avenues of evangelistic mission is entertainment which includes weekend events of musicals, concerts and theatrical plays. Performers share gospel-themed stories using everyday language that the youth speak and the musical tunes they are familiar with. Mavuno Church designs these weekends as a welcoming environment. Those young adults who attend one of these weekend services experience a completely different liturgy from what they have experienced elsewhere. Meticulous attention is paid to the choice of music, decorative props, and opportunities for people to make connections with others during the service. Youth who were *complacent* are drawn to church services by the invitational nature of these weekend events. Many move on from these weekends to become *consumers* of Sunday service content. They begin to attend services because of a need in their lives that can be addressed by elements of the church service. The weekend services are, for Mavuno Church, a step in the discipleship journey.

---

26. Some studies have made the connection between this demographic with such issues as religion, social engagement and even economics. See for example Rachel Spronk, "Exploring the Middle Classes in Nairobi: From Modes of Production to Modes of Sophistication," *African Studies Review* 57.1 (2014); Mthuli Ncube, Charles Leyeka Lufumpa and Steve Kayizzi-Mugerwa, "The Middle of the Pyramid: Dynamics of the Middle Class in Africa," *Africa Development Bank Market Brief* (2011). Pierre Jacquemont, "Africa's 'Middle Class" *Afrique Contemporaine* 244.4 (2012).

27. Kaunda, "Checking Out the Future: A Perspective from African Theological Education."

The goal is to educate *consumers* about their own journey of transformation and persuade them to take the next step of becoming *connected*.

The sermons delivered during the weekend services are a particularly potent form of theological education. While the weekend service is not designed to present a systematic articulation of Christian theology, it is consistent with the principle of meeting felt needs. Mavuno Church leadership seeks to follow the example of Jesus who often used parables to bring spiritual truths to life for his audience. Jesus made the faith accessible to his audience using the circumstances and dilemmas they were encountering as a touch point to make his message relevant.

There are those who have dismissed Mavuno Church's strategy of presenting the gospel in culture as being *worldly* and *carnal*.[28] Even pastoral staff who are new to Mavuno Church style of ministry often harbour similar concerns. To respond to this, Muriithi Wanjau, the visionary and founding pastor, uses letters and sermons to educate staff and church members on the theology of missions as it relates to human cultures. For example, to address concerns about the form and style of music used during the singing time in church, Wanjau gave a treatise arguing that the separation between the secular and spiritual spheres of life is a construct of Greek philosophy carried forward through our Western education. He gave an example of how popular hymns that are sang today in church were made popular by churches from a previous era in church history. Wanjau said that the gospel has always remained the same, but the packaging has changed with every culture and generation.[29]

Wanjau's example illustrates an ecclesiologically-driven, non-formal theological education where knowledge and attitudes regarding the gospel in culture reach lay people and ministers outside theological institution channels. The recipients of this knowledge are not just passive and disinterested observers. The education is happening in the context of ministry and addresses a real and emotionally-charged challenge. This form of theological education seizes upon unplanned yet opportune moments occurring in everyday life, to show students how orthodoxy (right belief) relates to orthopraxy (right action).

---

28. "Has Mavuno Church Taken It Too Far in Attempt to Draw Teenagers to Church?" KTN News Kenya, February 22, 2014, YouTube Video, 2:13, https://www.youtube.com/watch?v=Hx3P0gcQcPo; Kikhami Obayi, "Public Outcry over Mavuno Church 'Gerrit' Poster," The Star, last modified April 22, 2014, http://www.the-star.co.ke/news/article-156753/public-outcry-over-mavuno-church-gerrit-poster.

29. Muriithi Wanjau, "This Aint Your Grandma's Church," *Pastor M's Blog* (blog), accessed September 1, 2015, https://greatnessnow.wordpress.com/2007/10/18/this-aint-your-grandmas-church/.

Stage 2: From **Consumer** *to* **Connected**

The Mavuno Church weekend service seeks to get the *consumer* to become a *connected* person who is integrated into a vibrant community of faith. This is accomplished when the *consumer* participates in a ten-week discipleship experience called *Mizizi*.[30] The environment enables participants to connect with God, their purpose, and like-minded people who are also discovering and living out their faith. During the *Mizizi* experience, facilitators, who are more mature in the faith, use a workbook to guide discussions about foundational theological themes. These themes include the attributes of God, God's character and intentions, spiritual disciplines, and financial stewardship. *Mizizi* provides participants with opportunities to form close relationships with other Christians. They learn how to have a close relationship with God and get inspired by who God wants them to be. Experiential learning activities such as an evangelistic outreach, a community service event, and a final off-site retreat are included for participants to practice the concepts they are learning. The retreat serves as a transition or rite of passage to the next step in the Transformation Loop. Those who have committed their lives to Christ undergo baptism. The *Mizizi* group then transitions into a small group of believers, called a *Life Group*, who meet regularly for fellowship and outreach. *Mizizi* and *Life Groups* give young adults a sense of community which is an antidote to the alienation brought about by the weakening of traditional social support structures such as the extended family and neighbourhood.[31] *Mizizi* is a practical guide for the laity to engage with significant aspects of their faith in a nonformal theological education experience. Formal theological education should not be restricted to the study of religious literature, church history, and church doctrine.[32] It should also deal with the spiritual life and concerns of lay people. Elias concurs that small group faith sharing is an effective avenue for spiritual formation and theological learning because people find small groups supportive and non-threatening.[33]

---

30. *Mizizi* is a Swahili word which can be translated as "roots."

31. Elias, "Models of Theological Education for the Laity," 187–88.

32. This model was applied to theological education by John Elias, a veteran adult and religious education researcher. He used this within his model. Elias credits his approach to British educator Brian Wren's treatment of conscientization as theological education which "begins with an explanation of Freire's theory of conscientization as critical consciousness through dialogue, provides philosophical and theological reflection on justice, deals with issues of power, conflict, and cultural oppression, and ends with practical suggestions for putting this form of education into practice." Elias, "Models of Theological Education for the Laity," 187–88.

33. Elias, "Models of Theological Education."

Stage 3: From Connected to Committed

After *Mizizi*, participants join a *Life Group*. The church generally considers one who is part of a Life Group a *committed* person. *Life Groups* are the hub of other discipleship steps which encourage members to apply sermon content in their lives. The environment provides association and mutual accountability for members. Those who attend the *Life Groups* and regularly attend church services identify with Mavuno's vision as evidenced by their sacrificial and regular giving to the church. The church uses the collegial term "associates" to identify those who serve regularly in the ministries of the church. Associates attend forums where the leadership communicates and discusses strategic decisions about Mavuno Church.

In light of the foregoing, the approach used by Mavuno Church at this *Life Group* stage could be understood within the theological education through conscientization framework outlined by John Elias.[34]

The first step of the conscientization model was a six-week course in which Elias led church leaders through a philosophical and theological reflection on social justice as well as various approaches to pastoral action.[35] The second step was to establish an institute for training lay leaders with the end result being that each group would take some kind of social action in the community. The third step was a commission ceremony where graduates were charged to go and lead similar work in their religious communities.

This is quite similar to the steps that *committed* people take together with *Life Group* members in Mavuno Church. For example, they take one step called *Hatua*.[36] It is a curriculum developed by one of the former pastors, Dr. Linda Ochola-Adolwa. It takes participants through an in-depth study of the Old Testament with the aim of challenging them to begin to engage and transform structures of social injustice. In a study that Ochola-Adolwa conducted to better understand the civic participation of church members, she concluded that while most of the Life Group members were civically engaged, they hardly ever engaged structures and decision-making processes in society.[37] Thus, essentially, the *Life Group* is a platform where a non-formal approach

---

34. Elias, "Models of Theological Education," 189–90.
35. Elias, "Models of Theological Education," 189–90.
36. *Hatua* is a Swahili word which means to take action.
37. Ochola-Adolwa, "A Study of Macro, Social, and Psychological Factors That Influence the Civic Participation Practices of Christians at Mavuno Church, Nairobi, Kenya." PhD diss., Fuller Theological Seminary, 2017.

to theological education is advanced beyond *Mizizi*. Additional experiences deal with pertinent issues on the life of the Christian.

Stage 4: From **Committed** to **Compelled**

According to Mavuno Church's transformational discipleship process, the *compelled* person is passionate about God and his redemptive mission towards all creation. Such a person prays regularly for the extension of God's kingdom while sacrificing their time and money towards a Frontline Initiative in one of the six sectors of society. The initiative might be a business venture, a non-profit or any other kind of structure that seeks to transform one of the sectors of society to reflect God's original intent to bless.[38] The church leadership sees its responsibility towards the *compelled* person as: (1) providing leeway for them to exercise and represent Mavuno Church to the society; (2) connect them with people, resources, and networks; (3) help them mentor other leaders in the congregation; and (4) hold them accountable to their kingdom vision and high standards of integrity.

From her research, Wanjiru Gitau lists twenty Frontline Initiatives started by members. One ministry, for example, was created to rehabilitate ex-prisoners through discipleship, care, and a halfway house.[39] Church and mission is another sector of society in which both lay and clergy can engage in. According to Mavuno Church's discipleship process, it is not enough for the *compelled* person to know a lot about their faith. Their commitment to the Christian faith comes across through tangible impact on society.

Mavuno Church, which sees the church and mission sector as the centrepiece for impacting all other sectors, developed its own frontline initiative called the Mavuno Leadership Pipeline. Mavuno Church's Leadership Pipeline focuses on the engagement and growth of staff within the church as an intentional staff development structure. Gitau defines it as "a structural arrangement of staff according to the needs of the church and according to the maturing levels of these staff."[40]

---

38. Delanyo Adadevoh, *The Whole Gospel to the Whole Person* (Orlando: International Leadership Foundation, 2012).
39. Gitau, "Focusing Scholarly Discourse on Megachurches."
40. Gitau, "Focusing Scholarly Discourse on Megachurches," 33.

The Leadership Pipeline

A second training avenue is the Leadership pipeline, used as a framework to develop full time staff members within the church. The leadership pipeline is a concept adapted from Charan, Drotter and Noel's book by the same name.[41] While Charan *et al.* prescribed it for commercial businesses, it is applicable in non-business environments such as the church. It envisages an organizational hierarchy where people grow in responsibilities and influence. This theory has helped Mavuno Church to organize and train their leadership better for mission. The pipeline's entry point into the staff team is the *Discovery Program*. This is a one-year internship programme designed to expose candidates to the Mavuno Church environment. A rigorous recruitment process ensures that candidates possess key qualities such as a teachable spirit, a growing encounter with Christ, and leadership potential. Candidates learn to serve under more experienced leaders with the expectation that they will learn Mavuno values and skills such as management of self, time, and relationships. The second level is the pastoral trainee. It lasts two years and comes with an increased level of responsibility. Candidates receive theological grounding and the critical skills of self-leadership, leading others, leading teams and leading an organization.

The pipeline has been effective at raising pastors and church planters for the church plants in Uganda, Malawi, Ethiopia, and Germany. The Leadership Pipeline fits the description of Reed's ecclesiologically-driven model for theological education.[42] It is an attempt by the churches to assume major responsibility for training their own leaders rather than relying on the formal theological education institution.

The result of an institutionally driven theological education paradigm in the Western church as Reed puts it, has been threefold: (1) lack of leadership – formal institutions do not have the capacity to educate the number of leaders required; (2) lack of fully prepared leadership – acquiring wisdom is replaced with mastering academic disciplines; and (3) nominalism – practical theology to build up believers is lacking partly because ordered learning is removed from community life causing the average Christian to believe that theology is irrelevant. In contrast, the ecclesiologically-driven model entrenches core biblical values in leaders such as faithfulness in service, discipleship, spiritual disciplines, and character development within the context of community life.[43]

---

41. Ram Charan, Stephen Drotter and James Noel, *The Leadership Pipeline: How to Build the Leadership Powered Company*, 2nd edition (San Francisco: Jossey-Bass, 2010).
42. Reed, "Church-Based Ministry Training Which Is Truly Church Based."
43. Reed, "Church-Based Ministry Training Which Is Truly Church Based."

It is for this reason that we now turn to discussing the bridges between formal and informal theological education.

Formal verses Non-formal Theological Education

The story of Mavuno Church, just like the relationship between the apostle Paul and his protégé, Timothy, illustrates the benefits of a nonformal theological education. Timothy's education, as seen in 2 Timothy, included elements such as practical wisdom, community context, ministry context, evidence of progress and giftedness, community commending and discipline.[44] Timothy's developmental process was fully integrated with the real-life mission he and Paul participated in together. In contrast, Timothy's training was mission driven and consisted of "planting, establishing, and multiplying of churches."[45]

In case this is understood to imply the jettisoning of formal theological institutions, an understanding of the context shows otherwise. In a study by Mugambi involving eighteen church planters serving at Mavuno Church, all respondents indicated that theological education was important.[46] The concern, however, was the relevance of the theological education from a formal institution. This is consistent with the findings of the Global Survey on Theological Education conducted between 2011 and 2013.[47] Most African respondents indicated that practical ministry skills strengthened theological education. Leaders encounter experiences people are dealing with. Daily issues such as poverty, human rights abuse, unemployment, tribalism, corruption, and all forms of social injustice as opposed to abstract theoretical problems. Mugambi notes that despite Mavuno Church developing content and programmes to train its own emerging leaders, certain areas need content that the church is not structured to develop.[48] According to Mugambi, formal theological institutions must rise to the challenge and work with churches to develop this content to secure the theological future of the church in

---

44. Reed, "Church-Based Ministry Training Which Is Truly Church Based."
45. Reed, "Church-Based Ministry Training Which Is Truly Church Based," 9.
46. Kyama Mugambi, "Perceptions and Recommendations for Theological Education for Church Planters in Kenya: A Case Study of Mavuno Church," *Impact Journal* (2016).
47. Kaunda, "Checking Out the Future: A Perspective from African Theological Education," 124–25.
48. Mugambi, "Perceptions and Recommendations for Theological Education for Church Planters in Kenya."

Africa.[49] While the average person can make theological inferences through intuition, the conceptual refinement of those inferences requires training in both language and religious discernment. The clergy and lay leaders should know more than ordinary believers. It is less inadequate for them to rely only on intuition and inspiration on matters doctrinal and theological.[50] Mugambi concurs with the need for advanced theological education for clergy and lay leaders to cultivate theological articulation.[51]

Mugambi suggests a number of other ideas that a formal theological institution can partner with churches to align with the work of church planting.[52] The proposals include: (1) crafting programmes that are more affordable, more accessible, and more relevant; (2) developing opportunities for theological students to work alongside church planters to gain practical experience and mentoring; and (3) developing multi-disciplinary content that is useful for the academy and churches to safeguard Christian orthodoxy and addressing relevant national issues. Formal theological education is valuable. Indeed, non-formal theological education models such as the Mavuno Transformation Loop enhances its effects. In arguing for a more relevant theological education, Jusu asks educators to reconsider how the fourfold division of theological education (biblical studies, church history, systematic theology, and practical theology) is taught.[53] The fragmented theological curriculum was not designed for training church ministers. The theological education curriculum should combine both formal and non-formal training, where practical approaches to theology are not considered less rigorous. Rather, such practical theological approaches should serve as the unifying force for the once-fragmented curriculum. Mavuno's discipleship approach demonstrates how non-formal theological education is disseminated. It also highlights the need for integrative theological training methods that prepare leaders for such mission-oriented approaches.

---

49. Mugambi, "Perceptions and Recommendations for Theological Education for Church Planters in Kenya."

50. Mugambi, "Perceptions and Recommendations for Theological Education for Church Planters in Kenya."

51. Jesse N. K. Mugambi, "The Future of Theological Education in Africa and the Challenges It Faces," in *Handbook of Theological Education in Africa*, ed. Isabel Apawo Phiri and Dietrich (Oxford, United Kingdom: Regnum Books International, 2013), https://www.ocms.ac.uk/wp-content/uploads/2021/03/Handbook-of-Theological-Education-in-Africa.pdf, 120–21.

52. Mugambi, "The Future of Theological Education in Africa and the Challenges It Faces."

53. Heliso, "Africa and Christian Theological Education: In Preparing Saints for the Africa God Wants."

Conclusion

Further discussion needs to explore new models of relevant and contextual theological education, and how it is delivered particularly to church leaders and church planters. The enlightenment-era foundation which built Western theological education has also been called into question in the West. Its effectiveness is no longer as evident given the world-view shift to the postmodern and post-Christian society. Its efficacy in the African context also requires interrogation. For historical and structural reasons, formal theological institutions will continue to exist into the foreseeable future. The question arises as to the role and function of formal theological institutions in places where the church is growing so fast that the institutions cannot produce enough mission-ready leaders. This chapter shows how a church in Africa is adapting to the need for theological education in both church leaders and laity through an ecclesiologically-driven non-formal theological education. This model provides certain pointers towards the need for theological education and new ways of engagement and partnership between churches and theological institutions. Much remains to be explored about the connection between formal and non-formal theological models.

11

The *Pambio* in Mission

Meaning and Significance in African Christianity

William Obaga

It is easier to begin with the question: what is a *Pambio*? In a nutshell, the *Pambio* is a Christian music genre that has evolved since the late 1970s to early 1980s as a folk hymn in communities throughout sub-Saharan Africa. Etymologically, *Pambio* is the Kiswahili word for a "chorus" or "refrain" of a Christian hymn. In eastern Africa, especially in Kenya and Tanzania, this meaning has not changed. However, the same word has gained a second meaning as a term referring to a new genre of African folk hymn. In some parts of western Africa this folk hymn goes by the name "chorus hymn." In southern and other western African regions, it is known simply by the term "chorus." This means that the terms *Pambio*, "chorus," or "chorus hymn" refer to the same thing, that is, the new genre of African hymn composed mainly by lay Christians in churches and communities. As should be expected, this hymn functions in community life as a folk song of a Christian nature in various contexts – sacred and secular.

The *Pambio* is based on a simple, rhythmic, and folklike melody sung in call-and-response form. It allows anyone to lead the call: woman, man, youth, child, lay, clergy, and so forth. The leader extemporizes basic theological and biblical thoughts and the community responds with a short, often fixed response. Almost invariably, the community sings its *Pambio* with body movement, including dance, swaying, marching, clapping, or foot stomping, and with or without musical instruments. It allows for variation, reiteration, or extension of text, melody, or rhythm as the occasion or context suggests. The *Pambio* is usually amenable to appropriation and modification to suit new contexts, even in the secular arena. It further allows for the adaptation of African polyphonic singing style and the use of some Western ideas and musical instruments, notably guitars and keyboards.[1] It appropriates certain Western elements of texture and style, such as chordal harmony employed in oral and spontaneous African polyphonic style.

The Evolution of the *Pambio*

The practice of singing the refrains of hymns (*Pambios*) without verses began in the USA and was later imported to Africa through influential American evangelists. Just around the mid-twentieth century mass evangelical rallies were organized by pioneers who included Billy Graham, T. L. Osborne, Morris Cerullo and others. The first such mass rally by Billy Graham attracted 6,000 people in New Orleans in 1947. Such large gatherings required short memorizable songs in place of hymn books. In less than a decade, the mass rally tradition was exported to Africa and so was the singing of refrains (*Pambios*) without verses. This became customary in Africa over the next three decades. The *Pambio* (refrain) transformed into an idea of creating short songs of a similar kind. This evolved throughout the continent into the short but versed hymn that African Christians continued to call a *Pambio* or chorus and the practice of singing refrains from hymns was abandoned.

Three phases have been identified in the evolution of the *Pambio* in Africa. To illustrate these stages, we will use examples from East Africa. In the first phase, the renowned hymn in the Luganda language, *Tukutenderesa Yesu* ("Let us praise the Lord") is the first known *Pambio* in East Africa.[2] It emerged in Uganda at the birth of the East African Revival of 1933/34. Within a short time, it became the chief revival hymn as the revival spread quickly across East Africa – Rwanda, Uganda, Tanzania, Kenya. The second phase began with the advent of the mass rallies in Africa, the so-called "crusades," when T. L. Osborne (1923–2013) became the first American evangelist to hold such

---

1. Electronic keyboards, guitars and wind instruments are commonly used.

2. This *Pambio* remains popular in East Africa till today, especially among the current successors of the East African Revival Movement and in the general circles of East African Christianity.

a rally in Mombasa in 1957. From then on, similar rallies were frequently organized in Nairobi, Mombasa, Kisumu, Dar es Salaam and Kampala. The hymn refrains were easy for large crowds to memorize. The "crusade" idea caught local imagination and similar rallies soon sprung up in many urban centres of East Africa, while chorus singing was maintained and reinforced in these rallies.

The third phase came with the rise of neo-Pentecostalism in the 1970s.[3] The localization of "crusades" became the seedbed for the rise of neo-Pentecostalism in Africa. Consequently, the Africanization of the choruses gradually began to take a new shape. Choruses provided a platform for local expressions and contextualized biblical and theological thoughts. Thus, the rise of the *Pambio* genre contributed to the direct involvement of lay Christians in gospel inculturation and in the deepening of its meaning in the local context. By the 1980s, distinct African melodies with local texts in verse and chorus had emerged to replace the refrains of Western hymns. The new hymnic genre acquired the term *Pambio* in Kiswahili and "chorus" or "chorus hymn" in English. The new hymn featured in every region in vernacular languages and in Portuguese, French, and English.[4] The *Pambio* has since functioned as a heart song that expresses the deeper feelings and meets the spiritual needs of the Christian communities. It has also become the preferred medium of African gospel music making throughout the continent. Furthermore, it features very prominently in charismatic or neo-Pentecostal worship, while also being popular with the laity in mainline churches. As a contemporary genre, the *Pambio* of East Africa, the *ebibindwom*[5] of Ghana, and the *chorus* or *chorus hymn* are equivalent terms. They share several common characteristics: they are composed orally and spontaneously; their texture and form are in African folksong style; they are almost invariably performed with some form of body movement; and they emanate chiefly from the growing Christian communities.

---

3. Brian Siegel, "Neo-Pentecostalism in Black Africa" (Anthropology Presentation, Southeastern Commission for the Study of Religion Anthropology Presentations, Greenville, SC, 17th March 2013, http://scholarexchange.furman.edu/ant-presentations/1).

4. Portuguese, French and English have now been acquired as African languages. They, however, differ with the other vernacular languages in that the latter are invariably tonal which influences the melodic contours and rhythmic patterns in ways that differ from the colonial languages that have now been appropriated as new African languages.

5. J. Kwabena Asamoah-Gyadu, ed., *Christianity, Mission and Ecumenism in Ghana* (Accra: Asempa Publishers, 2009), 9–36.

Distinguishing the *Pambio*

The character of the *Pambio* has been described above, but it is helpful to distinguish it further from other genres of African Christian songs, particularly the older hymn of the AICs[6] and the *kwaya* or *makwaya*[7] music that had developed earlier. This implies that, as the *Pambio* has recently emerged, it has continued developing side by side with these older genres and other newer categories of African sacred music. We will briefly review the two named genres to help inform our understanding of the distinct character of the *Pambio*.

On the one hand, the older folk hymn is the oldest indigenous African sacred song which emerged throughout Africa among the AICs right from their founding. The hymn of the AICs markedly distinguished these churches from missionary churches. Their folk hymn style is distinct from the *Pambio*; it more closely resembles the traditional folk song. It is highly rhythmic and helps to facilitate the often exuberant and enchanted worship of the African Independent churches. On the other hand, there is the *kwaya* song, a type of African church anthem. Originally influenced by the style of German and Anglo-American hymns, it developed in the nineteenth and twentieth-century mission schools and later became an anthem for church gatherings. *Kwaya* music evolved and adapted some Western concepts like voice parts[8] and harmony, but the harmony was conceived orally in an African polyphonic style. Characteristically, it is in a modern African melodic style[9] resembling the Western hymn. At the beginning, it was in linear form but it is now often structured in call-response form, African rhythm, and performance style. A *kwaya* song is invariably composed and arranged by ear and then taught by rote and has a wider melodic contour than the *Pambio*. It further differs from the *Pambio* by its more elaborate lyrics. It was sung mainly a capella but later evolved to include accompaniments of guitars, keyboards and African percussion instruments.

---

6. AICs stands for African Independent (sometimes "Instituted" or "Indigenous") Churches.

7. In East Africa, *kwaya* is a Kiswahili word for choir, hence *kwaya* music. This type of choral anthem is known as *makwaya* in South Africa – see Ruth M. Stone, ed., *Africa: The Garland Encyclopedia of World Music*, vol. 1 (New York: Garland Publishing, Inc., 1998), 763–65. See also Markus Detterbeck, *Makwaya: South African Choral Music: Song, Contest and the Formation of Identity* (Innsbruck, Austria: Helbling Publishing House, 2011).

8. SATB (Soprano, Alto, Tenor, Bass) and the various formations related to it, e.g. SA, SSA, TTBB, etc.

9. Most of the time it is in "call-response" form.

Pambio as a Folk Hymn

We have categorized the *Pambio* here as a folk hymn. Like the traditional folk song, it comes out of anonymous authorship within communities where it plays an immense role as a Christian hymn. The hymn is a corporate, performative, and communicative genre of contemporary Christianity and now permeates a wide range of spaces and contexts. Furthermore, it has an unrestrained role in folk theologizing as an expression of the embodied gospel. The texts of the *Pambio* often express the experiences of daily life and give commentary to moral issues in society in the light of the lay understanding of Christian teachings. Again, as a folk hymn grounded in the creative imagination of lay Christians, the *Pambio* also fosters the lifting up of the corporate voice of Christian communities through song and dance in organized church settings and secular, religious and quasi-religious gatherings. Thus, African Christians have innovated the form and character of its melody and rhythm to mirror the style of an African folksong. It has particularly demonstrated flexibility to function in Christian and secular contexts and now plays a vital role, both central and peripheral, in Christian worship.

The *Pambio* features at the centre of neo-Pentecostal worship but peripherally in most mainline churches. However, it has become an essential song in the secular activities of Christian communities. The folk hymn has permeated African societies in such a way that Christians and non-Christians employ it in their informal, secular, and religious settings. In the latter case, the *Pambio* is patently missional due to its inherent power to permeate many contexts with or without liturgical instrumentality. Since this hymn inheres in the hearts and lives of Christians and non-Christians alike it has become an effective bridge in the inculturation of the gospel. In community life, the laity express and convey their theological notions through the *Pambio*. It is thus a vehicle of communicating the Christian faith in an African context, which demonstrates that Christianity is now rooted and embodied in the experiences of African communities.

There is, however, a general lack of recognition that the *Pambio* is a folk hymn. The clergy of mainline Protestant churches are increasingly open to allowing its use in the sanctuary. But they erroneously equate it with the classical hymn and then proceed to underrate it. Hence, it has not been well accommodated in the historic liturgies of mainline church worship. Consequently, its usage in that context is generally peripheral. A classical hymn is a distinctly different genre of song. It is an art song whose text and tune are composed by an expert theologian with poetic skills and a trained musician. In contrast, the *Pambio* is a hymn of the lay folk which embodies their faith and encounters with God within their cosmology. It should therefore be understood as the heart song of ordinary African Christians.

Claudio Steinert points out that the *Pambio* is a hymn of invaluable significance in African Christianity and criticizes those that despise or view it as a lesser, wild, or theologically juvenile hymn. Specifically, Steinert criticizes C. M. Johansson's view of this hymnic genre as undisciplined, spiritually immature, and inappropriate for worshipping.[10] Sadly, Johansson's view is echoed in the erroneous notions and attitudes among some mainline church clergy who do not understand the *Pambio*'s history and significance in the mission of the church. To appreciate its significance is to understand its origin, development, content, purpose, and socio-religious function in the public sphere. *Pambios* may be simple but not simplistic. They carry potent messages that furnish the believers with a spiritual foundation for life[11] in their individual and shared communal experiences. Christian folks in the communities produce *Pambios* for a variety of purposes. For instance, during corporate celebrations, such as commemorations, celebrations of success, events of adversity, mourning and funerals, political events, and so forth, *Pambios* help to foster common Christian values and community bonds so that interreligious encounters are not hindered by denominational/ecclesiastical barriers.

The Significance of the *Pambio* in Mission

In Africa today, the gospel is propagated by lay Christians in various ways, not least by the medium of the *Pambio*. During the missionary era, the gospel was shared orally among the people. It has been demonstrated that the local agency was responsible for the rapid expansion of African Christianity in the post-missionary era. As J. N. K. Mugambi notes,

> The work of preaching was carried out more by the local evangelists than by the missionaries themselves. The first groups of converts would be sent out to win more converts, and the process of conversion would continue spreading outwards from the mission station where the missionary would be based.[12]

---

10. Claudio Steinert, *Music in Mission: Mission through Music: A South African Case Study* (Pietermaritzburg, South Africa: Cluster Publications, 2007), 89. Steinert references C. M. Johansson, *Discipling Music Ministry – Twenty-first Century Directions* (Peabody: Hendrickson Publishers, 1992), 68–75.

11. Steinert, *Music in Mission*, 10.

12. J. K. N. Mugambi, *African Heritage and Contemporary Christianity* (Nairobi, Kenya: Longhorn Publishers [K] Ltd, 1998), 43.

Bengt Sundkler describes this phenomenon as the networking or ripple effect because "the message could spread as rings in the water"[13] as the received message was passed from individual-to-family-to-village and to the wider community through oral transmission, including hymn singing. Today, the *Pambio* has emerged as one of the key vehicles by which biblical and theological doctrines are diffused though these networks. It is also a tool for pedagogy, can function effectively in the liturgy, and has proved to be an effective medium of gospel inculturation.

In structure, melody, rhythm and performance, communities have modelled the *Pambio* on the traditional folk song while the gospel message it carries is nuanced in local linguistic forms interpreted via the African worldview. This is why it has also been adapted by the secular sectors of society. Music plays an indispensable role in all aspects of African life, including leisure and work, politics and socio-economic engagements, religious worship events and development activities, and in the people's moral and spiritual life.[14] In these events, the *Pambio* often features and enables lay people to express their biblical and theological thoughts and socio-religious norms while helping to inculcate these values among the young through hearing and performing. Steinert observes correctly that "Lively songs dwell in almost every corner of the building of African tradition!"[15] because "music constitutes the living nerve of the African life."[16] The *Pambio* in this context is listened to and/or performed at all times and in all places and situations.

Traditionally, African initiation rites, story-telling, economic activities, recreation, and other platforms provide endless opportunities for the instruction of the young via song. Thus, the youth are educated through songs and dances on family life, customs and practices as well as on obligations and responsibilities in the community where they grow up.[17] The *Pambio* is the contemporary means of educating the youth on Christian values by imparting to them the basic biblical and theological knowledge necessary for their faith formation. As a new genre of hymnody, the *Pambio* has missiological

---

13. Bengt Sundkler and Christopher Steed, *A History of the Church in Africa* (Cambridge: CUP, 2000), 89.

14. Celestine C. Mbaegbu, "The Effective Power of Music in Africa," *Open Journal of Philosophy* 5 (2015): 176–83, doi: 10.4236/ojpp.2015.53021.

15. Claudio Steinert, *Music in Mission*, 1.

16. Claudio Steinert, *Music in Mission*, 2.

17. Fred Warren and Lee Warren, *The Music of Africa: An Introduction* (Englewood Cliffs: Prentice-Hall, 1970), 6. See also Francis Bebey, *African Music: A People's Art* (New York: Lawrence Hill, 1975), 6.

implications which undergird its inherent value for basic theological pedagogy among the learning community. In addition, in the church's missional outreach to foster spiritual growth in the people's hearts and minds, the *Pambio* creates the appropriate environment. This enables a sacred encounter with "the living Savior alone who speaks to them through rhythm and rhyme."[18]

The pulse of the *Pambio*, therefore, is experienced in the whole fabric of contemporary African life. Furthermore, it is immensely useful for adaption into the church's hymn repertoire and for the chant of mainline church liturgies. Its current influences include appropriations by musicians for contemporary African gospel music, in global circles as material for choral arrangements,[19] and as a new repertoire to be found in contemporary global hymnaries. Furthermore, it is diffused worldwide via African immigrant churches in the Diaspora for which it is the core worship hymn.

The Significance of the *Pambio* in African Gospel Music

In recent years, the *Pambio* hymn has popularly become a basis for creating contemporary African gospel music. Many choirs and Christian "pop" musicians all over Africa use it to create an African genre of gospel music, much of which is used in charismatic church worship. Choirs adapt a *Pambio* melody and its text as a kind of *cantus firmus*[20] to build music around it. The music is arranged and rendered in *kwaya* style while its lyrics and melody are elaborated by improvisations of the solo singer in a way that is much more complex than its original form. The choir, however, renders its response in a choral *ostinato*[21] as the response to the solo's call – often an extended countermelody improvised by the solo singer accompanied by instrumentation.[22] All these forces act in concert to create vibrant music in ways that have profound spiritual effect on the individual and the worshipping assembly. Unlike mainline churches that

---

18. Steinert, *Music in Mission*, 2.

19. Hal H. Hopson (arr.), *He is Mine* (Ni Wangu): *A Swahili Song From Kenya* (Carol Stream: Hope Publishing House, 1999). Hal H. Hopson arranged the Kenyan *Pambio* into a choral setting for American and, indeed, global choirs.

20. This term refers to a melody used as the basis for a polyphonic composition. In this essay, I use it to refer to a *Pambio* melody that the soloist elaborates, modifies and embellishes while the choir usually sings a fixed response in *ostinato* or repeated fashion.

21. *Ostinato* is an Italian term used in music to refer to a short melodic phrase repeated throughout a composition. In this essay, the term is used to denote the constantly repeated choral response in voice parts (harmonies) against which extended improvisations are made by the solo singer.

22. Accompaniments usually comprise electronic guitars, keyboards and percussion.

treat it as a song of the periphery, neo-Pentecostal churches have brought the *Pambio* into the center of their liturgy, and the gospel music this hymn engenders has become quite attractive, especially among the youth. The *Pambio* often features at the "praise and worship" segment of worship – both as a congregational hymn and as a theme song of the gospel choir.

The *Pambio* as a Song of "Centre" and "Periphery"

In most mainline churches, worship is organized through the unfolding of the historic Western liturgical rite. Vital resources are brought into coordinated action in the worship space. The worship rite and its spatial location is what is meant here by "centre." When the liturgical ceremony is administered rigidly to control what is or is not allowable in the space, the singing of denominational Western hymns takes centre stage. This hinders the role the *Pambio* has at the core of that liturgical rite. Consequently, the ad hoc use of the *Pambio* to merely fill unforeseen gaps during worship makes it a peripheral hymn. However, when the *Pambio* gets integrated into the liturgy, it takes a central role as in the case of neo-Pentecostal church worship. In that case, this hymn offers an invaluable platform for the community's voice and spirit which is experienced in the corporate responses of praise, prayer, reflection, adoration, and thanksgiving.

We already argued that lay Christians have fuelled the evolution and development of the *Pambio*. In the community, they control the events that employ the *Pambio* as the context requires. In this setting, the roles of the laity and the clergy are reversed, for, the laity lead the singing of the *Pambio* in call-response and express their biblical and theological notions without restraint, while the clergy join in the response. In this way the latter affirm the proclamation rendered via the *Pambio*, even if the message may be theologically flawed.

Beyond Community and Church: *Pambio* in the Secular Sociopolitical Domain

There has been an increased appropriation of the *Pambio* for secular events. In contrast, the classical hymn is seldom used in these events partly due to its Western linear character and partly because it does not generate the heart rhythm of the people. The *Pambio* is short, rhythmic, memorizable and improvisable in its cyclical form. This folk hymn is in the rhythm and style of the people, and it invites them to participate in a familiar sense. It is often used in a secular context without altering its Christian content. However, it is sometimes modified to transmit intended political propaganda.

Some examples from Kenya can help to illustrate the latter observation. In the run-up to the 2002 General Elections, the opposition party appropriated a famous *Pambio* for its campaigns by modifying the Christian lyrics in the Kiswahili language to communicate the party's message. The text, *Yote yawezekana kwa imani* ("Everything is possible by faith"), was revised into *Yote yawezekana bila Moi* ("Everything is possible without Moi"). Since then, this *Pambio* became unpopular in religious settings. Previously, the incumbent president had been treated to a banquet of secular songs in *Pambio* form which showered praises on him at every turn. *Tawala Kenya, tawala, Rais Moi tawala Kenya, tawala* ("Rule Kenya, rule, President Moi rule Kenya, rule") was one of the political songs that featured frequently in his rallies during his dictatorial reign.[23]

In another example, a Kenyan Muslim woman from the coast region won a national parliamentary seat in 2017. She then led her Christian and Muslim supporters to sing in "call-response" the well-known *Pambio, Amenitendea, amenitendea, Immanueli amenitendea* ("He has done it for me, Emmanuel has done it for me"). They sang back the response with great enthusiasm. The Muslim MP understood the Christian meaning of the text and seemed to suggest that her victory was due to the power of Emmanuel, the Christ. This demonstrates the wide appeal of the *Pambio* and its influence beyond Christian circles. The excuse to celebrate the election result became an opportunity for the Muslims spontaneously to sing a Christian song. Unfortunately, her further appropriations of *Pambios* laced with potent political messages at subsequent public rallies[24] has betrayed a lack of respect for its Christian religious status and exposes the extent to which *Pambios* can be misused outside Christian circles.

In the final example, I was invited in 2015 to hear a motivational speaker at a secular meeting in Nairobi. One of the organizers, a Muslim woman, gave the opening remarks but requested to begin with a *Pambio*. She led the gathering in "call-response" to sing the popular Kenyan *Pambio, Hakuna Mungu kama wewe, ewe Mungu wangu* ("There is no other God like you, O Lord my God"). To everyone's surprise, she faultlessly led the hymn as everyone responded

---

23. Daniel Arap Moi ruled from 1978 to 2002.

24. See "Aisha Jumwa sings to praise Deputy President William Ruto, '*Hakuna wa kufanana na Ruto*,'" Standard Digital Videos, 20th May 2019, https://www.youtube.com/watch?v=JTNfyBIciPw.

warmly. These instances illustrate the *Pambio*'s universal appeal and its inherent power to break beyond sacred into secular spaces.

The Diffusion of the *Pambio* in Africa

Pambios have been diffused widely by oral transmission from one country to another across the continent. Whenever it spreads, its text may be received and sung in the original language or translated with new additional verses or substituted with new lyrics. In this way, *Pambios* are routinely contextualized in the new environment.

From the early to mid-1970s, Ghana's *Pambio O Nyame Womo* ("With God being present") was already being sung in that country. As a foreign student there during the late 1970s and early 1980s, I encountered it at campus crusades and Christian Unions. It was just one among other similar songs. In the late 1980s, its melody reached Kenya without the Ghanaian lyrics. New lyrics in Kiswahili were therefore adapted to it: *Yesu ni mwema, mwema, anipenda*. This text was also sung in English, "The Lord is good, good, and he loves me" and in vernacular languages. The appealing melody and rhythm were sung accurately, but any rhythmic variations were the result of aligning the new text to it. Interestingly, many Kenyans I have interviewed believe that it is an original Kenyan *Pambio*. Similarly, the Setwana *Pambio*, *Ga go na yo'tshwanang le Jesu* ("There is nobody who is like Jesus")[25] has been popular in Kenya since the 1990s. It is normally sung in Kiswahili to an exact translation of the original Setswana lyrics. However, again, it is normally thought to originate in Kenya. I have found that this phenomenon is common also in other African countries owing to the oral way it is transmitted across the borders.

In the DRC, many known Kenyan and Tanzanian *Pambios* are popularly sung in the original Kiswahili language. They are also translated into local languages and the Congolese people routinely assume them to be local in origin. This reveals how *Pambios*, usually transmitted orally, diffuse throughout the continent and then get contextualized. Among the widely known *Pambios* in the continent include Nigeria's "Winner eh, eh, eh, winner," South Africa's *Thuma mina* ("Send me Lord") and *Siya hamba ekukanyen kwenkos* ("We are marching in the light of God") East Africa's *Mambo sawasawa* ("All is well") and *Nimemwona Bwana* ("I have seen the Lord"), Mozambique's *Obrigado shikwembu sha matimba* ("Thank you Almighty God") and Congo's *Yo Nzambe na nguya* ("You are the Almighty God").

---

25. Steinert, *Music in Mission*, 9.

The *Pambio* provides a platform for lay creativity, invitation and participation in gospel inculturation. These local expressions have helped to anchor the Christian faith in the communal lifeworld. The depth of the *Pambio*'s short text and melody can be unpacked by understanding how metaphor, imagery, aphorisms, mnemonics and other linguistic forms of speech are employed to package the gospel message sung and interpreted through music, gestures and movement. The short texts often appear simple and straightforward, "but they carry [deep] layers of meaning and significance"[26] of an embodied gospel in the life of the singing community.

Pambio as a Global and Ecumenical Hymn

In its global diffusion, the *Pambio* can be located in two spatial contexts: namely, as the core hymn of African immigrant churches in the Diaspora and as a hymn of global worship in the ecumenical movement. Firstly, many charismatic African churches are now established in the West and in Asia. They have exported the *Pambio* to aid their vibrant worship style and to enable Africans in the Diaspora to feel at home.

Secondly, the *Pambio* has been globalized through the ecumenical movement since the early1990s.[27] Numerous *Pambios* from sub-Saharan Africa have since appeared in hymnbooks worldwide.[28] *Pambios* and classical African hymns began appearing in Western hymnals since the 1990s[29] but the *Pambios* are more accessible in the West where they are now employed in liturgical worship. Also, Western composers have used them to create choral arrangements and instrumental works. Such *Pambios* as Kenya's *Ni Wangu*

---

26. Michael C. Hawn, *Gather into One: Praying and Singing Globally* (Grand Rapids: Eerdmans, 2003), 162.

27. Lutheran World Federation, *Supplement to Laudamus: Hymnal for the Lutheran World Federation* (Geneva, Switzerland: Lutheran World Federation, 1989). This edition was used at 8th Assembly of the Lutheran World Federation (LWF) in Curitiba in 1990. In the previous LWF assemblies the hymnbook *Laudamus* – of which this was the *Supplement* – contained mainly Western hymns. For the first time, this supplement incorporated many African hymns of the *Pambio* type, as well as hymns from other non-Western regions of the globe. This was one of the earliest indications of the affirmation of non-Western hymns within the ecumenical movement. In this *Supplement* booklet are many *Pambios* from various African countries. Many of them later found their way into non-African hymnbooks around the world.

28. Dieter Trautwein, *Thuma Mina: Singing with Our Partner Churches: International Ecumenical Hymnbook* (Basel/Hamburg: Basler Mission/Evang. Missionswerk in Deutschland, 1995).

29. Evangelical Lutheran Church in America, *Evangelical Lutheran Worship* (Minneapolis: Augsburg Fortress, 2006).

("He is Mine")[30] and *Tunaomba Mungu Atawale* ("We pray that God reigns")[31] come to mind.

Conclusion

The evolution of the *Pambio* in African community settings, its significance in mission and gospel inculturation, its emergence as the primary hymn of charismatic churches, its global appeal and spread through the ecumenical movement, and its diffusion through African immigrant churches of the Diaspora draws our attention to this folk hymn as an important area of missional inquiry and of theological, ethnomusicological, and intercultural reflection. The *Pambio* is thus an invaluable medium of gospel inculturation and an essential instrument in pedagogy, communication, and the diffusion of the gospel.

Furthermore, the *Pambio* remains an effective instrument for liturgical worship and a vital vehicle for education, mission, theology, inculturation and the embodied gospel. These realities should compel African scholars and mainline churches to pay serious attention to this hymnic genre's multiple significances. The African academy too needs to include the *Pambio* in its theological inquiries and discourses for the posterity of African Christianity.

---

30. Hopson, *He Is Mine*.

31. John R. Paradowski, "Tunaomba Mungu Atawale *(We Pray God to Reign)*" (Dallas: Choristers Guild, 2009). It is noted on the score that the origin of this song is unknown. But I can confirm here that it is a well-known Kenyan *Pambio*.

12

Missiology for a Youthful Continent

Joseph Ola

In this chapter, I argue that there is a disparity between the youthfulness of African Christianity (judging by its age distribution) and its leadership – a disparity which, if left unchecked, has potential to undo the growth of African Christianity. This disparity therefore calls for a missiology that will further enable the missionary potential of African Christianity and foster the realization of its promising future. This extraordinary growth of African Christianity in the twentieth century is due to several factors. First, there have been a huge number of *conversions* from African traditional religions and Islam to Christianity, especially in the second half of the past century. Second, the *Africanization* of the Christian faith, especially, as Sanneh insightfully argues, through the translation of the Bible into vernacular African languages, has made it more accessible to the Africans south of the Sahara.[1] Consequently, this qualitative and quantitative growth of Christianity in Africa is now being perpetuated in the twenty-first century by Africa's demographic youthfulness and biological reproduction. Compared to Christianity in other regions across the globe, African Christianity has the youngest median age (19.5)[2] – younger than the median age for both global Christianity and world population (30).[3]

---

1. Lamin Sanneh, *Translating the Message: The Missionary Impact on Culture* (Maryknoll: Orbis Books, 1989).

2. David E. Kiwuwa, "Africa is young. Why are its leaders so old?," CNN, 29 October 2015, https://edition.cnn.com/2015/10/15/africa/africas-old-mens-club-op-ed-david-e-kiwuwa/index.html.

3. Pew Research Center, *The Changing Global Religious Landscape* (2017), 14, https://www.researchgate.net/publication/316861337_The_Changing_Global_Religious_Landscape.

Besides, while the fertility rate of global Christians is 2.6 children per woman, it is 4.2 children per woman amongst Christians in Sub-Saharan Africa.[4]

In a sense, it can also be argued that young people led African Christianity into its growth in the twentieth century. Using Nigeria as a case study,[5] the key figures of the *Aladura* movement that evolved into Nigeria's classical Pentecostalism were markedly young men and women. Garrick Braide started his journey into notorious leadership in indigenous Christianity in the 1890s while he was still a teenager.[6] Samuel Adegboyega, who is reputed to be one of the founding fathers of Pentecostalism in Africa, was first ordained as a pastor at the age of twenty-eight.[7] Joseph Ayo Babalola, a key figure in the *Aladura* movement received his call into ministry at the age of twenty-four and led the great revival of 1930 in south-western Nigeria when he was just twenty-six.[8] Sophia Odunlami was a founding member of the *Aladura* prayer group that was later called "Precious Stone Society" – she was just nineteen at the time.[9] Her contemporary, Christiana Abiodun Akinsowon, became a co-founder of the Cherubim and Seraphim Society at seventeen.[10] The explosion of neo-Pentecostal churches in the 1970s and 1980s have been attributed largely to revivals among the youth in universities and secondary schools.[11] Benson

---

4. Pew Research Center, *The Changing Global Religious Landscape*, 15.

5. It is noteworthy that Nigeria is one of Jenkins' favourites as to where the largest Christian populations will be by 2050. Other countries in his proposition include Brazil, Mexico, the Congo, Ethiopia, the Philippines, and China. Jenkins, *The Next Christendom*, 114.

6. Nimi Wariboko, *Nigerian Pentecostalism* (Rochester, New York: University of Rochester Press, 2014), 19.

7. Samson Adetunji Fatokun et al., *A Pentecost from Africa to Europe, from Europe to Africa: History and Distinctiveness of The Apostolic Church Nigeria, 1918–2017 (First Classical Pentecostal Denomination and Mother of Apostolic Churches in Nigeria)* (Ibadan, Nigeria: Global Estida Publishers, 2017), 526.

8. David O. Olayiwola, "Babalola, Joseph Ayodele," in *Dictionary of African Christian Biography*, https://dacb.org/stories/nigeria/babalola2-joseph/.

9. Fatokun et al., *A Pentecost from Africa to Europe, from Europe to Africa*, 14–15.

10. Israel O. Olofinjana, *20 Pentecostal Pioneers in Nigeria: Their Lives, Their Legacies* (Bloomington: Xlibris, 2011), 43–47.

11. Wariboko, *Nigerian Pentecostalism*, 26.

Idahosa,[12] Enoch Adeboye,[13] William Kumuyi,[14] and David Oyedepo[15] – to mention but a few – while they were between the ages of twenty-seven and thirty-two pioneered churches that have played a significant role in Nigerian Pentecostalism with the exception of Adeboye who, as opposed to pioneering, took over the leadership of RCCG at the age of thirty-nine.[16] The same trend of God calling and using young people tremendously in God's mission in the world is visible in the wider global church history. Jesus' twelve disciples,[17] Origen,[18] Martin Luther,[19] John Calvin,[20] John Paul II[21] and Billy Graham[22] among many others were all in their youth when God began to use them. The mission of God has always been championed by young people.

---

12. Benson Idahosa left Assemblies of God church to plant his own church – which became instrumental to nurturing many other neo-Pentecostal preachers in the continent – at the age of thirty. See Wariboko, *Nigerian Pentecostalism*, 20.

13. He is the General Overseer of RCCG. He gave his life to Christ at the age of thirty-one, was ordained as a pastor at the age of thirty-five. See Adedamola Osinulu, "A Transnational History of Pentecostalism in West Africa," *History Compass* 15.6 (2017): 7.

14. He founded Deeper Life Bible Church (with the headquarters reputed to be the largest church congregation in Africa) at 32. See Wariboko, *Nigerian Pentecostalism*, 20–21.

15. He founded the Living Faith Ministries (also known as Winners' Chapel) at 27. His church once had the world's largest church auditorium. See "About Us – Winners Chapel International, Dartford," accessed 09 July 2020, https://winners-chapel.org.uk/about-us/.

16. It should be emphasized, however, that this was eight years after he became a Christian.

17. It has been argued to a reasonable extent that the majority of Jesus' twelve disciples were teenagers and young adults. See Otis Cary and Frank Cary, "How Old Were Christ's Disciples?," *The Biblical World* 50.1 (1917): 3–12, https://www.jstor.org/stable/pdf/3136128.pdf.

18. Origen was eighteen years old when he was called by Bishop Demetrius to direct the catechetical school of Alexandria. See Thomas C. Oden, *How Africa Shaped the Christian Mind: Rediscovering the African Seedbed of Western Christianity* (Downers Grove: InterVarsity Press, 2007), 164.

19. Martin Luther was ordained as a priest at the age of twenty-four and was thirty-four when he nailed his ninety-five theses to the door of the Wittenberg Castle. See Scott H. Hendrix, *Martin Luther: Visionary Reformer* (New Haven: Yale University Press, 2015), 38 and 61.

20. Philip Melanchthon, John Calvin, John Wesley and Jonathan Edwards have been described as "eligious geniuses . . . who as children were precocious and early manifested a special interest in religion." See Cary and Cary, "How Old Were Christ's Disciples?," 8.

21. John Paul II was ordained as a priest at twenty-six. See "Karol Wojtyla (Pope John Paul II) Timeline," The Christian Broadcasting Network, accessed 09 July 2020, https://www1.cbn.com/churchandministry/karol-wojtyla-%28pope-john-paul-ii%29-timeline.

22. Billy Graham was sixteen when he became a Christian, twenty-six when he hosted his first radio show and thirty-one when he ran the Greater Los Angeles revival which lasted for eight weeks. See David Aikman, *Billy Graham: His Life and Influence* (Nashville: Thomas Nelson, 2010), 55, 48 and 65.

Background Research and Findings

In a background research for this chapter,[23] I asked one hundred young African Christians from different church traditions between eighteen and twenty-five years old questions to discover how they sustain their faith, their perceptions about the youth-consciousness of their churches, their imagination of what kind of church is youth-friendly and what kind of changes they would like to see in their respective churches. A questionnaire was administered via Google Forms to respondents who are all members of an online Christian mentoring platform for young adults. Ninety of them responded – all Africans. Sixty-one percent of the respondents admitted that young people are leaving their churches. They corroborated their response by highlighting some factors that are *absent* or *present* in their respective churches – factors that point to the disconnect between their generation and the older generation. What follows are some recurrent themes in their responses.

A Generation Crying for Acceptance

Some of the respondents who had left a church for another or admitted to an exodus of their peers from their churches, pointed to a feeling of being rejected as the motivation for the move. Some of them described this as inability to genuinely *feel like* a member of the church, as their opinions did not matter. Some pointed to a lack of confidence being placed in them. Some others pointed to outright condemnation received from the older ones. One respondent remarked,

> In my church, we (youths) are not being allowed to display our youthfulness in terms of dressing and musical preference . . . They (the older ones) just keep dulling our vibes.

Another respondent observed:

> We are not being involved in the dealings of the church and our opinions are not reckoned with; it is very obvious that so much preference is given to older people.

One young woman lamented, "in my church, ladies are not allowed to showcase their talents . . . and this fire in us is dying out. (Such gender marginalization is

---

23. While this chapter addresses the subject of youth and African Christianity, my experience of African Christianity has largely been in Nigeria. In addition, my observations are primarily limited to the Protestant churches – especially the Pentecostal and charismatic expressions.

still characteristic of some classical Pentecostal denominations.)[24] And another remarked:

> I left my parents' church because of too much criticism and condemnation which often come from the adults who wanted to remove the speck in my eyes, not minding the log in theirs.

Yet another respondent added:

> There are not enough activities for us to engage in. It's as though the pastorate can't trust us with any meaningful responsibility that will make us feel like an important part of the service. All they want us to do is sing, and when we do, they often complain we are being worldly. Many of us only keep coming because our parents insist.

In a similar response, another respondent wrote, "they (the older church members) don't really believe in us; they see us as the black sheep amongst the congregation."

These responses resonate with one of the key findings of Barna's 2019 global research on millennials (18–35),[25] namely: only one in three millennials feel that someone believes in them and the remaining two thirds desperately crave to be believed in, too.[26] The implication is clear – to secure the future involves believing in the younger generation. As they search for identity and trade their childhood dependence for adult autonomy, the church should position itself to influence that development by giving them a genuine sense of belonging. When they feel accepted, encouraged and motivated, they will thrive; but this will not happen until the young people in our churches can genuinely feel accepted and not condemned. The genuineness is as important as the acceptance; discerning genuineness from falsehood is one of the generational gifts common to most millennials. It is one thing, for instance, to give youths a sense of belonging when they are physically present in the church; it is another

---

24. For example, not until 2019 were women (young or old) allowed to attend prayer vigils in The Apostolic Church, Nigeria despite being arguably the first classical Pentecostal denomination in Nigeria. See "Women Now Free To Join Night Vigil," *The Apostolic Church Nigeria LAWNA News* (Lagos, Nigeria), May 2019, 1–2.

25. The research employed the use of interviews with more than 15,000 adults ages eighteen to thirty-five in twenty-five countries (including 750 South Africans, 512 Nigerians, 300 Kenyans, and 462 Ghanaians) asking them about their goals, fears, relationships, routines and beliefs, and thereby uncovering a number of key trends.

26. "Key Findings," Barna Group, 2019, accessed 09 July 2020, https://theconnectedgeneration.com/key-findings/.

to keep in touch with them while many of them travel far from home to study in tertiary institutions within their country or abroad. As such, one of the respondents lamented the "lack of communication between the church and the youths in colleges and tertiary institutions" as the reason why many of her colleagues were leaving the church. Young people seek acceptance and will settle where they find it – the biggest expression of which is to show a genuine interest in the things that interest them.

In Search of Spiritual Nourishment and Freedom

Many respondents pointed out their pastor's preaching as a major reason why the youths are leaving their churches. One respondent commented, "The sermons preached on Sundays don't relate with us as youths and our daily struggles." In a more elaborate response, another respondent shared:

> I have spoken with few of the youths of my current local church and I find that most of them are leaving, have left or are planning to leave because they've enjoyed being under the tutelage of other ministers of God who carefully teach the word of God ... they believe their faiths will grow and be built up under such environments unlike here where no one enjoys coming to church on Sundays or during the week.

This corroborates yet another respondent's submission that "some youths feel they need more of God than their church can offer at the moment." A young man added:

> Only few of the pastors under the body of my church as a whole are quality preachers of the Word. So, when we go out and listen to the quality of message been dished out by other pastors, we tend to be drawn away naturally. Most of the preachers restrict themselves to the knowledge base of the General Overseer. It's a shame.

As physical nourishment is significant to the health and wellness of children as they grow, the same significance applies to spiritual nourishment with respect to spiritual growth. One of the fascinating findings of this research is that many more youths claimed to get their spiritual nourishment from engaging with books or other resources from "White foreigners" (70.5%) and from online podcasts or videos (61.4%) than from other African ministers (36.4%) or from their pastor's sermons or books (60.2%, see Figure 1).

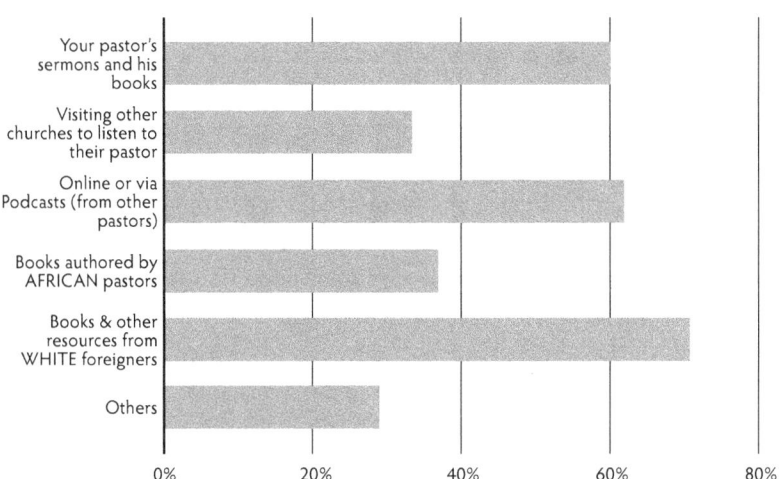

Figure 1: Sources of respondents' spiritual nourishment

If Western theological thought is shaping the spiritual worldview of these African youths, it makes one wonder what the future of African Christianity would look like. This is a painful reminder that African Christianity is yet to rid itself of Western theological dominance and framework. The demographic shift in the heartlands of Christianity, as Andrew Walls laments, is yet to match the thinking and praxis of the African church.[27] Yet there is no African Christianity without African theology. As Asante argues, African modes of conceptualization must be the crux of any analysis that involves African culture and behaviour so that Africans will never need to divorce their African culture in order to become Christian.[28] However, the forces of postmodernism and globalization – both of which millennials find alluring – are taking their toll on the younger generation. In many urban cities across Africa, it is increasingly becoming fashionable to raise *modern* children – children who grow up in homes where English language is the default language and where parents are liberal with the responsibility of handing down the cultural heritage they were raised with. To what extent this inter-generational shift in cultural emphasis is influencing the religious imagination of African youths is yet to be fully explored but

---

27. Andrew F. Walls, "Christian scholarship in Africa in the twenty-first century," *Transformation* 19.4 (2002): 220.
28. Molefi Kete Asante, *The Afrocentric Idea* (Philadelphia: Temple University Press, 1998), 2.

the inclination of respondents towards exotic spiritual nourishment spewing forth theology brewed in *un-African* pots is quite instructive: there is a need for effective communication of theological truths in African thought[29] and an intentional tradition of passing this on to the next generation. Upon these shall the future of African Christianity heavily depend. To this end, African preachers will need to learn to theologize in a way that still falls within the boundaries of African theology and stays relevant to the coming generation. Likewise, African scholars will need to start conceptualizing African cultural heritage in a manner that is consistent with what young people have come to know and affirm in their lives and substantiated by their contemporary experiences. All these recommendations need to be included in relevant and sound theological education for pastors and preachers in Africa such as is still missing largely on the continent.

Germane to the young people's attraction to books and spiritual resources by "White foreigners," as indicated in the research findings, is the recurrent issue of restrictive doctrines. One respondent submitted:

> Yes, I am young, but I am beginning to discover the liberating truth concerning the grace of God day by day, and the exact opposite of this is being taught in my church.

Another respondent agreed:

> Some of the doctrines emphasised in my church as rules of conduct come across as too stiff and too rigid for a typical "modern" youth. Why will you tell me that I am going to end in hell for wearing trousers as a lady? Is that in the Bible? That is why so many of us are leaving in a bid to find somewhere more suitable for us.

The issue of restrictions on female dressing and appearance is not an unpopular one in many Nigerian churches. The General Overseer of one of Nigeria's largest neo-Pentecostal denominations emphasized in an audio clip excerpt, that went viral on social media, the stance of his church against women wearing trousers or using any jewellery or make-up of any kind. In his words:

> According to our doctrine, certain things will no longer be permitted at our meetings . . . We are God-friendly, not people-friendly. Beginning from next Sunday, any woman who comes here wearing trousers will be stopped at the gates . . . Uncovered

---

29. Bénézet Bujo, *African Theology in its Social Context* (Maryknoll, New York: Orbis Books, 1992), 11.

hair for women is no longer allowed . . . We will not admit you into deliverance with jewelleries, with make-up, with all those things anymore . . . Dresses and skirts that are above the knees will no longer be allowed here.[30]

Today's youth culture, having been shaped by the forces of globalization and the media, has little tolerance for such restrictions.

Dynamic Leadership, Not Traditionalism

Some respondents flagged bad leadership as part of the reason youths are leaving the church – a finding which the Barna research on millennials emphatically corroborates.[31] The youth stage of life is a season of relationships and activities.[32] One of the significant relationships that youths are looking for is leadership. Good leadership is attractive to young people because it models for them a desirable picture of who they can be. One of the respondents posited that a major reason for the exodus of youths from her local assembly is "bad leadership from current youth leaders." Another respondent added:

> As youths, we are looking for a place where plans are acted upon and not just deliberated upon in various meetings. We love to be under result-oriented leadership.

This kind of leadership will look like *mentorship* and *reverse mentorship*. Gone are the days when discipleship was all about following a few lessons from a syllabus designed according to some systematic theology. Young people want Christian models and mentors – people who can relate with their fast-changing world and model for them how to live out their faith in that context of dynamic change. However, they also want leaders who are willing to learn from their youthful perspectives to life and religion too (reverse mentorship). They do not want a leader that has an answer for every question – Google does that for them – rather they will thrive in relating with a Christian leader

---

30. "Dr. D. K. Olukoya Bans Trousers, Earrings and Open Hair in Church" (YouTube, 07 December 2018). https://www.youtube.com/watch?v=po5Q1BP_Lys; Sam Eyoboka and Olayinka Latona, "MFM Bans Females from Wearing Trousers, Catholic Church Outlaws Headgears," *Vanguard News Nigeria* 01 September 2012, https://www.vanguardngr.com/2012/09/mfm-bans-females-from-wearing-trousers-catholic-church-outlaws-headgears/.

31. One of the most widely endorsed ideas in the research is that "there are not enough good leaders right now." Barna Group, "Key Findings."

32. Susan Shepler, "The Social and Cultural Context of Child Soldiering in Sierra Leone" (Paper, Workshop on Techniques of Violence in Civil War, International Peace Research Institute, Oslo, 20–21August, 2004).

whose job isn't to have all the definitive answers but to help create a hunger in them to chase their questions into the arms of Christ. It could be the reason many Christian parents struggle with raising their young children is that the youngsters are yet to see a harmony in the values their parents are preaching and the actual lifestyle of the same parents.

Besides good leadership, one of the most fascinating attractions for youths is dynamism. They want to stay trendy and associate with trends. Unfortunately, many African churches are still living in the days of their founders. As such, a respondent laments:

> My church is a church for old people as this can be seen in the old songs they sing, the language the services are conducted in (Yoruba), the Old Testament doctrines they practice and their silence on the gifts of the Holy Spirit.

Similarly, while one respondent inveighs his church's unwillingness to "accept the changes that comes with modern technological advancements," another is lamenting that her "church is not evolving." How then do we equip these younger generation to take African Christianity to another level?

The Young and The Old: A Missiology for a Youthful Christianity

> In the last days it will be, God declares, that I will pour out my Spirit upon all flesh, and your sons and your daughters shall prophesy, and your young men shall see visions, and your old men shall dream dreams. (Acts 2:17 NRSV)

"In the last days..."

We have established that African Christianity is a youthful Christianity. If the potentials locked up in this youthfulness is fully released, our world will not be the same in a few years. No doubt, the future of African Christianity is pregnant, but what manner of offspring(s) it shall produce is a function of how well the *young* and the *old* will come side-by-side in the mission of God. The Scripture above readily comes to mind when thinking of African Christianity. This prophecy by Joel found its first-referenced fulfilment on the day when the church was born, and it signalled the beginning of the end – and the beginning of the best. And this era in which we live is perhaps the beginning of the beginning of the very best. Andrew Walls rightly described the current reality of Christian history as "very exciting" in that "we have every justification to hope for greater things in the time to come."[33] This is the time, more than ever, when we can look forward to "something better" which God has provided, according to the writer of the epistle to the Hebrews.[34]

"... I will pour out my Spirit upon all flesh..."

Here is the crux of Joel's prophecy and therein is the missiological key for ministry to all ages. Between Edinburgh 1910 and Edinburgh 2010 global mission conferences, as Kirsteen Kim rightly observes, there has been a shift of missiological emphasis from "Kingdom" to "Spirit,"[35] as mission theology has evolved towards a pneumatological perspective.[36] Today, mission looks more like "finding out where the Holy Spirit is at work and joining in."[37] But even more exciting to me is the fact that this Spirit is available to *all flesh* – young and old, male and female alike. This prophetic message is highly instructive for African Christianity – and, indeed, world Christianity. We tend to forget that the gifts of the Holy Spirit are distributed equally and widely in the church. The Holy Spirit is not the exclusive preserve of a certain age group. Both sons and daughters, in the day of the Spirit, shall prophesy. As young men are seeing visions, old men are dreaming dreams – dreams and visions of the spread of God's kingdom till *all flesh* is reached.[38] The gifts and expressions of the Spirit is latent in every member of the body of Christ. Only when the Spirit is allowed to work through the entire community of God's people, from the oldest to the youngest, can the spirit of God prevail. When Moses was informed that Eldad and Medad are prophesying in the camp – an act that seems to usurp

---

33. Interview with Andrew Walls, "An Exciting Period in Christian History," *Faith and Leadership*, 5 June, 2011, accessed 09 July 2020, https://www.faithandleadership.com/andrew-walls-exciting-period-christian-history.

34. Hebrews 11:40 NRSV.

35. Edinburgh 1910 conference was tagged "Advancing the Kingdom of Christ" while Edinburgh 2010 conference was tagged "Joining in with the Spirit."

36. Kirsteen Kim, "Edinburgh 1910 to 2010: From Kingdom to Spirit," *Journal of the European Pentecostal Theological Association* 30.2 (2010).

37. Kim, "Edinburgh 1910 to 2010," 7.

38. It is interesting that in the rest of the book of Acts, references to dreams and visions are strategic missionary directives. Beginning with Ananias' vision directing him to go and commission Paul for his great missionary work (Acts 9); then Peter was instructed in a vision to take the gospel and the Spirit to the Gentiles – to those of Cornelius' household (Acts 10); Paul's journey into Europe was through a vision of a man saying, "Come over into Macedonia and help us" (Acts 16); and in Acts 18:9 and 26:19, Paul received divine encouragement for his missionary experience through visions.

Moses' authority – his response carries with it the spirit of Joel's prophecy. "Are you jealous for my sake? Would that all the Lord's people were prophets, and that the Lord would put his spirit on them!"[39] It is therefore essential, as Father Koshy notes, that "the spiritual experience and expertise of every member must be recognized and drawn into the common spirituality of the local congregations."[40] The youths need the wisdom and mentorship of the older generation as much as the older generation need the fresh expressions of the youths.

My Yoruba-speaking elders in Southwestern Nigeria have a knack for sharing their wisdom with us, the younger folks, through proverbs. Many times while growing up, I have heard my father say to me and my siblings, *Agba ki wa l'oja k'ori omo titun wo* which when translated, means "An elder cannot be in the market and a child's head will be allowed to drop." This is his way of letting us know that we can trust him and our mother to look out for us and cover our oversights and blind spots as we do life. However, occasionally, as we start to mature, my dad will present a family issue or a personal matter to my siblings and I, seeking our inputs as his children. At times like that, he says *Omode gbon, agba gbon l'afi da Ile-Ife* which when translated, means "The youths were wise, the elders were wise; on this basis was Ile-Ife founded."[41] Or he says *Owo omode ko to pepe; t'agbalagba ko wo akeregbe* which when translated, means "The hand of a child cannot reach the ceiling; the hand of an adult cannot enter a gourd." Proverbs like these remind us as his children that we have also got something to offer and that wisdom is not exclusive to the older generations alone. It is such mutuality that we need in African Christianity. Such mutuality recognizes the relevance of both the young and the old and makes both of them feel welcome in a church.

What will this look like? For one, it will look like some of the remarks I gleaned from 38.6% of the participants of the background research – those who admitted that youths are not leaving their churches. One respondent recalled:

> There has been a time when youths were leaving my church all in the name of finding a place where they will be accepted and appreciated because most elderly members were too judgmental. Now, things have changed as our youths are being involved in

---

39. Numbers 11:29 NRSV.

40. Vineeth Koshy, *Youth Envisioning Ecumenical Mission: Shifting Ecumenical Mission Paradigms for Witnessing Christ Today* (Edinburgh, 2010), http://www.wcc2006.info/fileadmin/files/edinburgh2010/files/conference_docs/Parallel1_Koshy_youth.pdf.

41. Ile-Ife is the cradle of the Yorubas.

leadership positions – leading both youths and older people – and this has brought new life to the church.

Another respondent commends his church's dynamism, "I think young people are involved in my church because most of the things in church are done in the modern ways and not following the conventional ways of old." It is noteworthy that the *Aladura* movement of the early twentieth century originated in part as a quest for such expression of Christianity that is relevant to the current reality and religious consciousness of the local people – a Christianity that could satisfy both "the spiritual and emotional yearnings" of the adherents.[42] Consequently, we must creatively rethink the mission praxis of African churches in a manner that will satisfy both the spiritual and emotional yearnings of their youths. In doing this, Kwiyani made an apt proposition of five non-negotiable features of discipling African youths growing up in the Diaspora. These features, in my opinion, are equally relevant and applicable on the African continent. He writes,

> I suggest here five characteristics of youth ministry that will help disciple the second generation to take their faith forward and reach out to their cities: *historically aware, spiritually empowered, contextually relevant, missionally shaped* and *biblically and theologically informed*. These youths face different kinds of challenges; they ask different kinds of questions and have different kinds of needs. This kind of youth ministry empowers them to be fully aware of who they are and what God has purposed for them.[43]

The one feature I will add will be "creative expression," however, not so much as an addition but the *how* for achieving the five features Kwiyani proposed. Any youth ministry model that gives no room for creativity has cancelled itself out. As Father Koshy noted at the Edinburgh 2010 conference, "the gigantic problems of youth of our church demand an unusual, imaginative and even fanciful response."[44] Novelty makes a young heart beat faster. Youth ministers will need to fashion creative ways to ground their youths in their

---

42. Samson Adetunji Fatokun, "'I Will Pour Out My Spirit Upon All Flesh': The Origin, Growth and Development of the Precious Stone Church – the Pioneering African Indigenous Pentecostal Denomination in Southwest Nigeria," *Cyberjournal for Pentecostal-Charismatic Research*, no. 19 (2010): 3, http://www.pctii.org/cyberj/cyberj19/fatokun2.pdf.

43. Harvey C. Kwiyani, *Our Children Need Roots and Wings: Equipping and Empowering Young Diaspora Africans for Life and Mission* (Liverpool: Missio Africanus Publishing, 2018), 78.

44. Koshy, *Youth Envisioning Ecumenical Mission: Shifting Ecumenical Mission Paradigms for Witnessing Christ Today*, 2.

historical awareness, spiritual empowerment, and theologically informed bible knowledge while teaching them to express their missional agenda in a contextually relevant manner. This will involve meeting the youths on their *playing fields* – be it social media, sports, performing arts, technology, education, social involvement, mentorship or youth leadership. Leveraging the interest of youths in these areas can become effective tools for engaging them while seeking to prepare them for the future of the church and global Christianity. Jesus met his disciples (mainly teenagers?)[45] in their respective worlds – in a fishing boat, at the tax office, in a mentoring platform – he had his way of reaching the ones he chose and then training and equipping them with such creative ingenuity that amazed the rabbis of his day. We should follow his example and unleash a new breed of African Christian youths who will cross boundaries and go beyond conventional approaches, by the Spirit, advancing the course of *missio Dei* in their days. May this be so.

Conclusion

The rapid growth of African Christianity and its youthfulness holds great potential for the future of global Christianity. However, African churches will need to be intentional in prolonging their life cycle by understanding that the church does not exist to meet the needs of any one generation. A healthy congregation should be constantly readdressing the concerns and perspectives of a continually evolving society with timeless truth, more so with an eye on the next generation. Employing a missiology that appreciates both the giftings and relevance of the youths will produce an even more vibrant Christianity in Africa with more churches looking more like a river that is kept alive by constant movement and energy, rather than an unadventurous and unperturbed lake. The youth ministries of African churches should be in that endless pursuit of freshness and adaptation to changes that will unleash a breed of Christian youths who are confident of their identity, proud of their heritage and ever-so-willing to contribute their quota to the advancement of God's mission in the world.

---

45. Cary and Cary, "How Old Were Christ's Disciples?"

13

African Women in Mission Challenging Gender-based Violence in East Africa

Linda Ochola-Adolwa and Harvey Kwiyani

This essay makes a rather bold attempt, at least in our opinion, to articulate a mission-theology from the perspective of the African woman who, in many ways, lives at the bottom of the social hierarchy. Using stories of East African women living out their Christian faith while experiencing constant poverty and violence, we seek to understand what difference Jesus makes to them and how they keep evangelizing and discipling their neighbours despite these difficult circumstances. We are informed largely by social theories about women's lives in Africa, but we look at those theories through missiological and, therefore, theological lenses. While we make use of the social sciences, our thoughts are profoundly shaped by the theological reflection of scholars like Mercy Amba Oduyoye and Emmanuel Katongole whose works on womanist and political theologies for Africa, respectively, do not shy away from the difficult issue of the plight of the African woman – even the *Christian* African woman – who is often the most affected victim of the violence that characterizes even the most Christian countries on the continent. We believe that an African woman's theology of mission is necessary not only for the African continent but also for the wider context of World Christianity. The world needs to hear of the missional fortitude of the African woman who, against all odds, continues to bear witness of Christ, shining his light and sharing his love. As a block, Black women form quite a significant portion of world Christianity. Their theology matters and, as we argue in this essay, their missiology should matter as well.

Mission in an African Woman's Eyes

In Chinua Achebe's great novel, *Things Fall Apart*,[1] a story is told of Okonkwo's seven-year exile among his mother's people – a very extraordinary arrangement among the Igbo people (of Nigeria) of the fictional community of Umuofia.[2] Okonkwo has to seek refuge among his mother's family because among the Igbos, whose culture is high up on the patriarchy hierarchy, people believe that *one's mother is supreme*. Indeed, Okonkwo named his daughter born in exile *Nneka* (which means "mother is supreme"). This belief that one's mother is supreme is the reason for Okonkwo, or anyone for that matter, to seek refuge in their mother's land. It is an assurance that they will be safe with their mothers. Even the strongest of men have their mothers to guide and protect them. This was commonplace in pre-Christian Africa when many cultures considered women in general – and *mothers* in particular – to be givers and sustainers of life. Many still believe this today. Lives (and bodies) of all women, but especially of those who have given birth, are sacred. This becomes even more evident in matrilineal cultures where a family's children and wealth primarily belong to the woman and her family. In such cultures, the supremacy of the mother defines the relationship between her sons and other females. Essentially, the plight of the Black woman – economic, emotional, physical, and otherwise – is a mishap that needs to be dismantled and her God-given dignity restored and missional potential realized. If mother is indeed supreme, there is a significant amount of reckoning for our theologies (and missiologies) to do in order to recognize the place and role of the African woman in Christianity on the continent.

A missiology according to African women must exist because, of course, African women have played a key role in the spreading of Christianity not only in the continent but also around the world. It is common knowledge today that Africa has more Christians than any other continent. It needs to be emphasized just as much that a majority (sixty to sixty-six per cent) of all Christians in Africa are female. Allan Anderson suggested back in 2004 that seventy-five per

---

1. Chinua Achebe, *Things Fall Apart* (New York: McDowell, 1959).

2. Okonkwo is the main protagonist of the story. He is a leading warrior of his community, and has little to no regard for women, including his wives. Yet, when in trouble, he had to go back to his mother's people because, of course, men can never really be without women. If they despise their wives, they still must respect their mothers, and the mothers have a way of keeping them safe.

cent of the members of the Pentecostal movement are women.[3] It would not surprise us to hear that about half of that seventy-five per cent are in Africa. If anything, if that figure still holds today when one third of all Pentecostal and charismatic Christians are in Africa,[4] it is quite possible that even upwards of seventy per cent of African Christians are female. We cannot deny that women are the backbone of African Christianity. Their voices have sung – often through tears and heartaches – songs of redemption in choirs and worship teams in every city in the continent. Women have prayed in vigils and prayer mountains, lamenting and crying out to God for the salvation of the continent. Not only have they taught the story of Jesus in Sunday School, where they have formed the majority of teachers, but also in schools in public education, where many of them have worked as teachers. At home, the mother has been the primary discipler who has prayed for and taught children about the love of God. Thus, African women have engaged in God's mission for as long as the gospel has been preached in Africa. As our examples below demonstrate, African women have always been key agents in the spread of Christianity. However, there are also a rising number of African women who choose to become missionaries (in the professional sense of the word), migrating from their home region to other parts of the continent – and in some cases, the world – to serve God.

As Africans, we know beyond any shadow of doubt that to effectively empower a community economically, special attention must be given to the community's women. In most African cultures, women are the custodians of a community's life and welfare, and for this reason, it is usually said across sub-Saharan Africa that the only way to uplift a people's livelihood is to educate their women.[5] We argue in this essay that this is also true about Christianity, evangelism, and salvation. The best way to evangelize a community is to disciple its women. We understand, in hindsight though, that the conversion of the majority of sub-Saharan Africa has been largely to the response of African women to the gospel. Women's ministries, whether located in larger

---

3. Allan Anderson, *An Introduction to Pentecostalism: Global Charismatic Christianity* (New York: Cambridge University Press, 2004), 11. We believe that this figure may have risen considerable in the 15 years between 2004 and 2020.

4. Tapiwa Mapuranga, "Bargaining with Patriarchy? Women Pentecostal Leaders in Zimbabwe," *Fieldwork in Religion* 8.1 (2013): 74–91.

5. A common saying suggests that when a man gets an education, it is only an individual who is educated, while when it is a woman who gets an education, the whole village gets an education too.

denominational networks or run as para-church prayer movements, have played a very significant role in the transformation of the continent.

African Women in Mission: Historical Glimpses

African women have been engaged in God's mission in the continent for as long as Christianity has existed. African Christianity, from its early days in Egypt and the Maghreb to its current dominance in sub-Saharan Africa, has been undergirded and carried forward by the ministry of female Christians. Thus, the lineage of African female evangelists is long. In this two-thousand-year history, we could find thousands of names, but three stand out, showing us only a few of the different ways in which African women have participated in mission. The first was a young woman called Perpetua (AD 182–203) who – with Felicitas, her maid – was martyred at the age of twenty-two for refusing to denounce her faith. She was arrested together with four other catechumens for defying the Emperor's edict preventing people from converting to either Christianity or Judaism. She kept a diary that has been in circulation since her death as a book entitled *The Passion of Saints Perpetua and Felicity*.[6] Her father begged her recant her faith for the sake of her young child and for their decent family name. She refused and was consequently led into the arena to be mauled by wild animals on 7 March AD 203. She died by a gladiator's sword having survived an attack by a wild cow.[7] As a result, Perpetua stands as a towering example of an African woman in mission. She gave her life away at a time when martyrdom was the ultimate mission strategy – as is still in some parts of the world today. Just a few years before she was martyred, Tertullian had written in his *Apology* that "we [Christians] multiply when you mow us, the blood of the martyrs is the seed of the church."[8] The same is true of Perpetua. By refusing to denounce her faith, she gave her blood as a seed for the mission of the church, and therefore, asserted her place (and that of many African women) as bearers of Christ's witnessing even to the death. In addition, by documenting her own

---

6. Thomas J. Heffernan, *The Passion of Perpetua and Felicity* (Oxford: Oxford University Press, 2012).

7. Heffernan, *The Passion*, 134–35.

8. See Terrot Reaveley Glover, Gerald Henry Rendall and W. C. A. Kerr, *Tertullian, Apology, De Spectaculis*, vol. 250 (Cambridge: Harvard University Press, 1953), 227.

story, Perpetua becomes the agent of her own story, and thereby sets up an example that many African women theologians ought to follow.[9]

Second among these towering African women missionaries is Monica (AD 332–387), St. Augustine's mother.[10] Monica gave birth to Augustine in AD 354 in Carthage when she was 23 years old. When Augustine seemed to lose his way, Monica tearfully prayed that he would return to the church. She later undertook a dangerous journey, crossing the Mediterranean, to be with Augustine in Milan where he had settled. In Milan, Monica came to know Ambrose, the bishop of the city. When Augustine turned from his sins, Monica rejoiced to see her prayers answered. She continued to live with her son after his conversion. Augustine and Monica later moved to Cassiacum, where Monica was active in the philosophical discourse that Augustine authored. The two planned to return to North Africa together, but before they returned Monica died in Ostia outside of Rome.[11] She remains an exemplary mother who raised one of Africa's most revered theologians. Her prayers and philosophical discourse with Augustine are evident in his works. This work that she did well is no doubt missionary service. Her sacrifice for the sake of the faith and ministry of her son invites African women today to be missionaries in their own families as well as those beyond them.

Our third outstanding African woman in mission is prophetess Doña Beatriz Kimpa Vita (1684–1706).[12] Beatriz was born in a royal family in the Kingdom of Kongo in what is now Northern Angola. She grew up a Christian and, in 1704, she had a vision of Saint Anthony of Padua. She has been called the female Anthony of Africa – pointing to Saint Anthony of Egypt. Her prophetic charisma inspired a political movement that emphasized the Africanization of Christianity and political unification. She assembled thousands of followers in the ruins of the former capital city, developing a Christian cult – Antonianism – that would become the basis for the first attempt south of the Sahara to establish a national church independent of Rome. She was condemned as a heretic by the Christian King Pedro IV and as a witch by common law and was burned alive

---

9. The authorship of *The Passion* is complex, containing the voices of Perpetua, another male martyr and that of a subsequent editor. For full details, see Heffernan, *The Passion*, 4–16. Heffernan is convinced on balance that the first-person sections of *The Passion* were written by Perpetua.

10. For Saint Monica's biography, see Gillian Clark, *Monica: An Ordinary Saint* (Oxford University Press, 2015).

11. Clark, *Monica*, 22.

12. For further information about Kimpa Vita, see John Thornton, *The Kongolese Saint Anthony: Dona Beatriz Kimpa Vita and the Antonian Movement, 1684–1706* (Cambridge: Cambridge University Press, 1998).

in 1706. After her death, a majority of the kingdom continued to adhere to the sect she founded. Her ministry foreshadows significant aspects of Pentecostal movements that can be found throughout Sub-Saharan Africa. She embodied the African woman missional leader *par excellence*. Together with Monica and Perpetua, she exemplifies the kind of engagement that African women have with God's mission. They demonstrate that African women have indeed been part of God's mission on the continent over the centuries. In addition to these many ways of participating in mission, in the current context of postcolonial Africa, we discuss two key ways through which African women are engaging in mission. First, we will look at the missiological implications of the work of the Circle of Concerned African Women Theologians.[13] Second, we take the Circle's work of theological reflection and use it to discuss how African Christians can *missionally* engage the problem of violence against women in the continent.

The Circle of Concerned African Women Theologians

It is part of our foundational argument that the Circle's theological work is of significant missiological import for the continent of Africa. A great deal of the female theologizing in the three decades between 1990 and 2020 has been spearheaded by the Circle, initiated and originally led by Mercy Amba Oduyoye.[14] Elsewhere, Oduyoye describes her experience working at the University of Ibadan's Department of Religious Studies when she became painfully aware that the male theologians were developing an African theology with a male face in their minds. She became convinced that there could not be a comprehensive understanding of the nature of humanity without a feminist perspective.[15] This is why she initiated for the Circle. It started in 1989 when a group of eighty African Christian women theologians gathered in Accra, Ghana.[16] Their goal was to make a theological contribution to male-dominated theologies that were coming out of Africa at that time. They observed that African women had largely been ignored in the ecclesial discourse around the quest to transform society. In response, they resolved to embark on a journey of

---

13. Hereinafter, the Circle.

14. Oduyoye's extensive biography can be found at https://www.biola.edu/talbot/ce20/database/mercy-amba-oduyoye.

15. Kwok Pui-lan, "Mercy Amba Oduyoye and African Women's Theology," *Journal of Feminist Studies in Religion* 20.1 (2004).

16. Teresia Hinga, *African, Christian, Feminist: The Enduring Search for What Matters* (Maryknoll: Orbis Books, 2017), 3.

theological reflection through research and publishing to ensure that the voices and experiences of African women were heard. They began a seven-year cycle of research and publishing that sought to raise awareness about and begin to address women's issues from an African woman's theological perspective. They challenged each other further to develop platforms for action in their local contexts to move beyond just naming and denouncing the various injustices encountered by women. In so doing, the Circle allowed African women to play a significant role in providing theologically informed solutions to the problems that they were facing.[17] Their work has had great missiological impact in Africa. First, they helped make theology pay attention to the issues faced by African women. Both African men and Western theologians could not do this. Second, they made theology accessible to other African women. Many women gained confidence to articulate their theology because they saw other women do it. Third, in making theology accessible to African women, by empowering them to talk theologically to their families and neighbours, they also encouraged African women to engage in mission.

Mission Amidst Gender-based Violence

Teresia Hinga, one of the Circle theologians, dedicated a great deal of her work to naming of gender-based violence against women as the root problem of the continent. She rightly noted that African women become double victims of violence when men declared war on one another. Women suffer the general consequences of the war along with children, but many also suffered extra violence when soldiers assault them sexually.[18] This is the kind of violence that Katongole decries in his masterful work, *Born from Lament*, in which he discusses the effects of war in the Democratic Republic of Congo (DRC), and highlights the damage caused by sexual war among women in the country.[19] He tells, rather sadly, of how many soldiers weaponized rape and in one instance,

---

17. Hinga, *African, Christian, Feminist*, 15.

18. Hinga, *African, Christian, Feminist*, 175. Also Sara Meger, "Rape of the Congo: Understanding Sexual Violence in the Conflict in the Democratic Republic of Congo," *Journal of Contemporary African Studies* 28.2 (2010).

19. Emmanuel Katongole, *Born from Lament: The Theology and Politics of Hope in Africa* (Grand Rapids: Eerdmans, 2017). The DRC is an extraordinarily painful example because, on the one hand, it is suggested that more than ninety-five percent of its population is Christian and, yet, the plight of Congolese women is ineffable. See, for instance, the impact of the sexual violence executed against women in the Congo at https://www.smh.com.au/interactive/2009/congo/index.html.

killed a priest and raped nuns in a Catholic parish.[20] Wider discourse on sexual violence against women in the DRC documents well how hundreds of thousands of women have suffered rape in the aftermath of the Rwandan Genocide (when Rwandese soldiers crossed over into the DRC). United Nations statistics suggest that well over one million women in the Congo have suffered rape in what has been called "sexual warfare." North-east DRC has been called the "Rape Capital of the World" where rape has been used as a weapon of war.[21] In Kenya, during the 2017 elections, the Kenya National Human Rights Commission reported 201 cases of gender-based violence, including individual and gang rapes, often in the presence of the children of victims.[22] Most of this violence against women took place against the backdrop of protests between civilians and security agents. In most cases, the perpetrators were security agents who were otherwise supposed to protect the women.

How then are African mothers engaging in mission in the context of the hopelessness of violence in the twenty-first century? We employ the metaphor of an African mother without excluding those who have not borne children, because while as Hinga notes that the general societal perception of women contributes to the indiscriminate abuse of women,[23] the societal imagery associated with motherhood is one that demonstrates the capacity of women to use their role and status to access certain resources and pathways to action.[24] For instance, we are reminded of the mothers of political prisoners who mounted a protest against the Moi government in the 1990s in Kenya for the release of their sons. They did this by staging a hunger strike and then maintaining a protest in the basement of the All Saints Cathedral in Nairobi for over a year. These women – these mothers – are at the forefront of the fight against gender-based violence. Many of them work in healthcare such as nurses, midwives and community health service providers, working in their various capacities to show God's love to the victims of violence. Some are working in advocacy, fighting for the rights of the victims of the violence. Others are working in the government seeking justice on behalf of the victims. For instance, the Kenya

---

20. Katongole, *Born from Lament*.

21. Galya Ruffer, "Testimony of Sexual Violence in the Democratic Republic of Congo and the Injustice of Rape: Moral Outrage, Epistemic Injustice, and the Failures of Bearing Witness." *Oregon Review of International Law* 15.225 (2013): 235.

22. Kenya National Commission on Human Right, "Silhouettes of Brutality: An Account of Sexual Violence During and After the 2017 Elections" (Nairobi, KNHCR, 2018). See http://www.knchr.org/Portals/0/KNCHR_Silhouettes_of_Brutality.pdf.

23. Hinga, *African, Christian, Feminist*, 178.

24. Alexandra Tibbetts, "Mamas Fighting For freedom in Kenya," *Africa Today* 41.4 (1994).

Women Judges Association was quick to call for prayer for the nation on behalf of those affected in post-election violence in the country. In November 2018, the Kenya Women Judges Association celebrated their silver jubilee, beginning with a prayer breakfast. In praying for the state, and especially for the women affected by violence, the Kenya Women Judges Association is participating in God's mission in Kenya. Commenting on this turning to prayer, Justice Okwengu noted that:

> We felt there was need for prayer because . . . as women, if God does not enable us, we cannot manage. Women are the backbone of the society. The role of praying for the family is the mother's. As women in the Judiciary, we feel we must fill that space . . . If the Judiciary is not working, then the ordinary citizen has no hope. In issues of election violence, the people who suffer the most are the women.[25]

Another response that we find worthy of consideration comes from Rwanda (more than 20 years after the genocide). Uwineza, Pearson and Powley point out that during the genocide, between 250,000 and 500,000 women were raped and the testimonies of survivors recorded various forms of gender-based violence.[26] Ambani observes that sexual violence was used both as a tool of gender oppression and ethnic and political intimidation. Of course, in political conflicts, it is common for women to be raped simply for being a woman. This is often intended to enforce a society's power structures and inequalities. While gender-based violence is present both in times of peace and war, it intensifies in times of political conflict.[27]

More than twenty years after the genocide, Peace Uwineza, as coordinator of the Ladies Ministry at Christian Life Assembly Church in Kigali, along with other women, created the Ladies Shine Conference where women had opportunities to give expression to their experiences by praying for one another

---

25. Hannah Okwengu, the president of the Kenya Women Judges Association and Jessie Lesiit initiated the thanksgiving and prayer service that launched the silver jubilee celebration week for the KWJA.

26. Peace Uwineza, Elizabeth Pearson and Elizabeth Powley, "Sustaining Women's Gains in Rwanda: The Influence of Indigenous Culture and Post-genocide Politics" (Washington DC: Institute for Inclusive Security, Hunt Alternatives Fund, 2009).

27. John Ambani, "The Roots and Effects of Electoral Sexual and Gender-Based Violence on Women's Political Participation in Kenya," in *Gender Equality and Political Processes in Kenya: Challenges and Prospects*, ed. J. Beigon (Nairobi: Strathmore University Press, 2016). The TJRC report defines sexual violence as acts including gang rape, sodomy, defilement and mutilation of sexual organs. The perpetrators take advantage of the breakdown of the social order and general lawlessness to commit these acts with impunity (2013).

and worshipping God together. In this space, the women actively reflected on passages of Scripture in which women are the key actors and characters. This was done to help the community of women create or access their social memory in order to continue in the process of their healing from the wounds of the past.[28] This practice is reflected in Katongole's theory of social memory. He argues that for Christian teaching and values to make a difference, there is a need to engage layers of memory through the stories told by the society, including its various institutions. Katongole notes that who we are and can become, depends very much on the stories that we tell, stories that we listen to, and the stories that we live. He points out that the task of the Christian faith is not just to improve the way politics works but also to change the stories a community tells itself. Thus, when the women attended the conferences at Christian Life Assembly, it is not merely about women congregating. It was primarily an opportunity for the women to begin to tell a different story – a story that would produce different characters with different values. For Uwineza, the Ladies Shine Conferences are an engagement in mission where women tell the stories of women from the Bible. In these stories women are cast as actors and not just victims and as leaders and providers of hope and solutions to the brokenness in society.[29]

Further Explorations

While we acknowledge some of the significant ways in which African women are participating in mission, especially in the fight against gender-based violence, we propose that it is particularly important for African women to keep on in this fight. Their work in this mission brings our attention to other areas that African Christianity must shine God's light in mission. First, there is the simple challenge that as African Christians, we have a hard time talking about this important subject of gender-based violence. This is evident in that gender-based violence is usually underreported when compared with other kinds of violence. For instance, in Kenya in 2017, various religious groups reporting on election violence and election-related deaths observed that silence around sexual violence was audible even though it was common knowledge

---

28. Emmanuel Katongole, *The Sacrifice of Africa: A Political Theology for Africa*, The Eerdmans Ekklesia series (Grand Rapids: Eerdmans, 2011), 2, 10.

29. At the helm of organizing a three-day conference for women was Peace Uwineza. She and the other women of the Christian Life Assembly, are examples of women engaging in mission through the workplace in the areas of justice, healing and reconciliation. Peace Uwineza has also distinguished herself in the area of inclusive security in Rwanda.

that many women were violated in the post-election season.[30] It is very likely that within Christian communities, the subject of gender-based violence is still not paid sufficient attention. Further data gathered by the Kenya National Commission on Human Rights demonstrated that most victims did not turn to the church or their pastors for help. Thus, the missional role played by women in speaking about and to other women about violence becomes even more important. Hinga concurs and challenges the existing situation by saying that:

> The church has to be consistent with its own vocation of being the champion of justice in society. The church has to be in solidarity with the women. These efforts should be made out of genuine concern for justice for women and the restoration of their dignity, a prior condition to the effective education of society on the issue of women and violence, the church to be seen to treat women with justice and uphold their dignity.[31]

To a great extent, this silence on issues of gender-based violence is an outworking of sexism in Christian communities. Kameri-Mbote explains that when gender is discussed, it is not merely about the physical or biological differences between male and female, but also about the social structures around what it means to be male or female.[32] She makes the point that it is these socially ascribed structures that determine the rights, duties, obligations and status assigned to men and women. In the context of patriarchy – as is in many African cultures – these socially ascribed structures seem to determine what the church does or does not speak about and, generally speaking, those decisions are made by men.

Second, there is the challenge of the reluctance of the church to engage with the issue of state-sponsored violence. This dates back to the relationship between the missionaries and the colonial powers. In *The Sacrifice of Africa*,

---

30. Three groups spoke out to sound the alarm on the number of election-related deaths five days after the election. The Multi-Sectoral Forum, a group of religious leaders drawn from various faiths put the figure of those dead at eighteen. The Anglican Church of Kenya Archbishop, Jackson ole Sapit spoke up noting that the church had its own network of people providing information on the number of those who died, contradicting the government's claim, that no protestor had been killed and that police had not used excessive force to quell disturbances (Nation, 2017). The Inter Religious Council of Kenya published a statement acknowledging that the election had taken place in less than ideal circumstances in terms of violence and controversy(Convocation, 2018).

31. Hinga, *African, Christian, Feminist*, 180.

32. Patricia Kameri-Mbote, "The Quest for Equal Gender Representation in Kenya's Parliament: Past and Present Challenges," in Japhet Biegon, ed., *Gender Equality and Political Process in Kenya*, 39–66.

Emmanuel Katongole notes the silence of the missionaries amid the brutality of the colonialists. He provides an example of the Catholic Sisters who took care of hundreds of orphaned children in the Belgian Congo region without raising the questions about the brutal raids throughout the territory through which these children were becoming orphaned.[33] This approach resulted in limiting salvation to the spiritual and pastoral to the exclusion of the material and temporal. Katongole's view agrees with the perspective offered by Ambani who sees gender-based violence as the symptom of a much bigger problem of state-sanctioned violence, impunity, and ethnic and economic marginalization.[34] Considering this, it is possible that the church finds itself unable or unwilling to confront sexual gender-based violence because if it does so, it must confront something much larger and more difficult to respond to.

Samuel Kobia presents the challenges faced by the church in confronting the state. First, it must face the dilemma of the duty to obey rulers as stated in Romans 13. Second, it must address the dilemma of how to engage without being fully drafted into the political agenda. Third, the church must deal with its own denominational and ethnic differences before it can speak and act ecumenically and nationally. Of course, Christians have a tendency to tilt towards ethnicity in times of crisis.[35] It is worth noting that in both the election violence of Kenya in 2017 and the genocide in Rwanda in 2004, ethnic overtones played a significant part in the political conflict. It is Katongole who, in his book *Mirror to the Church*, suggests that "the blood of tribalism runs deeper than the waters of baptism."[36] It may be that the church is unwilling or unable to confront the ugly divisions within it before it can confront the societal institutions around it.

It is only when the church resolves these issues that it can play the role of watchdog and support victims of violence by being visible and audible. Kamaara observes that besides the media, the church is perhaps the most powerful institution in terms of civic thought and action in Africa. Since the church has the unique opportunity of gathering people together regularly every week, it has the potential to effectively shape the attitudes and practices of

---

33. Katongole, *The Sacrifice of Africa*, 18.

34. Ambani, "The Roots," 115.

35. Samuel Kobia, "The Nation-State in Africa: Violence and Quests for Life with Dignity," in *Church-State Relations: A Challenge for African Christianity*, ed. J. N. K. Mugambi and Frank Kuschner-Pelkmann (Nairobi: Acton Press, 2004).

36. Emmanuel Katongole and Jonathan Wilson-Hartgrove, *Mirror to the Church: Resurrecting Faith after Genocide in Rwanda* (Grand Rapids: Zondervan, 2009), 47.

Africans in almost every arena of life.[37] Only then can the church respond pastorally to the challenge of sexual gender-based violence.[38]

Conclusion

This chapter has set out to articulate a mission theology from the perspective of the African woman. It has explored the missional fortitude of African women who continue to be a witness for Christ amidst their various challenging realities. In conclusion, African women are engaging in mission. They are the backbone of the church and they are also the anchor of society. As such, they have to engage in mission in the context of gender-based violence, both to challenge it and to *minister* to those affected by it. The resilience of women themselves, in hearing and addressing the concerns and voices of other women, stands out as a way in which African mothers are engaging in mission. Within women's fellowship groups, conferences, and professional associations, women play a very important role in naming and unmasking the evils that diminish the lives of other women in their societies. This is mission. In many cases, women are being pastors to themselves by supporting one another unequivocally when tragedy strikes. They provide counsel in helping one another resist abuse and violence when it threatens them. These women represent and exemplify countless other African women courageously engaging in mission by documenting and by voicing the female perspective through prayers and through biblical teaching in the context of gender-based sexual violence.

---

37. E. Kamaara, "Religion and Socio-Political Change in Kenya: 1978–2003," in *Church-State Relations: A Challenge for African Christianity*, ed. J. N. K. Mugambi and Frank Kuschner-Pelkmann (Nairobi: Acton Press, 2004), 129.

38. Linda Ochola-Adolwa, "Study of the Macro, Social and Psychological Factors that Influence the Civic Participation Practices of Christians at Mavuno Church, Nairobi, Kenya." (Doctor of Intercultural Studies thesis, Fuller Theological Seminary, 2017), 102.

14

African American Presbyterian Mission Work as an Exercise in Recognizing and Redefining Identities, 1916–1935

Kimberly Hill

The topic of civilizing missions within studies of Christian history in the nineteenth and twentieth centuries often focuses on European and American cultures as catalysts for change abroad. Yet the expansion of non-Western independent church movements since the 1960s has inspired a more recent scholarly interest in Christian institutions that flourish while embracing indigenous leadership, languages, and traditions. The theologian Lamin Sanneh characterized these new congregations, particularly those founded by Africans, as potential evidence that "colonialism was an obstacle to the growth of Christianity" in the global South.[1] Though the field of World Christianity emphasizes religious developments that multiplied after the decline of European colonialism, its significance remains linked to a contrast with Western norms from previous decades. Part of the key to understanding the current roles of African immigrant churches involves noticing how African Christians overcame obstacles to their religious expressions during the early twentieth century. Spiritual practices that aid in the recent expansion of African immigrant churches continue historic patterns of community focus and transnational identity formation. For example, interactions between African

---

1. Lamin Sanneh, *Whose Religion is Christianity? The Gospel Beyond the West* (Grand Rapids: Eerdmans, 2003), 18.

Christians and African American missionaries in the Belgian Congo guided these missionaries toward holistic interpretations of religious responsibility.

This essay highlights two African American Presbyterians, Alonzo Edmiston and Althea Brown Edmiston, who developed ministries that came to reflect the perspectives and interests of their African neighbors in the central Kasai region of the Belgian Congo. African American missionaries were central to the historical basis for World Christianity; whether or not they worked for separate Black organizations, their persistence in spite of widespread racial prejudice reinforced perceptions that Western acculturation was not the only viable option for diverse populations.

Starting with the founding of Sierra Leone, support for the development of local Black leadership accompanied the work of African American missionaries in West Africa.[2] The Black emigrants who fled the United States and Nova Scotia in 1791 included preachers who established meeting houses with supervisory positions for certain members.[3] Following generations of settlers attended the mission-affiliated Fourah Bay College in Sierra Leone, and several graduates applied their Western-style education to producing regional linguistics, historical, and political studies.[4]

Black settlers and missionaries expanded on this trend after the establishment of the Liberia colony in 1821. Lott Carey, the best known early African American missionary, accepted political and administrative appointments in addition to his ministerial role with the African Baptist Missionary Society.[5] Carey participated in two revolts against the White leadership of the colony and criticized the American Colonization Society for opposing evangelistic outreach among Africans who lived far from the coastal settlements.[6] A later American emigrant from the West Indies, Edward Blyden, advocated for Liberia College to become a model for African studies curriculum on the continent.[7] Meanwhile, African Methodist Episcopal Church

---

2. Akintola J. G. Wyse, "The Sierra Leone Krios: A Reappraisal from the Perspective of the African Diaspora," in *Global Dimensions of the African Diaspora*, 2nd ed. (Washington, DC: Howard University Press, 1993), 343.

3. Lamin Sanneh, *Abolitionists Abroad: American Blacks and the Making of Modern West Africa* (Cambridge: Harvard University Press, 1999), 100.

4. Joseph E. Harris, "Return Movements to West and East Africa: A Comparative Approach," in *Global Dimensions*, 53.

5. Sanneh, *Abolitionists Abroad*, 209–11.

6. Sanneh, *Abolitionists Abroad*, 208–10.

7. Harris, "Return Movements to West and East Africa," 54.

co-founder Daniel Coker established a congregation in Sierra Leone, which became one of the primary A.M.E. mission fields in the 1880s.[8]

As noted by missiologist Jehu J. Hanciles, it would be oversimplified to argue that the concept of civilizing missions was disrupted completely by the intervention of the relatively small number of African American appointed missionaries who traveled before 1900.[9] Most of these individuals traveled through White-led organizations and did not question the denigration of non-Western cultures.[10] Racial restrictions adopted by denominational administrators and colonial officers combined to prevent all but a few African American missionaries from having long careers on the African continent.[11] The Black co-founder of the American Presbyterian Congo Mission, William Henry Sheppard, fit these patterns during his almost twenty years abroad. He recruited five other African Americans to join the mission before 1900, and his close interaction with regional African leaders did not prevent him or his colleagues from challenging some local traditions as "wicked customs."[12] By 1916, Sheppard and all of his first recruits had been dismissed from the Congo Mission. Hanciles finds the significant influence of African American missionaries not in their attitudes or in their longevity, but in the political ideals and professional alliances that Black missionaries and their supporters helped to facilitate.[13]

Historically Black colleges and universities accepted students from the African continent, providing the only means to specialized medical training

---

8. James T. Campbell, *Middle Passages: African American Journeys to Africa, 1787–2005* (New York: Penguin Press, 2006), 53; Daniel Alexander Payne, *History of the African Methodist Episcopal Church*, ed. Charles Spencer Smith (Documenting the American South), 485–89; Mark Ellingsen, "Changes in African American Mission: Rediscovering African American Roots," *International Bulletin of Missionary Research*, 36.3 (July 2012), 136.

9. In his book *Black Americans and the Evangelization of Africa*, Walter L. Williams estimated this number to be about 115 African American missionaries. Jehu J. Hanciles, "'Africa is Our Fatherland': The Black Atlantic, Globalization, and Modern African Christianity," *Theology Today*, 7.2 (2014), 217.

10. Ellingsen, "Changes in African American Mission: Rediscovering African American Roots," 137.

11. Kenneth James King, *Pan-Africanism and Education: A Study of Race Philanthropy and Education in the Southern States of America and East Africa* (London: Oxford University Press, 1971), 88–89, 91, 132.

12. William E. Phipps, *William Sheppard: Congo's African American Livingstone* (Louisville: Geneva Press, 2002), 106; King, *Pan-Africanism*.

13. Hanciles, "Africa is Our Fatherland," 217–18; Ellingsen, "Changes in African American Mission," 137.

after British institutions adopted race restrictions in the early 1900s.[14] The establishment of A.M.E. and National Baptist churches in Western and Southern Africa gave newly appointed African pastors access to international donor networks and helped local young men and women receive scholarships to American institutions.[15] Enrollment of African students at the premier Black universities in the United States started to increase after 1877, and the cultural exchange also increased through missions. Ten Fisk University students and alumni (including Althea Brown) served in overseas ministry between the following year and 1937.[16] Two African American missionaries to Malawi went abroad in 1902 specifically to help develop an industrial school under the leadership of John Chilembwe.[17] But, even in regions where no African Americans were present, news of Black colleges like Tuskegee Institute spread among African leaders and inspired the creation of local schools and colleges following a similar model.[18] Some students who attended the A.M.E. college, Wilberforce Institute, later shaped theories of African nationalism.[19]

African American Presbyterians continued the emphasis on education, leadership, and community building that African Christians and African American missionaries had developed together since the early nineteenth century. When William Henry Sheppard and a White minister named Samuel Lapsley started the American Presbyterian Congo Mission (A.P.C.M.) in 1891, they entered a volatile political context spurred by the global rubber trade. King Leopold II of Belgium controlled the region as his personal financial venture, and the local people were expected to provide labor and resources at the request of rubber companies owned by the king or other European investors. Local villages were disrupted by government-sponsored raids in search of workers and tax revenue. Displaced people, most of them of Luba or Lulua ancestry, relocated to mission stations in search of physical protection.[20] By recruiting five other African American missionaries before 1900, Sheppard hoped to

---

14. Adell Patton, Jr., "Howard University and Meharry Medical Schools in the Training of African Physicians, 1868–1978," *Global Dimensions*, 109.

15. Kings M. Phiri, "Afro-American Influence in Colonial Malawi, 1891–1945," *Global Dimensions*, 393–97.

16. James A. Quirin, "'Her Sons and Daughters are Ever on the Altar': Fisk University and Missionaries to Africa, 1866–1937," *Tennessee Historical Quarterly*, 60.1 (Spring 2001), 27–28.

17. Phiri, "Afro-American Influence in Colonial Malawi, 1891–1945," 390–91.

18. Phiri, "Afro-American Influence in Colonial Malawi, 1891–1945," 398. Andrew Barnes, *Global Christianity and the Black Atlantic* (Waco: Baylor University Press, 2017).

19. Phiri, "Afro-American Influence in Colonial Malawi, 1891–1945," 396–98.

20. Jan Vansina, *Being Colonized: The Kuba Experience in Rural Congo, 1880–1960* (Madison: University of Wisconsin Press, 2010), 90–92.

create and manage an additional mission station that served villagers who identified as Kuba.[21] The first A.P.C.M. station in Kuba territory (Ibaanche) and the first A.P.C.M. station founded in the colony (Luebo) were based so far inland from coastal ports that by 1900 colonial authorities had yet to exert full control over the region.[22] The location meant that the resident missionaries could play a mediating role between the rulers and chiefs of the isolated Kuba kingdom, the European traders, the Belgian representatives of King Leopold II, and the Southern Presbyterian Church.[23]

Community-based Mediation Strategies at the American Presbyterian Congo Mission

Althea Brown and Alonzo Edmiston started serving with the A.P.C.M. in 1902 and 1904 respectively. As part of the second wave of African American Presbyterian missionaries supervised by Sheppard, they sought to expand the Ibaanche mission station that he had designed in 1898. Brown and Edmiston married in 1905 and worked together for about thirty years utilizing the ministry strategies and social networks they had developed among the Kuba people. Brown specialized in linguistics, teaching, and nursing while Edmiston focused on church leadership, agriculture, and industrial education. Their first major challenge was to rebuild Ibaanche after a 1904 anti-colonial revolt. The newly married couple staked their security and their reputations on expressing the concerns of their African neighbors, with Brown arguing publicly that the Kuba fighters had been provoked to violence by negligent Belgian officials.[24] After a prolonged furlough from 1908 to 1911, the couple returned to Ibaanche at the start of the colony's political transformation into the Belgian Congo. Edmiston helped to negotiate with the new government for the potential expansion of Presbyterian outreach throughout the surrounding villages while Brown prepared for that expansion by researching the Kuba language.

Before 1919, none of the African evangelists or church members who affiliated with the American Presbyterian Congo Mission were invited to speak

---

21. Phipps, *William Sheppard*, 112–20.
22. Phipps, *William Sheppard*, 115.
23. Spelling of this mission station name in publications varies: Ibanche, Ibaanche, Ibaanj, Ibanj, and Ibanc. This chapter uses the spelling "Ibaanche" as used in several American Presbyterian Congo Mission records.
24. Althea Brown Edmiston, "Missions in Congo Free State, Africa," *American Missionary* (Dec. 1908), 110.

at its business meetings.²⁵ The Edmistons disrupted that pattern of neglect by foregrounding local perspectives in their ministry goals. Alonzo Edmiston kept a journal featuring extended transcripts of negotiations with regional chiefs and rulers written in dialogue style.²⁶ He expressed special concern when the Congo Mission policies shifted away from encouraging missionaries to learn the Bushoong language spoken by most of the Kuba people because he worried that negotiations with Kuba leaders would suffer as a consequence.²⁷ Althea Brown continued the tradition of promoting multiple languages at the Congo Mission by writing the first Bushoong grammar and dictionary.²⁸ That publication distinguished itself from the earlier translation work published by Presbyterian mission supervisor William Morrison by emphasizing the beauty of the language and the unique characteristics of the Kuba political structure that predated the missionaries' arrival.²⁹

Both Brown and Edmiston embraced some aspects of the civilizing missions rhetoric common to the American women's missionary movement from the 1880s through the 1920s, which focused on providing education and domestic skills training to uplift potential female converts.³⁰ However, they tended to seek changes that incorporated African students' interests in paid positions and the developing urban colonial economy.³¹ At the most basic level, observing local people taught these African American missionaries to value the survival skills of local people in addition to their capacity for religious change.

For a year, Brown and Edmiston managed the Presbyterian agricultural college. Their original plan for this programme included regular conferences for regional chiefs and a cross-cultural museum. The missionaries hoped to

---

25. Edmiston, *A. L. Edmiston Diaries*, African Collection, Talladega College Library Archives, Talladega, AL 13 November 1919.

26. A.L. Edmiston, *A. L. Edmiston Diaries*, 10 August 1916.

27. Edmiston, *A. L. Edmiston Diaries*, 10 May 1918.

28. Althea Brown Edmiston, *Grammar and Dictionary of the Bushonga or Bukuba Language as Spoken by the Bushonga or Bukuba Tribe Who Dwell in the Upper Kasai District, Belgian Congo, Central Africa* (Luebo: J. Leighton Wilson Press, 1932). To review a digitized copy, see https://library.si.edu/digital-library/book/grammardictionar00edmi. Accessed 13 May 2021.

29. Ira Dworkin, "On the Borders of Race, Mission, and State: African Americans and the American Presbyterian Congo Mission," *Borderlands and Frontiers in Africa*, ed. Steven Van Wolputte (Berlin: Lit Verlag, 2013), 199–202; Robert D. Bedinger, "Althea Brown Edmiston: A Congo Crusader," *Glorious Living*, 268.

30. See Peggy Pascoe, *Relations of Rescue: the Search for Female Moral Authority in the American West, 1874–1939* (New York: Oxford University Press, 1990), 33–34; Dana Lee Robert, *American Women in Mission: A Social History of Their Thought and Practice* (Macon: Mercer Univ. Press, 1996), 25–26, 35–37.

31. Brown Edmiston, "Missions in Congo Free State, Africa," 310.

make their college a repository for arts and crafts that represented African and African American traditions while also hosting dialogue about African leaders' current and future concerns. Those plans were abandoned out of overriding concern to help students survive the flu epidemic of 1918.[32]

After closing their agricultural college in 1919, the couple relocated to teach at three other A.P.C.M. mission stations in the Kasai region over the next eight years. In each location, Alonzo Edmiston learned different strategies to address students' concerns about the lack of variety in the boarding school meals. Because the residents of the girls' school complained about over-reliance on boiled cassava roots for their daily meals, Edmiston started offering meal allowances and planting more fruit trees to supplement the students' diet.[33] Adding produce like peas and watermelons also created new outreach ideas.

When African evangelists attended the annual missions conferences in the 1920s, Edmiston offered agricultural exhibits and other farm-related activities. Each evangelist left with packets of seeds from his farm's yield of fruits and vegetables, and Edmiston gained enough expertise in local agriculture to produce two textbooks that he taught to Bible College students in the 1930s.[34] His experiments with local cassava, sugar cane, and berries supplemented the diets of the mission station residents and created marketing opportunities. These innovations drew on his observations of African villagers' cooking techniques and their agricultural preferences.[35] While Belgian officials were crafting a plan for mandatory cash crop cultivation throughout the colony, this missionary heeded the preference of African farmers who foresaw the incompatibility of cotton planting with subsistence farming.[36]

The Edmistons also learned about community building as recipients of effective mediation strategies. The ways that they embraced and passed down a broader understanding of "family" provide evidence of this learning

---

32. Alonzo Edmiston, "Aims and Policies of the Agricultural School to Be Started at Luebo for the A.P.C.M.," June 1918, 4, PCM Records, RG 432, box 21, folder 1, Presbyterian Historical Society, Philadelphia, PA, 3; Edmiston, *A. L. Edmiston Diaries*, 13 March 1919.

33. Edmiston, *A.L. Edmiston Diaries*, 9 December 1924, 19 August 1924, 6–22 January 1927.

34. Edmiston, *A.L. Edmiston Diaries*, 19 December 1918, 4–5 March 1919, 30 March 1923; "Reverend A.L. Edmiston Missionary to Africa," typed career abstract, undated, Althea B. Edmiston Collection, MSS 883, box 1, folder 1, Manuscript, Archives, and Rare Book Library, Emory University.

35. For example, Alonzo Edmiston devoted a few pages of his journal to the local method for capturing and grilling white ants. See Edmiston, *A. L. Edmiston Diaries*, 12 January 1920.

36. Edmiston, *A.L. Edmiston Diaries*, 16–17 February 1916; Osumaka Likaka, *Rural Society and Cotton in Colonial Zaire* (Madison, Wisconsin: University of Wisconsin Press, 1997), 13, 16–18.

process. In 1917, Alonzo Edmiston recorded a Kuba tradition about ancestral spirits inhabiting the bodies of those who travelled to or from America.[37] This tradition hinted at contemporary beliefs that African Americans could represent a supernatural force destined to liberate the colony from Belgian rule.[38] Though the Edmistons did not seem to know the political implications of this belief, its relational benefits inspired them to feel invested personally in the interests of local people. Like their Congo Mission colleagues, the Edmistons received new names in a local language and grew accustomed to students calling them "mother" or "father."[39] Like her mentor Maria Fearing, Althea Brown Edmiston grew so close to the local Christian girls and women that she included them in her last will and testament.[40]

The family's transnational identity formation continued across generations. Kuba princes followed traditional practice by bestowing their own names on both of the missionaries' sons (Sherman "Kueta" and Alonzo Leucourt "Bope") at birth. Despite working in regions outside the Kuba kingdom for most of their last twenty years of ministry, the missionaries passed down their interest in that kingdom to the next generations; the Edmistons' great-grandchildren still refer to their grandfathers exclusively by their Kuba names.[41]

Conclusion

A common thread in the work of the Edmiston family in the Belgian Congo was that the perspectives of local people needed to be considered in Presbyterian ministry. By the time that Althea Brown Edmiston died and Alonzo Edmiston retired (in 1937 and 1941 respectively), the era known as the peak of the American missionary movement had started to wane. After 1960, the retreat of American missionaries from the newly independent Democratic Republic of Congo placed the future of the African synod founded by the Edmistons and their mission colleagues under the control of local believers. That

---

37. A. L. Edmiston, *A. L. Edmiston Diaries*, 2 August 1917.

38. Wyatt MacGaffey, "The West in Congolese Experience," in *Africa & the West: Intellectual Responses to European Culture* (Madison: University of Wisconsin Press, 1972), 56–59.

39. Muambi Luongoso (Alonzo Edmiston), "Mama Tshitolo: Madame A.L. Edmiston," *The News of the Kasai People* (August 1937), 7–9. Vass Family Papers, RG 476, box 2, folder 6, Presbyterian Historical Society, Philadelphia, Pennsylvania.

40. Patricia Sammon, *Maria Fearing: A Woman Whose Dream Crossed an Ocean* (Huntsville: Writers Consortium Books, 1989), 121; Edmiston, *A. L. Edmiston Diaries*, 3 June 1937.

41. Althea Edmiston Cousins, Evelyn Edmiston Easton, Herbert Edmiston, Dr. Kimberly Cousins Trent, and Lisa Edmiston, conversation with the author, Philadelphia, PA, 20 April 2018.

Presbyterian community continues to exist, and its ongoing collaborations with the Presbyterian Church in the U.S.A. are similar to the global influence of African immigrant churches.[42] The expansion of African immigrant churches beyond the continent has been dubbed "reverse missions," though sociologist Rebecca Y. Kim notes that it is a problematic phrase since "there is no set direction for missions."[43] Likewise, the contrast inherent in this phrase obscures the continuities in historic African Christianity. Given the evidence of long-term African influence at the Congo Mission, modern Christian mission work from central and western Africa can be interpreted as a continuation of the religious strategies that helped sustain local churches despite political and social instability.

The Communauté Presbytérienne au Congo (Presbyterian Community of Congo) still uses a broad coalition to withstand the consequences of political exploitation. The repression of political protesters in 2017 escalated into ethnic clashes within the Kasai Province where the original American Presbyterian Congo Mission was based. Yet the ministries of local Presbyterians continue to operate and draw international support. Within Kasai, the church members set themselves apart from the recent conflict by continuing to represent various ethnic groups in their community service. Their network of schools includes a building named after the Zappo Zap ethnic group though the church continues to reflect its roots in Luba communities.[44]

A similar approach is evident during annual meetings of the Congo Mission Network. This gathering of current missionaries, descendants of American Presbyterian Congo Mission staff, and church administrators from the Democratic Republic of the Congo includes workshops on current projects and goals that Christians are pursuing within the country. Though the group has roots in the overseas ministries of American southerners, "outreach" is not the operative term for the Network; instead, it is a team with common interests. The plans to build and manage schools, hospitals, and church buildings originate with partners who live in the D.R.C.[45] Congolese Presbyterians

---

42. Akintunde E. Akinade, "Non-Western Christianity in the Western World: African Immigrant Churches in the Diaspora," *African Immigrant Religions in America*, ed. Jacob K. Olupona and Regina Gemignani (New York: New York University Press, 2007), 90–91.

43. Rebecca Y. Kim, *The Spirit Moves West: Korean Missionaries in America* (New York: Oxford University Press, 2015), 3–4.

44. Tammy Warren, "'Build Congo Schools' Improves Education Quality in the DRC," *Mission Crossroads* (Spring 2016), online version. https://www.pcusa.org/news/2016/3/21/building-congo-schools-improves-education-quality-/. Accessed 13 August 2018.

45. "About the Congo Mission Network," Congo Mission Network, http://www.congopartners.org/about.asp. Accessed 13 August 2018.

who emigrated to the United States stay updated on affairs in their home country by supporting the Network and leading affiliated churches. The active missionaries and the descendants of the early Congo Mission staff offer prayer, finances, and logistical support to these projects. In the process, they maintain personal connections with the relatives, friends, and protégés of the African Christians who helped found the Presbyterian Community of Congo alongside their ancestors. Though they are distinguished from one another by language and nationality, the American and Congolese Presbyterians share a drive to understand their mission history and keep it relevant.

The past and present activities of the American Presbyterian Congo Mission analyzed here suggest that the principles of incorporating local perspectives and avoiding dichotomies will continue to help African churches produce innovative ministry projects. Brown and Edmiston crafted inventive missions careers partly because they worked on some of the projects that were most significant to local people. A similar dynamic is apparent in the work of African immigrant churches in the twenty-first century when ministers and congregants define each aspect of their communities as part of the sphere for their activism. These aspects often include concerns about visa applications, racial disparities in policing, and other issues that could be dismissed as secular in a different theological framework.[46] It is likely that these congregations will continue to grow dramatically in the United States as long as they address congregants' spiritual needs without minimizing or ignoring their sociopolitical concerns. The second sign of a promising future for African immigrant churches can be found in their capacity to bridge disparities between multiple groups. Gwinyai Muzorewa characterized this trait in Black theology as a refusal to limit one's public identity to the racial "minority" label; he encouraged readers to recognize the empowerment within defining one's self and one's worth more generously.[47] At the congregational level, African immigrant churches retain their alliances on the African continent while declaring transnational identities and goals. They serve members of African descent while offering a gospel message with broad charismatic appeal. Scholars note that African churches

---

46. Jacob K. Olupona, "Communities of Believers: Exploring African Immigrant Religion in the United States," *African Immigrant Religions in America*, ed. Jacob K. Olupona and Regina Gemignani (New York: New York University Press, 2007), 29; Elias K. Bongmba, "Portable Faith: The Global Mission of African Initiated Churches (AICs)," *African Immigrant Religions in America*, ed. Jacob K. Olupona and Regina Gemignani (New York: New York University Press, 2007), 115–17.

47. Gwinyai H. Muzorewa, "The Meaning of a Minority in America," *Know Thyself: Ideologies of Black Liberation* (Eugene: Resource Publications, 2005), 93.

tend to operate as missions to Americans on the assertion that their theology champions biblical principles that are neglected in the West.[48] The missional appeal in this message is based on inclusiveness: groups of Christians helping immigrants and each other navigate new communities while sharing a spiritual mandate that transcends borders. By continuing this kind of ministry, the churches testify to the enduring power of leaders understanding and investing in their neighbors.

---

48. Akinade, "Non-Western Christianity in the Western World: African Immigrant Churches in the Diaspora," 90–93.

15

African Christians and Missionaries in Europe

Harvey Kwiyani

This chapter explores the missional potential of African Christians and their churches in Europe. It makes use of the author's long-term involvement with many of these churches and their leaders both in Europe and North America.[1] The first section of the chapter explores some of the general factors behind the rise of African migration to Europe, and the consequent growing presence of African Christians in Europe. The second section focuses on mission and the missional role that African Christians could play in Europe. Holding the chapter together is the argument that non-Western Christians *are* in the West today, and that their presence reinvigorates Christianity in many ways. However, for African and other non-Western Christians to succeed in mission work to re-evangelize Europe, they must learn to contextualize their ministries, and this will require intentional partnering with European Christians. Re-evangelizing the mission field of Europe calls for collaboration among all Christians resident in it – including all non-Western Christians.

---

1. An earlier version of this essay was published under the title, "Blessed Reflex: African Christianity in Europe" in *Theologica Reformata*, 60.1 (2017), 13–27.

African Christian Presence in Europe

There are currently around ten million Africans living in Europe, with most of them living in France and the United Kingdom.[2] Many of them come from West African countries like Nigeria, Ghana, Mali, Senegal and North African countries including Egypt, Libya, and Tunisia, and are living in France, the UK, the Netherlands, Germany, Belgium, Portugal, Spain, Italy, Denmark, Norway, Sweden and the Republic of Ireland.[3] However, a census of African residents in Europe will reveal people from all countries of Africa scattered as migrants in all major European cities. In cities like London – where 14 percent of its 12 million inhabitants are of African descent – it is quite likely that every African tribe and tongue is represented. Every major city, from Dublin to Helsinki, from Oslo to Bern, from Lisbon to Athens, has a considerable resident population of Africans. Most of the Africans from sub-Saharan Africa are Christians, and the easy evidence to their presence is the existence of many African churches. A majority of these churches have been started in the twenty years between 1990 and 2010. A small percentage of them are growing – though slowly – mostly through migration of their fellow nationals to Europe and the evangelism of other Africans (also especially of their fellow nationals) already resident in their cities. Most of them are struggling to grow – their target audience is too limited and their market too saturated. Many have started and closed for the same reasons.

The Blessed Reflex

Two hundred years ago, in the early 1800s, as the Protestant missionary movement gained momentum in the wake of William Carey's work when many hundreds of European and North American missionaries left the comfort and the confines of their homelands in the West to serve in what were at the time unevangelized lands, some spoke hopefully of the day when Christians from those unevangelized lands would come to help invigorate Western

---

2. I use the term "African" to describe the peoples of African origin – sons and daughters of the African civilization – who racially speaking, will generally have a brown skin and are politically described as "Black" people. However, "African," here, also includes all those persons who may not racially identify as Black but were born or raised in the continent of Africa, or for one reason or another, they culturally identify as African. Included here are people groups like White South Africans, Kenyan Indians, Arab Africans from North Africa, and many others.

3. Some have come from the West Indies, but this essay focuses on those that have come directly from Africa and are thus called African migrants – a label that is not used for the West Indian people of African heritage.

Christianity.⁴ This, they called the "blessed reflex."⁵ It would happen when Christians from lands like Africa and Asia which had no Christian population at all at the time would come to be part of the Christian presence in the West, and thereby strengthen Christian witness in Europe and North America. It is not clear how they envisaged this happening but, before any serious fruit of their missionary efforts had registered, the conversation had shifted from the hopeful expectation of non-Western Christians coming to reinvigorate Western Christianity to Western domination of the world, made much more possible by the industrial revolution, and leading to colonization of parts of Asia and Africa. For the following century, between 1814 and 1930, more than twenty percent of Europe's population would migrate to the rest of the world as colonial farmers, traders, and government agents.⁶ Now, more than two hundred years after that conversation, and several decades after the end of European colonization of Africa and parts of Asia, the blessed reflex is finally here. The concept itself never took off back then. It remained a subtext in mission history for two centuries. However, the prophetic seeds of that hope never died. Today, numerous non-Western Christians from all over the world are living in Western cities. Latin American, African and Asian Christians living in the Western cities of Europe, North America, Australia and New Zealand are an answer to the prayers said by European Christians more than two centuries ago.

Back in the early 1800s, the chance of such a reflex happening was unthinkable. The possibilities of Christianity catching on in the other lands were next to nothing – we know that, in Africa for instance, conversions to Christianity accelerated greatly once European colonialism was in place. Nevertheless, the talk about the blessed reflex undergirded the hope that the lives that were lost at sea and in the unevangelized lands were not being lost in vain. This, also, was its basis – should a time come in the future when European Christianity would need to be strengthened, Christians from other parts of the

---

4. William Carey published his essay entitled *An Enquiry into the Obligations of Christians to Use Means for the Conversion of the Heathens* in 1792 and left for India in 1793 after forming the Baptist Missionary Society (BMS). His impact was immediate, within ten years of the formation of the BMS, there were more than a dozen mission societies formed on both sides of the Atlantic.

5. See Kenneth R. Ross, "'Blessed Reflex': Mission as God's Spiral of Renewal," *International Bulletin of Missionary Research* 27.4 (2003). Also see Harvey C. Kwiyani, *Sent Forth: African Missionary Work in the West*, American Society of Missiology Series (Maryknoll: Orbis, 2014), 70–72.

6. Dudley Baines, *Emigration from Europe, 1815–1930*, New Studies in Economic and Social History (New York: Cambridge University Press, 1995).

world should be able to help. Many of those missionaries, like William Carey in India and Ludwig Krapf in East Africa, endured long lives on the mission field and managed to catch a glimpse of the potential impact of their work. Others, like David Livingstone in Central Africa, saw only small breakthroughs in converting locals to the faith but nevertheless contributed to mission through other means, such as geographical exploration. Whatever their work, it was not until the end of the Second World War that the light of world Christianity began to show on a distant horizon. Now, world Christianity is here, and it had found its way to Europe due to two main factors, both of which gained a great deal of momentum in the second half of the twentieth century, even more in the last quarter of the century, and these are the exploding of Christianity in Latin America, Africa, and some parts of Asia, such as, South Korea, and changing global migration patterns. Let us take a brief look at each of these two factors.

The Rise of World Christianity

The missionary movement that so effectively took many thousands of missionaries from Europe and North America to the rest of the world in the 1800s and early 1900s found itself in a crisis in the immediate years after the Second World War. In the late 1940s, the colonial empires began to crack as many colonies agitated for independence. Of course, the Western missionary movement had, generally speaking, taken advantage of colonialism and used it as a vehicle for spreading Christianity, therefore the collapse of colonialism would have significant implications. By the 1970s, over seventy-five percent of the colonies had become independent and many missionaries had returned home – some feeling rejected by their own disciples (as a number of freedom-fighters had been educated in mission schools, of whom a prime example is Robert Mugabe of Zimbabwe, who was educated in Marist and Jesuit schools).[7] The close alliance between mission and colonialism made it difficult for Africans to separate the two.[8] When political colonialism collapsed, where the missionaries continued to lead, a moratorium was called for. Some Asian

---

7. Andrew Norman, *Mugabe: Teacher, Revolutionary, Tyrant* (Gloucestershire: History Press, 2008), 16, 35, 36.

8. For further reading on this, see Chinua Achebe, *Things Fall Apart* (New York: McDowell, 1959). Another interesting read on this part of the history of African Christianity, see Mongo Beti, *The Poor Christ of Bomba* (Long Grove: Waveland, 1971). Both these are fictional books. However, they are helpful as they paint an unflattering image of the public perception of the relationship between missionaries, colonizers, and Africans.

and African leaders demanded that the missionaries go home and that the West should stop sending missionaries for a while.[9]

Difficult as that may seem, the withdrawal of Western missionaries led to an emergence of local missionaries and evangelists who went on to evangelize their countries with a type of effectiveness that foreign missionaries could not manage. Western missionaries had, in many places, translated the Scriptures into local languages. This turned out to be all the local missionaries and evangelists needed to reach their communities.[10] In the case of Africa, by the 1970s, Christianity was exploding in ways not seen before. African evangelists were converting millions of people every year. Similar revivals took place in Latin America and in some parts of Asia. By the end of the twentieth century, world Christianity had become a reality, and with it came the possibilities of a worldwide missionary movement. This growth of world Christianity has made possible something that could not happen before; people from virtually every nation, tribe, and tongue, partaking in God's mission in the world. Most of them work in their own localities, but many others have engaged in cross-border missionary work. Many have crossed continents, even to continents that sent them missionaries two hundred years ago. Mission is finally from everywhere to everywhere. For Africa, the rise of Christianity makes possible the emergence of an African missionary movement. Many African missionaries work in the continent of Africa, but many others have found their way to other continents, especially Europe.

Reverse Migration

For the four hundred and fifty years between 1500 and 1950, global migration patterns were dominated by the movement of Europeans to different parts of the world, first to the Americas and then to Asia and Africa.[11] This great

---

9. John Gatu, *Joyfully Christian, Truly African* (Nairobi: Acton Press, 2006), 163–76. Also, Gerald H. Anderson, "A Moratorium on Missionaries," *The Christian Century* 91.2 (January 1974): 43–45. And see Kwiyani, *Sent Forth: African Missionary Work in the West*, 64–66.

10. Lamin Sanneh, in his book, *Translating the Message*, has shown that it was actually this translation of the Scriptures that enabled African Christianity to blossom. See Lamin O. Sanneh, *Translating the Message: The Missionary Impact on Culture*, American Society of Missiology Series no. 13 (Maryknoll: Orbis Books, 1989), 164–66.

11. See Frieder Ludwig and J. Kwabena Asamoah-Gyadu, *African Christian Presence in the West: New Immigrant Congregations and Transnational Networks in North America and Europe* (Trenton: Africa World Press, 2011), 408. Millions of people were kidnapped from Africa and formed a significant part of this migration, mainly to facilitate the settlement of Europeans in the Americas by providing free labour.

European migration accelerated in the nineteenth century when, as Dudley Baines has suggested, over twenty percent of Europe's population relocated elsewhere, mostly for economic reasons.[12] While most of them moved to the Americas, Australia, and New Zealand, others moved to parts of Africa and Asia. This massive migration enhanced the expansion of the colonial empires and, in most cases, colonialism made the migrations necessary. The outcome was the spread of Christianity around the world as it was Europeans who were also largely Christians who migrated. When political colonialism began to crumble, the migration of Europeans to the rest of the world slowed down to a trickle and, starting in the second half of the twentieth century, migration patterns changed. Regional migrations in different parts of the world increased exponentially. By 2015, there were over 748 million internally displaced migrants and 232 million international migrants in the world.[13] As Castles and Miller wrote, "it is official, we live in the age of migration."[14] New migration patterns emerged that include the movements of Africans, Asians and Latin Americans to Europe and North America, thus reversing the old patterns.

Starting in the 1940s, non-Western migration to the West became a real possibility for many. Even more, for Europe, there was a need to import human-power to rebuild after the wars had destroyed a generation of young and productive men.[15] In some cases, European countries imported labour from their former colonies. Britain, for instance, invited some people from the West Indies to come help drive buses and dig the tunnels for the London Underground.[16] Now, in the early decades of the twenty-first century, Europe still needs to accept migrants in order to sustain her economy. This is partly because the birth rates of Europeans are lower than what it would take to keep their populations growing.

---

12. Baines, *Emigration from Europe*, 1.

13. International Organization for Migration, *World Migration Report 2015: Migrants and Cities: New Partnerships to Manage Mobility* (Geneva: International Organization for Migration, 2015), http://publications.iom.int/system/files/wmr2015_en.pdf.

14. Stephen Castles and Mark J. Miller, *The Age of Migration: International Population Movements in the Modern World*, 4th ed. (New York: Guilford Press, 2009).

15. Mark Sturge, *Look What the Lord Has Done!: An Exploration of Black Christian Faith in Britain* (Bletchley: Scripture Union, 2005).

16. The first group of 492 arrived on 22 June 1948 on SS Windrush from Jamaica and, with many others who followed in the 1950s, they have been referred to as the Windrush Generation. For the next two decades, many people from the Caribbean Islands arrived in Britain, and since then, the population of African-descent people in Britain has continued to grow.

African Christianity in Europe

Religion plays a very big role in the life of African societies. John Mbiti's declaration that Africans are notoriously religious is still true today for most African cultures as it was when he first published it in *African Religions and Philosophy* in 1969.[17] When Africans migrate, they bring their religions (whatever they are) with them. For instance, most Francophone Africans living in France have come Mali, Senegal, Gambia, and other Muslim-dominated West African countries and they bring Islam with them. Africans migrating from Christian-dominated countries like DRC, Ghana, and Ethiopia also bring their own expressions of Christianity to the Diaspora. Others have brought African religion along. However, it is Christianity that has been exported the most in African migration. This may be because, as Jehu Hanciles and others have suggested, immigration laws in many Western countries tend to favour Christians.[18]

African Christians exist in Europe because of this general migration pattern that sees thousands of Africans enter Europe every year. Just like the Europeans who left Europe in the nineteenth century, most African migrants have come to Europe for economic reasons; to work, to study, and to have better standards for their families. Apart from a handful of occasions, we are yet to see the African Christians come to Europe as missionaries, sent by an African mission agency. We are also yet to see many African churches in Europe engage their new contexts in a relevant manner, missionally speaking. Nevertheless, the presence of African churches is growing in Europe. The Redeemed Christian Church of God (RCCG), for instance, a Pentecostal denomination from Nigeria, has close to 1000 congregations scattered all over Britain, and continues to plant more than 10 new churches each year. The Church of Pentecost (CoP), another African Pentecostal denomination (from Ghana), has about 160 congregations in Britain and plants, on average, five churches every year. Both these denominations planted their first congregations in Britain in the 1980s, and as such, are growing rapidly in a context where Christianity is generally in decline. The RCCG and the CoP are the two largest African denominations operating outside Africa. There are many other smaller networks and denominations that are growing their churches in the Diaspora, for example, the Deeper Life Church, Christ Embassy, Christ Apostolic Tabernacle and Lighthouse Chapel. A typical African congregation in Europe will be fairly small, having twenty to

---

17. John S. Mbiti, *African Religions and Philosophy* (Garden City: Anchor Books, 1970), 1.
18. Jehu J. Hanciles, *Beyond Christendom: Globalization, African Migration, and the Transformation of the West* (Maryknoll: Orbis, 2008), 307–8.

thirty members, with the pastor's family inclusive. Very few African churches in Europe will grow beyond 150 members except in large cities like London where several African churches have a few thousand members. For many of them like the RCCG, having small churches are part of a strategy. They intend to have many small churches instead of few large churches and, in doing so, saturate Europe with their churches. The RCCG's mission statement suggests that it seeks to "plant churches within five minutes walking distance in every city and town of developing countries and within five minutes driving distance in every city and town of developed countries."[19]

African Christianity in Europe is in its fifth decade. The first African churches appeared in Europe in the 1960s.[20] Yet, African congregations in Europe continue to remain an exclusively African phenomenon, especially as the numbers of Africans in Europe increase. Almost all African denominations in Europe have more than ninety percent of their membership come from Africa. They are even divided along national identities and tribal languages; there are Ghanaian churches, Nigerian churches, Kenyan churches, as well as Akan churches, Yoruba churches and Luo churches. For example, ninety-seven percent of the 16,000 members of the Church of Pentecost in the UK in 2015 identified as Ghanaian, with an Akan majority. The statistics for the Redeemed Christian Church of God in the UK are not dissimilar where over ninety percent of the 150,000 members were Nigerian (and mostly Yoruba) at the end of 2015.

Nevertheless, as Africa's Christianity grows and as Africans continue to migrate to other continents, the continent of Africa will contribute greatly to world Christianity. In some cities in Europe, Africans are slowly becoming the most visible Christians. In Britain, the presence of African Christians is pronounced in almost every city. More than 50 per cent of church attendance in London since 2010 is attributed to African and Afro-Caribbean Christians – most of whom are members of African churches or other African Majority

---

19. See "Mandate," Redeemed Christian Church of God, http://www.rccguk.church/mandate/. Accessed 20 August 2020.

20. Yes, there have been some African-led churches in Europe since the early decades of the twentieth century. A good example of these is that of Thomas Kwame Brem-Wilson, a Ghanaian businessman and schoolmaster who started his own Sumner Road Chapel in South London in 1906. Another is that of Daniels Ekarte (1896/7–1964), a Nigerian, who established the African Churches Mission and Training Centre in Liverpool. See Harvey C. Kwiyani, *Sent Forth: African Missionary Work in the West*, American Society of Missiology Series (Maryknoll: Orbis, 2014), 77.

Churches.[21] Thus, people of African descent – who form only 14 percent of London's population – make sixty percent of church attendance in the city. The largest congregation in the UK, which is also the second largest congregation in Europe, is Matthew Ashimolowo's Kingsway International Christian Centre in London. It claims to have over 12,000 members. In Europe as a whole, the largest congregation is the Blessed Embassy of God Church in Kiev, Ukraine, which is led by Sunday Adelaja, a Nigerian. It claims over 25,000 members. Its impact in Ukraine and surrounding countries has been tremendous.

Mission and African Christians in Europe

African churches in Europe have *so far* been very successful only in evangelizing fellow Africans. A very small number among them have made inroads reaching Europeans. Here in the UK, many argue that it is too difficult to reach out to British people because it forces them to do things *differently*, which they find too uncomfortable. By "doing things differently," they mean having shorter worship services or having to embrace relational evangelism or indeed, speaking English at church – basic efforts they would need to be able to contextualize their ministries to connect with Europeans. Generally speaking, it is a big challenge for African Christians in the West to imagine contextualizing their ministries. Part of the reason is that many of them lack the training that would enable them to understand what cross-cultural mission to Europeans should look like.[22] Another reason may be that their understanding of mission is largely shaped by Western colonialism. Of course, most African pastors in Europe talk the language of mission fluently. They are clear in their intentions to evangelize Europeans. However, they carry out their weekly ministries as if they are only interested in reaching Africans. Some African pastors have made up their minds to reach Africans only, saying God has called them to evangelize only Africans in the West. Some feel called to specific ethnic groups in the Diaspora. A friend of mine insists that God brought him the England to minister to Yorubas in England, and no one else. Pastors like him see no need to contextualize their ministries. The hard work of cross-cultural ministry is of no interest to them. They live in a bubble of African Christianity in Europe

---

21. Harvey C. Kwiyani, *Multicultural Kingdom: Ethnic Diversity, Mission and the Church* (London: SCM Press, 2020), 13–14.

22. In response to this need for context-sensitive cross-cultural mission training, we have put together an initiative called *Missio Africanus* whose focus is to provide such training to African as well as other non-Western missionaries working in Europe. More on this at www.missioafricanus.com.

and have no plans to connect with even the wider Body of Christ in their neighbourhoods. Many in this camp focus their ministries on church growth and have embraced Donald McGavran's homogenous unit principle.[23] For them, it is easier to grow churches if they focus on their fellow nationals and, if necessary, other Africans. They do not even need to try engaging Europeans because, as they say, "the success rate is too little, it is negligible."

The cross-cultural challenges of reaching out to Europeans explain why most African churches in Europe have no non-Africans in their membership. This reality has serious implications on how we talk about mission in the African Diaspora. Giving up on mission to Europeans is nothing but abdicating the future of their own churches in Europe. Of course, migrant congregations generally do not survive more than two generations. Already, the greatest challenge currently facing African church leaders in Europe is the "faith of the second generation." While many African pastors manage to establish small vibrant churches that are shaped by their African cultures and that attract other first-generation African immigrants, their styles and strategies make reaching and discipling their own children almost impossible. Consequently, once the children leave their homes – for university or just moving out to be independent – they often leave their churches. Many of them stop going to church altogether. Yes, African children are secularizing in Europe just like all other young people – they are only secularizing later, generally after high school. If they do not quit the faith, they go to Western youth-oriented churches (like Hillsong) where they will feel more at home and meet other young people who share their passion and culture.[24]

This phenomenon that second-generation African immigrants are not staying in their parents' churches should not be a surprise. Young Africans in Europe *are* European, culturally speaking. They find it difficult to stay in African churches that are shaped for a different audience. When younger African migrants visit them, everything feels like they have entered foreign culture; the services are an immense cross-cultural experience for them. For many, their parents' African churches are usually the only mono-racial gatherings that they attend. Everywhere else they go, be it at school or at work, they experience life as a multicultural event. Therefore, they find their parents'

---

23. Donald A. McGavran, *Understanding Church Growth* (Grand Rapids: Eerdmans, 1970), 223–44.

24. This is a subject that I have discussed to a greater depth in another book; Harvey C. Kwiyani, *Our Children Need Roots and Wings: Equipping and Empowering Young Diaspora Africans for Life and Mission* (Liverpool: Missio Africanus Publishing), 2018.

churches quite strange. Consequently, African church leaders in Europe will do well to notice that their Christianity needs to be translated into something non-Africans can relate to, whether those non-Africans are their European neighbours, or their own children raised up in Europe.

What Would Effective African Mission in Europe Mean?

Africans must engage in mission in Europe, not just because the secularized context of Europe needs them to do so, but also because "the church is missionary by nature."[25] To stop engaging in mission means to deny themselves their identity as co-workers with Christ in the mission of God in Europe. They must choose the hard road of actually doing their best to engage Europeans in mission rather than following the homogenous unit missiology. They must do this because the legacy of their presence and ministerial work in Europe depends on it. They come to Europe bearing gifts that only they can bring and, when put to good use in a contextually relevant manner, they could help re-evangelize Europe. For the remainder of the essay, I will explore three ways in which African Christians could contribute to mission in Europe.

Evangelism

African Christianity is deeply evangelistic in nature. On the one hand, this is because most African Christians still live in close proximity with those who have not heard the gospel – relatives, neighbours, and others in indigenous religious traditions – and have the urgency to share the good news. On the other hand, there has been a great influence in Africa from Pentecostal and evangelical theology which places a great emphasis on the Last Judgment and hell and the need to save as many people as possible before it is too late. Such theologies emphasize that it is every Christian's duty to plunder hell and populate heaven by converting many people – getting them to be *born again* – from other religions or from nominal Christianity before death or the day of judgment.[26] Most African churches in Europe have brought this evangelistic zeal along. They distribute tracts on the high street. They engage in door-to-

---

25. David J. Bosch, *Transforming Mission: Paradigm Shifts in Theology of Mission*, American Society of Missiology Series no. 16 (Maryknoll: Orbis Books, 1991), 372.

26. This is a title of one of Reinhardt Bonnke's early biographies, Ron Steele, *Reinhard Bonnke: Plundering Hell and Populating Heaven* (Chichester: Sovereign World, 1986). It outlines his evangelism philosophy and strategy. It was written mainly for the African audience which, until its publication in 1986, was the focus of his ministry. It also reflects the general convictions

door evangelism. They pray for miracles. They engage in evangelism on a constant basis, but they use the strategies that were successful in Africa, and then get frustrated when they fail to see conversions like they did in Africa. To their credit, however, they do this in the European context where most Christians do not engage in evangelism at all. Of course, after centuries of seeing no need to evangelize within Christendom, most of Western Christianity lost its evangelistic edge. Today, even with the new ecclesiological/missiological conversations in Europe and North America (like missional church, emerging church, and fresh expressions), many still have no clue how to evangelize – especially how to evangelize fellow Westerners. This is one area in which missional partnerships between Africans and Europeans could be of much help. The Africans have the zeal to pray and evangelize while the Europeans may have a better grasp of the cultural gap that needs to be bridged in order to connect with the people. If we put these two together, we may have what we need for European Christianity.

Ecumenism and Engaging Other Faiths

Contemporary African Christianity (which has effectively emerged in the past century) has always existed in the milieu of other religions. For most of its existence, it has been a numerical minority – only in the 1980s did the number of Christians in Africa rise above that of Muslims. It knows what liminality feels like as both Islam and other Eastern and traditional religions have always competed for adherents in Africa. Thus, in the process of its growth, African Christianity has always had to deal with religious and cultural pluralism on a regular basis. For Europe, both religious pluralism and cultural diversity are fairly new – having become more pronounced in the second half of the twentieth century, in the context of post-colonialism and post-Christendom. Current political attitudes towards migration and diversity suggest many wish they could go back to the time before non-Westerners arrived (with their cultures and their religions). Even within Christianity, as Ben Lindsay and Azariah France-Williams have argued, racism against Black and brown people continues.[27] Most African Christian leaders will have experience in

---

of the many Pentecostal and charismatic Christians in Africa who were encouraged to evangelize to save as many as possible from the impending judgment.

27. Ben Lindsay, *We Need To Talk About Race: Understanding the Black Experience in White Majority Churches* (London: SPCK, 2019). Also see, Azariah D. A. France-Williams, *Ghost Ship: Institutional Racism and the Church of England* (London: SCM Press, 2020).

inter-religious dialogue. Many grew up with neighbours of other religions. Their experience and understanding of Islam, for instance, will be of great value as European Christians try to figure out how best to relate with their new Muslim neighbours. So, this is yet another area where Africans could play a vital role in mission in Europe.

A Return to Community

One of the greatest challenges facing Westerners is lack of community – which is one of the negative effects of individualism (which, of course, is not just an outcome of social disconnectedness in society, but also economic systems that capitalize on the individual to make maximum profit). Loneliness as a problem has reached epidemic levels in some parts of Europe, especially among the elderly.[28] In my work with an RCCG congregation that was trying to discern what God was calling them to do in their community in London, we discovered that within a half mile radius around their church, there were many elderly single people who lived alone and felt like the society had forgotten them. When we visited a few of them, we quickly realized that the primary need was companionship. The congregation worked with the City Council to authorize their members to visit some of the lonely elders, take them shopping or to other social events. Before long, the congregation had embedded itself in its community through what they called a "Befriending Ministry." In Europe, Africa's *communalism* will be the antidote to the individualism that shapes life. In our age of relational evangelism, one of the most important tasks of the church is to be able to form authentic missional communities of faith. Community and belongingness happen to be some of the major needs of Westerners – and we have Africans here who can help discern how best to do that. This, too, is an area where Africans can play an important role in mission in Europe.

Conclusion

The blessed reflex is here. Non-Western Christians are here to invigorate Western Christianity. As such, African Christianity, in one form or another,

---

28. For instance, see the Mental Health Foundation's report on the effects of loneliness in British communities, *The Lonely Society?* (London: Mental Health Foundation, 2010), https://www.mentalhealth.org.uk/sites/default/files/the_lonely_society_report.pdf. For an American perspective, Robert Neelly Bellah, *Habits of the Heart: Individualism and Commitment in American Life* (Berkeley: University of California, 1996).

will continue to exist in Europe, especially as long as African migration to Europe continues. However, a majority of African Christians in Europe have not yet successfully engaged Europeans in mission. They have not even engaged the faith of their children effectively seeing it requires cross-cultural efforts. For most of them, the work to do this is too difficult and yields minimal results. However, they cannot give up on mission among Europeans, as the same tactics will be needed to engage their own children – second generation African immigrants in Europe. To help them engage effectively in mission in Europe, there is need for European Christians to engage African Christians as partners in mission – something beyond renting out their church buildings for services. For instance, it may be possible for European and African Christians to collaborate in planting a church that is multicultural from the start. The two have complementary gifts, skills, worldviews, and theologies. If they work together, they may be able to try something in Europe that, I believe, has not been tried yet, and who knows, this may be a new key to the evangelization of Europe.

Conclusion

Tending and Attending to an African Missiology

Harvey Kwiyani and Angus Crichton

On the 7th April 1889, Mojola Agbebi made before the Native Baptist Church of Nigeria (one of the earlier expressions of African independency), the following prophetic proclamation:

> To render Christianity indigenous to Africa, it must be watered by native hands, pruned with the native hatchet, and tended with the native earth. A grave responsibility rests upon the shoulders of the Native Churches in Africa for the propagation of this Holy Faith among the untold millions of their brethren. It is a curse if we intend for ever to hold at the apron-strings of foreign teachers, doing the baby for aye.[1]

We will draw on Agbebi's image of a plant tended in African soil to explore the development of a missiology from Africa and for Africa and the wider world.

"Tended with the native earth" – the Soil that Nurtures African Mission

Taken together, these essays display the wide diversity of African missiological practice. Africa is a continent not a country: the second most populous continent on the planet; the home of linguistic and cultural diversity where more than two thousand languages are spoken; a continent of fifty-four nation states, each bringing together multiple ethnic, cultural and political groupings with their own unique histories and perspectives. Therefore, African

---

1. Quoted in E. A. Ayandele, *A Visionary of the African Church: Mojola Agbebi (1860–1917)* (Nairobi: East African Publishing House, 1971), 18.

mission is nurtured both by traditional proverbial wisdom (Kwiyani ch. 1, Ola) and globalized flows (Enyegue). Its expressions are found as much within congregations and leaders rooted in European denominations transplanted to Africa (Kritzinger, Marais) as in churches originating from within Africa (Asamoah-Gyadu, Kaunda, Maribei and Mugambi). The continent also has millennia-long ebbs and flows of connection to other continents across sea and sand, as great sections of its population leave and return under varying degrees of compulsion (Ola, Hill, and Kwiyani ch. 15). Indeed, we might suggest that it is an act of folly to express African missiological initiative within a single volume of essays. What does the introspective agonizing of the Dutch Reformed Church over its apartheid legacy have to do with the expansive materiality of the Shepherd Bushiri Ministries International?

Yet certain communalities connect these different essays, reflecting "the native earth" of the continent.

Dynamic movement and innovation: People and songs are on the move between countries and continents, jumping linguistic and immigration obstacles (Obaga, Hill, Kwiyani ch. 15). Joseph Ola criss-crosses continents with his youth mentorship programme that fully utilizes the digital space, as does Shepherd Bushiri and Emmanuel Makandiwa with their television stations (Kaunda). Ideas and images from the global stage are hammered out upon a local anvil (Enyegue). Wherever one locates the epicentre of Pentecostalism, it rapidly takes on distinct and diverse expressions on the continent. The similarities and differences are striking between the Pentecostalism of Mavuno Chapel (Maribei and Mugambi) and that of the United Family Interdenominational Ministries (Kaunda): both fully engage with African socio-economic realities yet provide very different responses. One feels the pent-up frustration of Africa's youth (Ola), which needs creative responses such as Mavuno Chapel to flourish (Maribei and Mugambi).

Increasing urban emphasis: While Harvey Kwiyani and Joseph Ola's reflection draws on Chewa and Yoruba proverbial wisdom, in their essays they have both travelled to urban centres, both within and beyond the continent. In this they reflect many other essays in this volume. While only one essay consciously proclaims its urban focus in its title (Ferreira and Bangura), at least another four profile expressions of Christianity that have flourished in urban spaces. For example African Christian women are resisting gender-based violence in downtown Nairobi as well as the villages of Eastern Congo (Ochola-Adolwa and Kwiyani).

Youthfulness: Africa is a profoundly youthful continent with a median age of nineteen. Joseph Ola's essay therefore is a particularly important contribution in exploring both the frustrations that youth experience and issuing a call for mutual respect, mentoring and utilization of youthful, distinctive gifting, as expressed in biblical and Yoruba proverbial wisdom. Peter Maribei and Kyama Mugambi's essay compliments Ola's, describing missional engagement with twenty-something, middle-class Nairobians who are disenchanted with institutional Christianity. In this sense Jean-Luc Enyegue's call for moving beyond a Westernization-Africanization polarity to Afro-Westernization is vital, for this is the soil that nurtures so many young Africans both on the continent and in the Diaspora.

Religio-cultural heritage: In one sense, the African missionary quest can be understood as the continuation of the continent's millennia old quest to secure wellbeing and ward off misfortune. It is a quest that is shared by all people in all times and all places, with the exception of Western modernity that pursues the same goal without empowerment by non-material beings and forces. This perspective is most clearly developed in Kwabena Asamoah-Gyadu's essay, where he highlights the continuity between what he describes as the primal imagination and contemporary African Pentecostalism.[2] Yet it can also be discerned in Mavuno Church's Transformation Loop which moves complacent, disconnected young adults first into community (*Mizizi* and *Life Groups*) and only then on into action (Maribei and Mugambi), reflecting the strong African value of *umunthu* (see Kiwanyi ch. 1). Three-quarters of a century previously the African American missionary Alonzo Edmiston embraced the same perspective, as he and his wife Althea worked with Baptist congregations in Congo (Hill).

Socio-economic marginalization and political mismanagement: While highlighting these realities is a cliché that bedevils narratives of the continent – hence we have placed this last in our list – it is also an inescapable reality for many. Consequently, Sarojini Marie demands development moves beyond charity to the holism of mission-as-development and development-as-mission, with her impassioned reading of the Rich Man and Lazarus particularly resonant. Asamoah-Gyadu, Kaunda, Ferreira and Bangura, Maribei and Mugambi demonstrate how the Pentecostal turn in African Christianity has offered a rationale and resources to many locked in socio-economic marginalization. Linda Ochola-Adolwa and Harvey Kwiyani recount how African Christian women have challenged gender-based oppression in both

---

2. In East Africa the more commonplace term is African Traditional Religion, while in other settings indigenous religions have been suggested. The term primal is not a reference to inferiority but anteriority.

their actions and their writings in the midst of Congo's "Great War" and the Rwanda Genocide. Klippies Kritzinger and Elias Opongo recount African episcopal leaders who spoke truth to power, in the case of Desmond Tutu to both a White minority and Black majority.

The above are but some of the contextual communalities that shape and nurture African Christian mission, while acknowledging the continent's significant diversity. Many of these factors are interconnected, for example youthfulness, urban centres and selective appropriation of global influences. So what missiological plants flourish in this rich soil?

"Indigenous" Mission Plants Flourishing in "native earth" – the Diverse Plants of African Christian Mission

What is immediately striking is the absence of the classic tenants of Western mission practice: dichotomized Christian/not-yet-Christian lands and professional Christian agents who move from the former to the latter sustained by missionary orders or societies – which Harvey Kwiyani finds within Latourette's *The Great Century of Christian Mission* (ch. 1). Instead, mission takes place both within and beyond communities and continents of origin. Therefore, African mission on the one hand is very local: the diminutive Desmond Tutu in King William's Town's Victoria Sport Stadium preaching into and beyond the deepest concerns of both Black and White listeners (Kritzinger); the mothers of the detained camping out for over a year in the basement of Nairobi's All Saints Cathedral, protesting against a predatory regime that had eaten their loved ones (Ochola-Adolwa and Kwiyani). Yet African mission is also transnational and intercontinental. Shepherd Bushiri and Emmanuel Makandiwa are originally from Malawi and Zimbabwe respectively, they acquired their anointing through the mediation of a Ghanaian prophet, Victor Kusi Boateng. Both Bushiri and Makandiwa have developed extensive ministries across Southern Africa (Kaunda). The Circle of Concerned African Women Theologians is a continent-wide, ecumenical initiative that has lamented and celebrated the experiences of African Christian women in presentations and publications (Ochola-Adolwa and Kwiyani). As has already been noted, the geographic movement of people is a facet of African Christian mission, but it is neither determinative, nor does it require the missionary society or order to facilitate it. Western mission agencies, now experiencing pensionable levels of income, have much to learn from their African sisters and brothers on doing mission with less scaffolding. Contrary to some hagiographic accounts, it is evident that African Christian mission must, as in every era, wrestle with the use of political and economic power in mission. Frederick Marais's chapter is a ruthlessly honest account of the Dutch Reformed Church's journey away from privileged political and social linkages to the wilderness of self-emptying awareness, repentance and service. We all need to learn with Maggy Barankitse the "politics of love," where political and economic power is used in the service of the many and the least, rather than the few and the powerful (Kritzinger).

Our second observation is the size and shape of these "indigenous" mission plants. Some could be likened to the luxurious pumpkin or squash that have proliferated far and wide. Others perhaps are more like a single, upright eucalyptus tree, buffeted by the strong winds of political mismanagement and economic degradation that is so characteristic of the African mission context (see above). The images of these two very different shaped plants are at each end of a continuum of the inspiration and execution of African Christian mission. At one end, the Spirit is blowing where he wills, across the grasslands and rain-forests, the deserts and lakes: the anointing falls upon an individual with signs and wonders following to overthrow this-worldly ills (Asamoah-Gyadu, Kaunda); a *Pambio* starts in Botswana in sung Setswana and ends up sung in Kenya in Kiswahili as if it had originated from there (Obaga); the quest for educational and employment improvement has swept a great tide of African Christians over the walls of Fortress Europe to refresh souls who, starved by secularism, are sampling multiple salvations (Kwiyani ch. 15). At the other end, conferences of Roman Catholic bishops speak truth to oppressive power on behalf of the many; a Circle of Concerned African Women Theologians politely but firmly make space around the cooking pot of African theological reflection hitherto tended by male hands (Ochola-Adolwa and Kwiyani). Mavuno Church consciously and creatively reimagines theological education away from seminaries to church-based programmes for disconnected twentysomethings in Nairobi to propel them out in sacrificial service (Maribei and Mugambi). Christian mission always requires a creative blend of Spirit-led initiative that bursts old wine skins *and* institutional structures that impel and empower (or constrain and constrict).

Third, these essays taken together reveal the danger of using theological lenses ground elsewhere. It is difficult to distinguish between African missiological and theological concerns: Joseph Ola's essay could as easily have been transplanted into a volume on African discipleship; William Obaga's uprooted into one on African Christian music; and perhaps most obviously Elias Opongo's essay would be as comfortable in a volume on African political theology. Both of us sat in an editorial meeting where the Jesuit priest and author Wilfred Sumani demanded that, if books were to be published on African theology for Africa, they must connect with the concerns of the woman selling roasted maize on a roadside *jiko* (charcoal stove) or the *jua kali* (informal sector) metalworker hammering out tin trunks. All theological reflection and writing must be missional, or it is nothing. It must connect with the lives of concrete communities to reveal how Christ and his kingdom is manifest among them (or hidden from/by them). We have little use in Africa for inherited silos that separate applied "missiology" from abstract "theology."

Fourth, we recognize that a continent-wide and Diaspora collection of essays can neither be fully representative nor fully inclusive. We would have wished for more essays authored by Francophone and female writers. We recognize there are notable omissions: African Christian interaction with Muslim communities – of such significance across the Sahel belt and down the East African coast – and environmental degradation whose consequences are falling upon the continent's most vulnerable. We now turn to this issue of silos and structures that limit cross-fertilization in our next section.

"Watered by native hands, pruned with the native hatchet" – Structures that Shape African Missiology

The conference in April 1965 on Christianity in tropical Africa and its published proceedings are often hailed as an initial landmark event in modern African Christian theology. Only around a third of its contributors were Africans.[3] Seventy years on there is a natural and right darkening of the hands watering and pruning. However, mission practice and reflection is shaped not just by reflectors and the subject matter, but the frameworks and structures within which that reflection takes place. Harvey Kwiyani in his opening chapter suggested *umunthu* as an integrating framework for an African missiology: God's restorative work to bring the entire created order, seen and unseen, back into its full personhood, its *umunthu*. Yet when reaching for an integrative missiological theme, a number of authors have settled on those that are also characteristic of and contained within missiological writing in the global north: for example prophetic dialogue or *missio Dei*. Binary thinking (Africa good, global-north bad) rarely encompasses complex realities. These integrative themes are rooted in Scripture, the Christian tradition and the wells of global-north theology most open to refreshment from the global South. We suggest

---

3. Christian G. Baëta, *Christianity in Tropical Africa: Studies Presented and Discussed at the 7th International African Seminar, University of Ghana, April 1965* (London: OUP, 1968).

this is more due to the relatively limited encapsulation *in published form* of reflection on African missionary practice and *in published form accessible on the continent*.[4] In earlier essays on African missiology, one author lamented the access on the continent to the works of African theologians, while another highlighted how global inequalities (or iniquities) underpin the production and consumption of African Christian thought.[5] Consequently, this volume's availability at an accessible price in East, South and West Africa, as well as in the global north, is to be welcomed. It stands alongside a small number of books and a handful of programmatic articles.[6] Common themes across these other publications include the corrosive legacy of European missionary thinking, speaking and acting towards African peoples and their cultures; the imperative of addressing socio-political and economic ills; the religiously pluralistic setting for Christian mission; the disorientating impact of urbanization and globalization; the ecological imperative welling up from African traditional and Christian spirituality and the ongoing quest "to render Christianity indigenous to Africa."[7]

---

4. The mission of this book's publisher, the African Theological Network Press, is that of "an ecumenical press serving the church in Africa and the Diaspora through affordable, high-quality, scholarly publications accessible on the continent and globally" ("About ATNP," African Theological Network Press, accessed 30th June 2021, https://www.atnpress.com/p/mission-and-vision.html).

5. Francis Anekwe Oborji, "Missiology in an African Context: Toward a New Language," *Missiology* 31.3 (July 2003): 335; Willem Saayman, "'Ex Africa Semper Aliquid Novi': Some Random Reflections on Challenges to Christian Mission Arising in Africa in the Twenty-first Century," *Mission Studies* 20.1 (2003): 64–67. We owe the wordplay on inequality in this context to Dr. Paddy Musana of the Department of Religion and Peace Studies, Makerere University, Kampala.

6. See the thirteen volumes in the series African Initiatives in Christian Mission edited by M. L. Daneel and Dana L. Robert, published by UNISA Press, details available at https://www.bu.edu/cgcm/research/africa/african-initiatives-in-christian-mission-book-series/. For multi-author works, see: Anne J. Nasimiyu and D. W. Waruta (eds.), *Mission in African Christianity: Critical Essays in Missiology* (Nairobi: Acton Publishers, 2000); Stephen Mutuku, Henry Mutua, Alemayehu Mekonnen, Steven Rasmussen, Mark Shaw, Josephine Mutuku Sesi and Caleb Shul-Soo Kim, *African Missiology: Contributions of Contemporary Thought* (Nairobi: Uzima, 2009); and the single-author volume by Timothy Kabulunga Nyasulu, *Missiology: A Study of the Spread of the Christian Faith* (Zomba: Kachere, 2004). For articles, see Tite Tiénou, "Themes in African Theology of Mission," in *The Good News of The Kingdom Mission Theology for the Third Millennium*, eds. Charles E. Van Engen and Dean S. Gilliland (Eugene: Wipf & Stock Publishers, 1999): 239–43. A volume on African approaches to mission was planned alongside the impressive thirty-five volumes in the Edinburgh 2010 Centenary Series, however, the volume did not reach the published light of day.

7. Again, in even listing and surveying prior publications on African missiology, one is immediately confronted with the difficulty in drawing a meaningful line between African theology, missiology and indeed Christian history – highlighting again inadequacy of using theological lenses ground elsewhere.

Allied to the accessibility to publications is an observation about a particular genre within African theological discourse. Tinyiko Maluleke has described this as the "double-sided balance sheet approach where the problems are listed on the one side and what needs to be done is listed on the other – with every sentence starting with the phrase 'the church should . . . .'"[8] There is a tendency towards high-altitude theologizing and prescriptive generalizing. In contrast, a good number of essays reveal the richness of missiological reflection when it is based on narrating embodied African experience at the grass-roots: Maggy Barankitse kneeling with Geraldo (Kritzinger); the actual voices of African youth crying to their elders for space (Ola); the *Pambio* as a central instrument of biblical and theological instruction and expression (Obaga); chronicling the ministries of Pentecostal pioneers beyond the tired lens of "the prosperity gospel" ills (Asamoah-Gyadu, Kaunda); the African American Edmistons learning their ecclesiology from their Congolese brethren (Hill). Both of us are currently resident in Europe, where we have experienced more than enough writing on the African continent that is long on theory and generalization and short on grass roots, grounded reality in all its rich diversity, splendour and tragedy. These essays suggest that we are still journeying together towards Mojola Agbebi's prophetic vision of "indigenous plant(s) . . . watered by native hands, pruned with the native hatchet, and tended with the native earth."

---

8. Tinyiko Sam Maluleke, "Christianity in a Distressed Africa: A Time to Own and Own Up," *Missionalia* 26.3 (Nov 1998): 336.

Langham Literature and its imprints are a ministry of Langham Partnership.

Langham Partnership is a global fellowship working in pursuit of the vision God entrusted to its founder John Stott –

> *to facilitate the growth of the church in maturity and Christ-likeness through raising the standards of biblical preaching and teaching.*

Our vision is to see churches in the Majority World equipped for mission and growing to maturity in Christ through the ministry of pastors and leaders who believe, teach and live by the word of God.

Our mission is to strengthen the ministry of the word of God through:
- nurturing national movements for biblical preaching
- fostering the creation and distribution of evangelical literature
- enhancing evangelical theological education

especially in countries where churches are under-resourced.

Our ministry

Langham Preaching partners with national leaders to nurture indigenous biblical preaching movements for pastors and lay preachers all around the world. With the support of a team of trainers from many countries, a multi-level programme of seminars provides practical training, and is followed by a programme for training local facilitators. Local preachers' groups and national and regional networks ensure continuity and ongoing development, seeking to build vigorous movements committed to Bible exposition.

Langham Literature provides Majority World preachers, scholars and seminary libraries with evangelical books and electronic resources through publishing and distribution, grants and discounts. The programme also fosters the creation of indigenous evangelical books in many languages, through writer's grants, strengthening local evangelical publishing houses, and investment in major regional literature projects, such as one volume Bible commentaries like *The Africa Bible Commentary* and *The South Asia Bible Commentary*.

Langham Scholars provides financial support for evangelical doctoral students from the Majority World so that, when they return home, they may train pastors and other Christian leaders with sound, biblical and theological teaching. This programme equips those who equip others. Langham Scholars also works in partnership with Majority World seminaries in strengthening evangelical theological education. A growing number of Langham Scholars study in high quality doctoral programmes in the Majority World itself. As well as teaching the next generation of pastors, graduated Langham Scholars exercise significant influence through their writing and leadership.

To learn more about Langham Partnership and the work we do visit **langham.org**

www.ingramcontent.com/pod-product-compliance
Lightning Source LLC
Chambersburg PA
CBHW070315240426
43661CB00057B/2650